MINISTRY OF CULTURAL AND ENVIRONMENTAL ASSETS
NATIONAL COMMISSION FOR THE CELEBRATION OF THE QUINCENTENNIAL
OF THE DISCOVERY OF AMERICA

NUOVA RACCOLTA COLOMBIANA
ENGLISH EDITION

ISTITUTO POLIGRAFICO E ZECCA DELLO STATO
LIBRERIA DELLO STATO
ROMA

MINISTRY OF CULTURAL AND ENVIRONMENTAL ASSETS

NATIONAL COMMISSION FOR THE CELEBRATION OF THE QUINCENTENNIAL
OF THE DISCOVERY OF AMERICA

NUOVA RACCOLTA COLOMBIANA

GAETANO FERRO

THE GENOESE CARTOGRAPHIC TRADITION AND CHRISTOPHER COLUMBUS

Translated into English by

HANN HECK

and

LUCIANO F. FARINA – Ohio State University

ISTITUTO POLIGRAFICO E ZECCA DELLO STATO
LIBRERIA DELLO STATO
ROMA

Originally published as *La Tradizione cartografica genovese e Cristoforo Colombo*
Translation © 1996 by Ann Heck and Luciano F. Farina

© ISTITUTO POLIGRAFICO E ZECCA DELLO STATO - LIBRERIA DELLO STATO

PREFACE

The title of this book differs little from that of the 1937 work by Paolo Revelli entitled Christopher Columbus and the Genoese School of Cartography. *Why then come back to a subject already treated with such breadth and depth by the late master?*

In the first place, because historical cartography has made advances that should be accounted for in the more than fifty years that have passed since then. Also, the time seems right to give a comprehensive view of the subject while at the same time expanding our field of vision so as to include, on the one hand, the recent contributions of geographic theory, and, on the other, explore how technical maps, linked as they are to navigational techniques, were used.

These considerations have led us to include in the present volume the most important aspects of the cartographic works made in Liguria (or used by Ligurian navigators) in the period before Columbus and even much earlier, although I make no claim to treat this subject exhaustively. I make some references to the post-Columbian era as well.

This broadened perspective is justified by the very existence, as will become clear, of what is more properly called a "tradition" than a "school" of Ligurian cartography. In this book I intend to present the various grounds for believing that this tradition existed and to study the cultural motivations that sustained cartographic activity, its eminently practical objectives, and the various characteristics of its end products.

A specific objective of this book is to situate in this cartographic tradition the formation and preparation that Christopher Columbus could, or rather must, have received in his native land before the well-known events of his life took him to the Iberian Peninsula and put him in contact with navigational practices and commercial circles there. In this way the present volume also hopes to help shed light on Columbus's cartographic knwoledge as one aspect of the many-faceted figure of the Discoverer of the New World.

CHAPTER I

THEORIES AND REPRESENTATIONS OF THE EARTH
IN PRE-COLUMBIAN TIMES

1) *The image of the earth*

Historical cartography, because it is concerned with the evolution of ways of depicting the earth's surface, is but an aspect of the history of ideas and skills possessed by groups of human beings, as they apply to the representation of the world around us. When one speaks of the history of thought and human skills, the scenario becomes extremely broad. On the one hand, it involves cosmological and geographical conceptions in all their complexity, together with the persistence of a certain number of traditional ideas. On the other, it includes the humble and more or less rich reality of the experience of commonly known places that become familiar either directly through travels and first-hand observation, or sometimes mediately by way of contemporary culture and second-hand narratives.

But there is more: the history of cartography is also that of methods of surveying and techniques of representation. Surveying methods amounted first to bare visual observations, limited by what the human eye can perceive, then quickly encompassed the most elementary astronomical references before finally involving triangulation with the help of instruments, and today's most sophisticated systems of aerial and satellite photography. The techniques of representation range from the rock carvings of the oldest depictions and the rudimentary sketches contained in assemblages of shells and bamboo sticks, to the parchment manuscripts of medieval nautical charts and the first engravings cut into wood or copper or stone, later reproduced on paper in relatively limited quantities, gradually giving way to modern printing techniques and their infinite variety of applications. Such an overview will afford us the opportunity to consider the enormous success story of maps-how widespread cartographic documents and works were and still are, and how influential they have been on geographic thought (and beyond it, since advances in the various branches of the sciences are linked together).

Cartography and geography in particular are closely connected, as various examples will show, since the former, as everyone knows, is concerned with depicting the facts that the latter studies. Cartography makes very useful contributions to our understanding of geography, illustrating graphically the territorial distribution of phenomena. Thus the history of cartography is closely linked to the history of geographical exploration and the history of geographical thought and theories. It builds on their results, while also making possible further developments or actually stimulating new initiatives. The historical development of cartography itself contributes considerably to geographical science as a whole, through its own constant updates and modification as it advances. Without the depictions made possible by cartography the comparisons that constitute the soul of geography could not be realized.

Nowadays there is often talk (possibly too often, in my opinion) of the image of the territory created by the people who live there or travel through it, and much space is given to the related discussions about the means through which such an image is formed and passed on by way of the most diverse experiences. Thus we end up discussing so-called mental maps of contemporary humans in the field of what is called the geography of perception, logically linked to semiology, that is the science of signs, of which the symbology of maps is only a part.

I do not deny that dwelling on reflections and meditations of this kind, as for any intellectual activity, can serve some useful purpose in today's human geography. On the other hand, advances in geography, as in any other science, cannot leave unexplored any of the lateral or related branches, from which helpful contributions may come at any time. I personally do not believe, however, in a typology of exceedingly specialized geography, nor in the mania for novelty, nor in the resulting abstractions, distilled in one's study with such elaborate sophistication.

On the contrary, I am convinced that cartographic documents of the past cannot be adequately studied and understood unless one first takes into account the culture that they express (and the methods by which they were constructed), on the one hand, and the aims and objectives for which they were intended, on the other. In other words, the depiction of the earth, and its evolution, are part of a system of thought and communication that is tied to, and a function of, the different eras and their means of expression. Within this perspective it is possible to overcome the ancient and deep-rooted habit of appraising the cartographic document of the past only according to whether it corresponds to geographic reality as we know it today, or better yet, whether it conforms to the mathematical rules of modern science, which governs how such a reality is to be represented.

This is not to deny that the point of departure for any investigation, obviously, ought to be an examination of the documents, which constitute the irreplaceable primary material in the case of studies of the past (and especially in this case, concerning what is called — not without chronological uncertainties — the Columbian era). Obviously, we are dealing with graphical works from various centuries depicting the planet as a whole or, more often, more or less extensive parts of it; alongside of which may appear the literary texts that elucidate them, or which set forth the ideas and theories that inspired such representations.

In the pages that follow I shall hold to these criteria — based above all on the rigorous examination of documentary sources — and with some specific caveats. In the first place, and to the extent possible, I will try to overcome any nationalistic or regionalistic interpretation of the various works and other evidence, in the conviction that the evolution of cartography, and more generally of the earth sciences, is only one aspect of a more general process of development of culture and civilization. This development, even though it had its more active centers in particular places and times, was also tightly linked to similar movements that were occurring elsewhere and had consequences and influences in other areas as well.

In addition it should be pointed out that when dealing with cartographic works intended for practical purposes, such as nautical charts, it is often difficult and sometimes impossible to find a way to check them against theoretical premises, so that in many cases one must resort to conjectures and suppositions. In reality, as so often happens in many realms of human activity, the inspirations arising from a need to satisfy immediate everyday requirements are not rooted in elaborate theories, and at times actually anticipate them.

There is no doubt that the cartography with which we are dealing in this book should be classified as predominantly the fruit of the labors of individuals, one that gives much room to decorative elements and to the views and subjective choices of their authors. The geographical or topographical information is likewise provided occasionally in a precise and exhaustive fashion, and at other times with many distortions and gaps. However, we must also take into account the fact that a large part of this cartography was derived from memory, or from illustrations of voyages of discovery, that is, from travel experiences of which the cartographer had direct or indirect information. Here it is worth remembering that travel at that time was both more limited and generally covering shorter distances compared to today, but it was also slower and therefore more conducive to personal analytical observations.

Still, the greater amount of information was obtained at second hand, by waiting on the docks in harbors or in the marketplaces of the larger cities for sailors and merchants, and after listening to their reports the writer would put together an account of their enterprises and adventures; only in rare cases did they enjoy the opportunity to read letters and documents drafted by the travelers or by missionaries, who also had an important role in broadening the geographical horizon of the past.

Finally, a few cartographic works exhibit particularly original characteristics, being expression and synthesis of the geographical theories prevalent at the time in which they were put together (if not in an effort to prove them). In studying and appraising them this specific aspect of such works needs to be taken into consideration.

2) *Elements of the classical tradition that persisted into the Middle Ages*

An erroneous affirmation, often echoed by popular culture (though sometimes cradled even in higher circles), is the belief that gives credit to Columbus's enterprise for having proved that the world is round.

This is untrue, for at least two reasons. To begin with, the first empirical demonstration that the world is round belongs to Magellan's circumnavigation of the earth, about thirty years after the discovery of America. In the second place, the idea that our planet is round goes back to early times and the well-established classical tradition that was accepted in all the cultured circles of Western Europe in Columbus's time. But theories in this regard were varied, interconnected, and sometimes contradictory; the disputed questions were very complex, as we shall see later. Several of these had to be faced by Columbus in the period when his plan to sail the Atlantic was taking shape, and was the object of elaborate discussions.

In fact, if truth be told, the Mesopotamian peoples had already conceived of the universe as spherical in structure, although within it the earth's surface looked like a flat disc. The Bible (which took over the knowledge of such peoples, though it nowhere describes the design of the earth) reflects ideas corresponding to what has been called the cosmography of appearances, so that the earth was seen as flat and quite limited in size. Though poor in geographic content, the beliefs of Holy Writ, conveyed through the Christian religious message, were widely accepted by the culture of the Middle Ages, whose cosmography, as we shall see, would long preserve a number of notions, albeit naive, derived from such beliefs.

The idea of a round earth, within a rational, logical system, goes back — as far as we know — to the fifth century B.C. and is to be credited to Greek thinkers of the Pythagorean school. Luzzana Caraci has emphasized that they came to formulate this idea not "by reason of astronomical observations, but by starting from a geometrical postulate, that is to say, from the consideration that the sphere is the most perfect geometric form." In the same way the spheres of the heavenly bodies that moved around it were determined to add up to the sacred number of ten.

Classical culture subsequently remained always faithful to this idea, especially after Eudoxus of Cnidos (fourth century B.C.) worked out a theory according to which the universe was formed of a series of spheres with the earth at the center. The spheres were arranged in eight systems, with differing movements for the heavenly bodies (we will not allude here to the intuition some thinker seems to have had of a helio-centric system, without, however, finding support at that time). This theory was accepted and developed by Aristotle (fourth century B.C.), whose thought pointed to air, water, fire, and earth as the constituent elements of our world within the sublunary sphere beneath the incor-ruptible ether. This theory was extremely widespread and enjoyed undis-puted prestige for many centuries.

The concept of a round earth posed (and would afterwards pose ever more forcefully) the problem, among others, of how to represent on a flat plane the surface of the planet or more or less extensive portions thereof. No trace of such concern is found in the cartographic work of Dicaearchus (late fourth century) or Eratosthenes (third century), even though both of them introduced mathematical elements (but not projec-tion) into mapmaking, and both made measurements of the circumference of the earth, based on the idea that it was round. Another measurement, calculated earlier by Eudoxus, seems to have resulted in an estimate much greater than reality. We know little or nothing of the conclusions Dicaear-chus reached, except that they had no effect on the way he made his maps. Eratosthenes, however, as we know, arrived at an extraordinarily exact measurement, indeed very close to actual fact.

This thinker introduced into the map of the known world a system of reference lines; these were at unequal distances, coinciding with parallels that passed through known sites, and were intersected by perpendicular lines, also spaced unequally. This system approaches the modern idea of a geographical grid and was useful for fixing the position of places. But, since he procedeed to represent a spherical surface on a flat plane without using a system of projection, the result led to significant distortions between geographical reality and its cartographic representation.

This problem must, however, have been on the mind of Crates of Mallos if it is true, as seems certain, that he built a globe (or several globes) precisely in order to represent better the surface of the whole world. It is certain that Hipparchus, who, like Crates, lived in the second century B.C., deserves credit for devising two projections for representing a sphere on a flat plane (though it seems that they were applied only to the heavenly spheres). Moreover, he maintained that cartography ought to be based on precise calculations of latitude and longitude so as to indicate the location of places, but he recognized that not enough data were as yet available.

The representation of the earth adopted by Crates showed its surface as covered, for the most part, with bodies of water (which would also be called "islands" or "spots"), on which "floated" (or among which stood) four small continents, diametrically opposed: our world (the *oikumene*), the *perioikoi*, the *antipodes*, and the *antoikoi*. In Christian times, when Crates' theory continued to be accepted, as Randles has so well shown, it was believed by medieval culture that the vast extent of the oceans prevented communication among these four worlds, and it was believed that the human race lived in only one of them, it being impossible that the others were inhabited. Thus the Christian *oikumene* was pitifully small compared to the surface of an immense sphere; precisely because of its small size it could be represented as flat. In this way the Greek idea of an astronomical sphere, or of a series of spheres, could be harmonized with the biblical suggestion of a flat, inhabited world.

In opposition to this conception, and in part alongside it, still in the Middle Ages, was the vision inspired more or less directly by Aristotle and his theory of the various spheres. The depiction of the earth entailed determining the relationship between its sphere and the sphere of water above it, especially since the culture of the time could not ignore the biblical passage, in which was recounted the story of divine intervention on the third day of creation to gather the waters into a single place or to one side, leaving the other part of the sphere as dry and habitable land.

In the Middle Ages it was a commonly accepted principle (assumed to go back to Aristotle, who in reality never formulated it clearly) that there was a ratio of one to ten between the volume of one sphere and that of the next. The part of the earth left uncovered by the waters must

Plate I

Examples of schematic world maps from the Middle Ages.

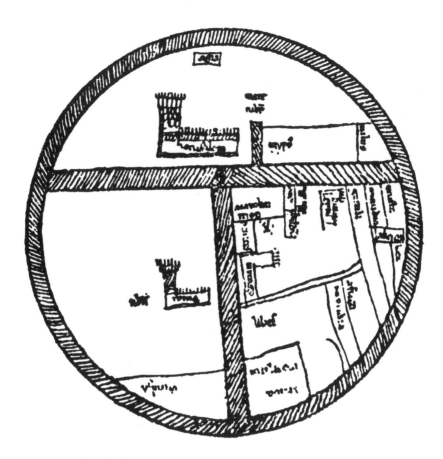

In the Sallustius manuscript, of the thirteenth century
(Vatican Apostolic Library, Rome).

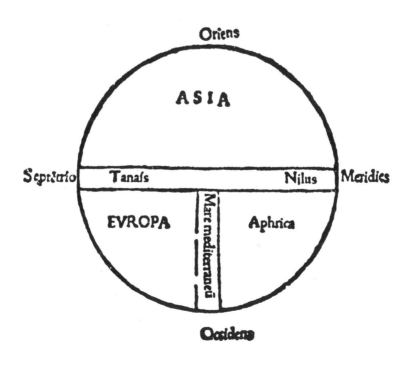

From the edition of Zacharias's *Orbis Breviarum*,
printed in Florence, 1483.

Plate II

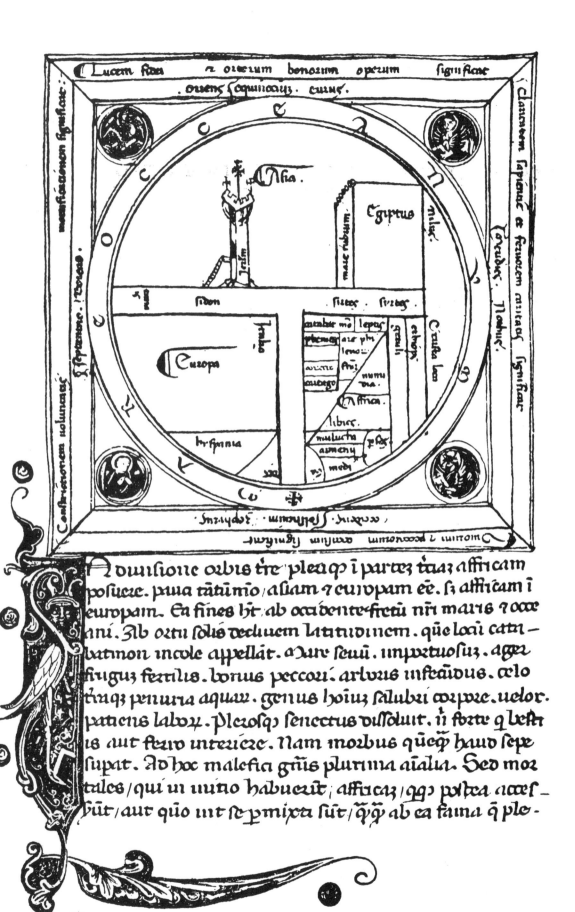

A T-O of scheme world map, from a Sallustius manuscript of the fourteenth century
(Marciana Library, Venice).

Plate III

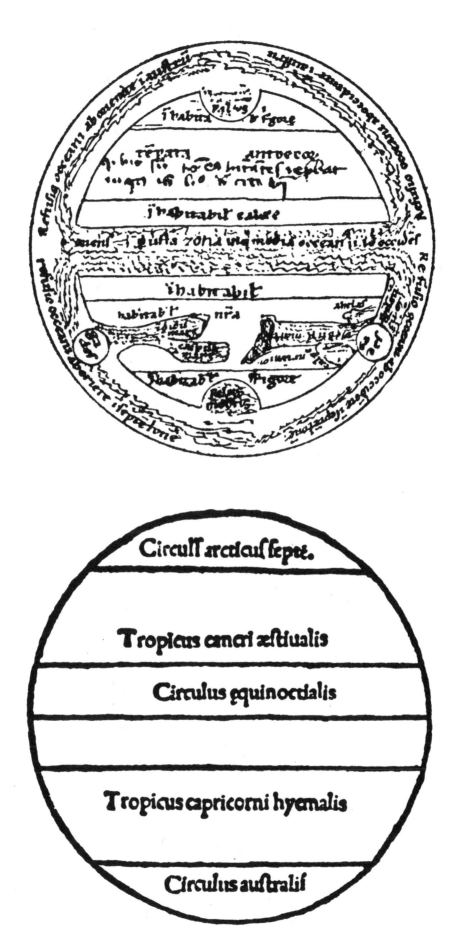

Two world maps with climate zones: top, from a thirteenth century manuscript by Macrobius; bottom, from the edition of Zacharias's *Orbis Breviarium* printed in Florence, 1483.

therefore have had a much smaller surface than the waters did. In this case, also, the inhabited *oikumene* known to Christians must have had dimensions small enough to be very well represented on a flat plane, though this was still within a single sphere (Plates I-II).

Cartography, in the meantime, which by now tended to depict only the habitable part of the earth as known from direct observation or from the fairly reliable information available in the Christian era, was now able to take advantage of the works of Marinus of Tyre and Ptolemy (both from the second century A.D.). They introduced radical innovations in the form of projections, as well as a determination of the size of the above-mentioned *oikumene* and the specific location of places according to measures of latitudes and longitudes expressed in degrees, rather than the earlier units of linear measurement (*stadii*).

Marinus of Tyre, whose work, now lost, deserves mention inasmuch as it was known to the Arabs of the Middle Ages, conceived what was to be the first projection used for maps of the earth. This projection entailed great distortions, especially in the depiction of peripheral areas. Other shortcomings were due to the small number of astronomical data available to him concerning various locations. Still it was he who determined that the *oikumene* extended 225° from the first meridian (at the Fortunate [Happy] Isles) to the easternmost edge; he thereby greatly exaggerated the dimensions of Asia to the east. This will have to be taken into consideration when evaluating Columbus's ideas about the size of the earth and the feasibility of crossing what he believed to be a single ocean in the middle.

Ptolemy, as we know, reduced that figure to 180°. Having at his disposal quite detailed information about the location of an adequately large number of places, he was able, based on these, to make a real drawing on a flat surface of a graticule of geographical coordinates according to true projections, albeit elementary ones (for regional maps one may speak, using modern terminology, of flat-rectangular projection, and for the map of the whole *oikumene* of simple-conic projection; yet Ptolemy also knew the modified-conic method). In subsequent cartography, which thus assumed a completely mathematical basis, the location of places came to be expressed by latitude and longitude. But only for the former was there a fair number of figures available (about 400 perhaps), and these were approximate. For longitudinal values one had to resort to estimates, which, as we may suppose, were based on distances since, for that time, we know of only one application for this purpose of the principle of time differential between two places; it relied on the observation of eclipses and consequently produced quite inaccurate results.

13

This explains the many errors in Ptolemy's cartography. In his works, including the well-known *Almagest*, he is nonetheless famous for having perfected and elaborated, on a rational basis, the geocentric system of the universe now known as the "Ptolemaic system." This is not the place to cast judgment on this thinker's cartography, which, like all ancient cartography, was imperfect mainly because the astronomical and geographical data on which it was based were lacking or inexact, mostly on account of deficient instruments. Moreover, all the manuscript versions of his *Geography* that have come down to us date from many centuries later (they seem to be derived from a text redacted in Byzantine circles in the tenth to eleventh centuries), and the number of maps contained in them varies. It has even been suggested that maps inserted in the original text were lost (this supposition, too, has been called into question), and other maps were drawn thereafter, based on codices and unreliably transcribed (like the one, for example, made by a Greek monk around the year 1300). The planisphere, however, is dated back to the fourth or fifth century A.D.

Ptolemy's work, preserved by Arabs and Byzantines, was introduced into the West by a translation made at the beginning of the fifteenth century, but it began to be widely distributed only with the various printed editions, which followed one after the other beginning in 1475-1477. His *oikumene* [inhabited world], conceived as spherical, was equal to only a quarter of the earth's surface, since that was the size and limit of the regions known in his time. In such a representation the seas and oceans did not connect at all with each other, since they were all surrounded by dry land, which also comprised the then unknown portion of the world.

In such an arrangement, of course, a spirit of mathematical rationalism prevails, whether applied to astronomy or geography, in a way perfectly consistent with the principles of Greek thought (and later with many ideas of Humanism). The part of Ptolemy's work that survived the crisis of classical civilization in the Eastern Mediterranean was very compatible with the Aristotelian *Summa*, which in turn was incorporated by the West into the inviolable corpus of theories, notions, and precepts of Scholasticism. Despite the numerous debates and differing points of view, and even though many aspects of nature and features of our planet remained unknown or disputed in the last century of the Middle Ages, the system of spheres, and the theory of the roundness of the earth, was accepted and widespread in the Christian world.

In fact such a teaching fit in well with the principles of orthodox theology with which it harmonized, as Lago, among others, has noted.

The celestial region, consisting of ethereal and incorruptible matter, was the most obvious place to be the seat of the Deity. In the sublunary region, however, the four constituent elements of our planet, which are in constant transformation among themselves, were defined as corruptible substances (in agreement with the Christian disparagement of earthly things). Finally, the position of the earth, firmly fixed at the center of the universe, was not basically at variance with the concepts of the Bible. And the part of the earth that was known, given its dimensions, could still be represented as flat.

* * *

If these were the theories that were taught and learned in Western Europe at the end of the Middle Ages, that is, in Columbus' time, the cartographic representations of the earth that were produced or in current use in such an environment had undergone changes that were perhaps even more problematical. This was all the more true because the medieval period, or at least the first part of it, was decidedly negative for geography, which virtually ceased to exist as a science, being replaced at that time, though not for ever after, by cosmography (or, better yet, geography became a part of cosmography).

Indeed, the dogmatic culture of the Church Fathers — which was barely, or not at all, receptive to observations of the natural world and to scientific interpretations — held sway during this first period, which lasted until around the year 1000, though there were also significant later manifestations of this attitude even into the fourteenth century; in addition, relations between countries situated any distance apart had become rare or intermittent. With geographical horizons shattered and restricted, it was to be expected that all speculation about the shape and characteristics of the earth as a whole, and all reflection about what takes place on its surface, would be reduced, and every attempt to depict it would be schematic, with religious and fantastic elements prevailing according to the inspiration and sentiments of the author.

In the field of cartography, if the products of these centuries can be said to belong to it (given the obvious imperfections and distortions that mark them — not to mention their almost invariably symbolic nature), the criterion of "appearances" mentioned earlier tends to prevail. We are dealing here, obviously, with documents that have come down to us in small numbers compared to the total quantity that must have been produced during the period (though Destombes has counted and published at least eleven hundred of them). Very simple and crude, they are characterized by stereotypical designs, which alternately incorporate a mix of real and fantastical elements.

Some of the *mappaemundi*, which is the form in which cartographic depictions generally circulated during this period, recall the biblical theory of the earth as a flat disc. These generally belong to the type referred to as "ecumenical." They go back to the ideas held by, among others, Saint Isidore of Seville, whose geographical or parageographical works were very popular in the Middle Ages up until Columbus's time. Isidore, in turn, leaned on the authority of Saint Augustine.

In these *mappaemundi* the earth was represented as it would appear to an ideal observer standing in eminent position in the center of the *oikumene*, whether the earth was shown in the form of a T inside an O, or subdivided by three radii, or as a rectangle, inside which the dry lands were arranged in the form of a V. Alongside these works, another group aimed to portray the known world, still conceived as a flat disc, with great preeminence and always with the customary tripartite division between Europe, Asia, and Africa. This group deserves to be considered separately because it gives a hint, though vague and indistinct, of the existence of a southern continent.

The later *mappaemundi* (relatively speaking, of course) that Quaini, following in the footsteps of Skelton and Destombes, defines as characterized by detailed geographical configurations and abundant place names, are still tied to the idea of a flat earth. Thanks to the additional details the schematic division of the world into continents is overcome, and the most diverse pieces of information, not strictly geographical, are accepted and repeatedly included.

Indeed, in these cartographic works all the elements that made up the culture of the time come together, and they tend to predominate, by a large margin, over the experiential data (indeed quite limited). This results in an image of the world not as it must have been known, at least in part, to geographers, travelers, and sailors, but rather as it was interpreted, as a sort of encyclopedia of nature (the best known examples are the *mappaemundi* of Ebstorf, Hereford, and Vercelli, all from the thirteen- or fourteenth century; in the first the representation of the *oikumene*, surrounded by the ocean, is constructed over a crucifixion scene, with Christ's head at the top, his feet at the bottom, and his hands to the sides). In such a representation, as Airaldi has pointed out, there is room not only for everything in existence — or at least everything known to exist — but also for whatever places one might have expected to find, based on theories, reasoning, or imagination. In other words, these late medieval *mappaemundi* are a synthesized cartographic equivalent of the summas or encyclopedias that were such a typical cultural product of those centuries.

An examination of these works confirms the conclusion that, compared to the classical period, there was considerable backward movement in cosmographic conceptions. This can perhaps be explained by the fact that observations were limited to very small areas. A more likely explanation, however, is that a complete and entire representation of the round earth, using *mappaemundi* of the so-called "hemispherical" type, would have required depicting the area below the equator as well, which would have meant facing the problem of whether these areas were habitable by the *antipodes* (which then reserved to people, not to a place).

"Hemispheric" *mappaemundi* of the type have come down to us in much smaller numbers than those of the "ecumenical" type. One example is found in the works of Pierre d'Ailly, with which Columbus was acquainted, as we know. For this reason, as well as because of the correlation between this way of depicting the earth and geographical discoveries, it is worth mentioning the theory of the five climatic zones that these *mappaemundi* generally illustrate (Plate III).

As it is, Parmenides (fifth century B.C.) had divided the terrestrial sphere horizontally into five zones: two around the North and South Poles, which were uninhabitable because of the cold; one astride the equator, uninhabitable and untraversable by humans; and two temperate zones in between. In the Middle Ages the acceptance of this layout led to a simplification of Crates' theory. The four areas of dry land were reduced to two: our northern "oikumene" and the southern one of the "antipodes," which virtually all the scholars and theologians of the time considered uninhabitable (among the exceptions were Roger Bacon and Albert the Great). They referred back to the principles stated by Lactantius (third to fourth century A.D.) and Saint Augustine (fourth to fifth century) and emphasized the repellent characteristics of the equatorial zone, which was untraversable because of "excessive heat." Those world maps that have been improperly classified as "ecumenical" and yet contain a southern hemisphere, even though vague and indistinct, take these ideas into account, while, at the same time, revealing the caution of mapmakers who did not wish to make any judgments concerning these lands.

In reality, Lactantius rejected the roundness of the earth and Aristotelian physics (and therefore also the principle that heavy objects fall toward the center of a sphere). Saint Augustine, on the other hand, did not deny the roundness of the earth, but declared that its lower part was entirely covered by water. Randles reminds us that at the beginning of the fourteenth century there was a conviction that humans could live in the part of the Indian Ocean that was south of the equator, as well as along its coasts and on its islands. Evidence of this belief is in a fourteenth century work that circulated widely in the fifteenth century and must therefore have been known to Columbus, namely that of Sir John Mandeville.

Nevertheless the torrid zone, even in the mid-fifteenth century, could appear to be out of reach to human beings this side of the Atlantic. It was precisely to this area that Columbus turned his attention, as did those who disputed his ideas during the discussions that took place at the court of the Catholic Sovereigns about the feasibility of his project.

In this regard there are two points to keep in mind. Portuguese ships had already entered the waters between the tropics (sailing throughout that area with a certain frequency and regularity) by the end of the period of Prince Henry the Navigator (that is, before 1461). Columbus himself had been perhaps more than once to Elmina [La Mina], a place that was known to be in the Gulf of Guinea, not far from the equator. The latter had been reached before 1475 by another Portuguese expedition, that of Francisco Gomes. And later, in 1481-1486, Diogo Câo went almost as far as the Tropic of Capricorn. Experience had thus proved the groundlessness of the theory that the torrid zone was uninhabitable.

Then, too, Columbus knew well that in order to respect the clauses of the Spanish-Portuguese Treaty of Alcaçovas-Toledo (1479-1480), which had been included in a papal bull, his routes of discovery to the west in the service of the Spaniards had to stay north of the parallel of the Canary Islands. These northern latitudes are much higher than those for which questions about "excessive heat" and the *antipodes* were raised. If the objections made to Columbus were about these issues, then he had a strong hand for demolishing them with ease. But perhaps in these matters the historiographic tradition surrounding Columbus has deliberately distorted or exaggerated the truth.

* * *

Other questions also occupied medieval geographic thought and were reflected in cartography. Among these was the issue of where to situate the Earthly Paradise, which according to Christian tradition must have been located to the east in a high place with plentiful water. Hence the occasional depiction of strange swellings on the earth's surface, from which descended abundant rivers. In other cases one finds of a very high mountain, drawn in some cartographic documents in such a way as to imply an insuperable obstacle to humans, to the east, almost symmetrically opposite the obstacle represented by the Atlantic Ocean to the west.

One could see how Columbus, however, convinced by his discoveries that he had reached the lands of Alpha and Omega, that is, where the far west is one with the far east, thought of situating in the New World of the Blessed the Earthly Paradise, near a great river with abundant waters, such as the Orinoco.

Other questions and theories discussed in those centuries — which we need mention only briefly here — concerned first the hilly nature and sponginess of the dry land (sponginess being a way to explain the existence of springs and the flow of continental waters) and then the more general issue of the relationship between the continental masses and the surface covered with water (and their respective heights/depths).

It is common knowledge that Columbus always maintained that his project was not hard to carry out because the actual extent of the watery surfaces was, according to him, less than what many authorities supposed. But opinions in this matter were divided. Objectors and detractors on either side could find arguments in the theories of scholars and the Fathers of the Church. Almost certainly this was one of the topics most hotly disputed before the Catholic Sovereigns in the debates of which Alessandro Geraldini speaks.

Finally, the passage in which Columbus claims that the earth is not a perfect sphere and that there are hills and swellings on its surface need not be interpreted as prescient anticipation of the now generally accepted geoid theory. It is merely an echo of themes related to the existence and location of the Earthly Paradise (as we have seen); to the possible difference between the depths of the waters and the heights of the dry land; to the structure of the latter; and to the swelling of the sphere due to the effect of the rising of the waters' surface — all recurrent issues in geographical and cosmographical discussions during the Middle Ages.

What is certain, and more relevant for the history of cartography, is the fact that these centuries' representational models of the earth that were far from accurate proved very persistent. They found expression in illustrations and miniatures in books (reproducing texts of classical or later authors) or in works of a theological and religious nature, as well as in pictures of various kinds.

In addition to these models (it is very difficult to say, given what we know, whether or not there were also examples of regional cartography), there were the innumerable rumors and legends about unknown or little known lands. Some of these were held to be uninhabited and uninhabitable, as stated earlier (although, once doubt was cast upon the principle of Aristotelian physics that heavy objects fall toward the center of the earth, it became easy, if not necessary, to admit either the existence of human beings at the *antipodes*, or the possibility of ships sailing to the southern hemisphere and returning from there). Other lands were held to be inhabited by strange and monstrous people.

This occurred particularly in the West, at the popular level and in religious circles, since the Church had repudiated much of the classical cultural tradition — especially the scientific tradition — partly in order to combat more effectively the ancient pagan religions and their rites. The Byzantines in the East, on the contrary, had contributed much to the preservation of the Alexandrian scientific heritage. In addition to Hellenic sources, the learned men of that world made use of Egyptian, Syrian, Hebrew, and Arabic ones (the latter had begun to spread in the ninth century, after the Arabs went back to the Greek culture of the Alexandrian period and therefore took up again the astronomical and geographical theories of that era, including the theory that the earth was round).

The works of the Byzantines, however, were written in Greek, and those of the Islamic in Arabic — two languages hard to understand, which impeded or limited to a great extent the spread of these writings in the West. Therefore few borrowings from sciences like astronomy, cosmography, and geography made it from the Eastern to the Western Mediterranean after the year 1000. Very succinctly, one could state that one of the strong suits of non-Western scholarship was the discovery and revisitation of Aristotle's works (which in the twelfth century would be translated into Latin). Such borrowings, like others (albeit not many), arrived directly from Arabic culture, and were accepted into scientific thought, which Scholasticism strove to systematize in a way that was compatible with the truths of the Christian faith which, rooted in Revelation, had no need of demonstration, but were open to scientific corroboration, thus letting the ancient authorities retain their full worth.

Hence the ambiguity, not to say the backwardness, of cartographic works about the earth in the last centuries of the Middle Ages: they were unable to break away from the stereotypical models established by tradition even though contemporary culture accepted new factors, arising from the experiences of travelers (especially in Asia) and from the reading of nautical charts. Because of the difficulty, or even the impossibility, of reconciling these "novelties" with the general principles affirmed by Aristotelian theory as well as Church doctrine (which accepted and justified many medieval prejudices), the findings of travel and navigation experiences could only be expressed in a radically new kind of cartography, based on the concreteness of direct observation, a cartography that would, among other things, allow, or at least facilitate, the transition from a worldwide scale to a chorographic, that is, regional, one.

3) *Innovations in nautical cartography*

From a certain point of view one can say that medieval nautical charts were still substantially wedded to the idea that the earth is a flat disc. Or rather, since maps were intended for eminently practical use, this issue was simply ignored; map makers had no interest in systems of projection and knew very little about them, or perhaps nothing at all. In other words the cartographer's objective was to represent whatever he, or rather the navigator, had seen, basing his work on this information. Further considerations would arise later at various times, whenever the material of nautical charts was to become part of *mappaemundi* or representations of very large expanses of the earth's surface.

The bibliography of medieval nautical cartography is extremely large, and it becomes even larger if we include publications that refer to subsequent production in modern times. There are a good many questions concerning various bibliographic topics, and some, wholly or in part, are still open. It will be necessary to make fairly detailed references to these questions, either because of the close connection between this kind of cartography and navigation, or, especially, because Columbus made use of it, and even worked at producing it himself, as we shall see.

In the past century and in the early years of the twentieth, decisive contributions to the study of medieval nautical charts were made by Lelewel, Peschel, Breusing, Fiorini, Wagner, Gelcich, D'Albertis, Steger, Kretschmer, Magnaghi, and De Reparaz, among those authors who treated this subject from a general point of view, discussing its various problems. And before the middle of the nineteenth century excellent collections of reproductions were first provided by Santarem, followed by Jomard, Marcel, and Nordenskiöld. In Italy the catalog of Uzielli and Amat di Sanfilippo was, for the time [1882-4], carefully edited.

Among the more recent works the contributions by Almagià, Caraci, and Revelli should be mentioned. Outside Italy, even the shortest reference list should include the works of La Roncière, Skelton, and Pelletier. Finally, the writings of Baldacci and Quaini are most recent, while Randles provides a useful, though perhaps too rapid, synthesis of the major problems still open today.

It seems expedient to mention right away those topics that do not pose particular problems (or about which consensus has been reached). Others will be barely sketched at this stage, and considered at greater depth in later discussions.

There is little uncertainty, for instance, about the materials used and the techniques of execution. Nautical charts were hand-drawn on sheep vellum. The larger ones took up an entire pelt, preserving all of its characteristics and dimensions, i.e., a rectangular shape longer on one end (corresponding to the animal's neck), where it forms the so-called *linguetta* [small tongue] or *umbilicus*; the opposite end was generally attached to a stick around which it was rolled (this explains the tears now visible, caused by forcible attempts to detach it). Of course smaller charts, depicting less extensive areas of sea and land, have other shapes (though still generally rectangular). These were mounted on wooden tablets or cardboard and met a different fate as far as preservation is concerned.

Following the tanning process, the parchment was treated and prepared in a timely manner, according to a procedure that was fully illustrated around the year 1600 by Crescenzio in his *Carta da Navigare* [*Chart for Sailing*], later inserted into the *Mediterranean Navigation*. (It has been summarized more recently by Magnaghi). To bleach its inner side (the side on which the design was to be traced) and to make it smooth, the vellum was rubbed with white lead and dried with a white cloth. Then the left-over skin bits were boiled in water until the mixture became thick and viscous. Another cloth (or a sponge) soaked in this fluid was then passed all over the well-stretched parchment. Once dry, this was rubbed with white lead a second time so as to render the surface perfectly white and smooth, eliminating any unevenness that might impede drawing or writing. The outer side, on the other hand, was left thick and rough, thus serving to protect the chart, at least partly, from temperature variations, humidity, and salinity.

The largest charts are those that depict not only the entire basin of the Mediterranean and Black Sea but also the eastern coasts of the Atlantic Ocean, insofar as they were known. As Magnaghi pointed out, these could reach as much as 130-150 centimeters [4-5 feet] in length by 70-90 [2-3 feet] in width. Often times, however, a map would be subdivided among different pages (often four and sometimes more), so that the collection amounted to a veritable small atlas (a term that would come into use only around the end of the sixteenth century). It is possible that the larger charts — which were rolled up, as was said earlier, and thus liable to curl, tear, and in general deteriorate — survived in smaller numbers than the atlases and the minor, casual collections of single-sheet maps, which were not rolled up and could be better protected.

Coastal outlines were drawn in black ink (more or less oxidized today, as it is natural) and contrasted on the inside by a thin color strip. The continents must have been done originally in yellow-gold (all colors have undergone alterations) with green or red reserved for some of the peninsulas. Islands, however, were consistently colored over their entire surfaces and in such a way as to distinguish them clearly from each other and especially from the mainland. Therefore they appear in green, blue, red, or gold, as the case may be, and the color differentiation allows one even to separate the islands belonging to Christians from those belonging to the Muslims.

The charts used to be drafted by copying from earlier prototypes, in most cases by tracing, which almost always resulted in a distortion of the coastline. The best and most accurate works, therefore, are the oldest ones, because they were copied fewer times. We have been able to reconstruct the rather complicated procedure by which the tracing was done. Crescenzio, at the beginning of the seventeenth century, reports that coastal outlines and the locations of the main geographical sites were traced with a very thin needle onto a scrap of paper laid over the example to be copied. The paper was then covered with a fine indigo powder. The sketch obtained in this manner was transferred by pencil onto the parchment — which was mounted on a frame with stretched lute or guitar strings — by holding it up to the light of the sun. The resulting pencil drawing was then redone in ink.

On the whole, the course of the shoreline ends up as a geometric, arch-like succession of protrusions and indentations. All river outlets along the way are shown as short parallel lines into the interior. All the details of the coast are generally enlarged so as to be quite evident. It is a matter of controversy, as we shall see, whether the network of "rhumb lines" and the wind roses were inserted before drawing the coasts of the mainland and the islands or afterwards, as the majority of scholars today maintains.

Similarly, there is much discussion about toponymy. For now it is sufficient to note that it was very abundant, but only along the coast, where the names of the most important sites were written in black or red. The writing is perpendicular to the coast (it reads from the sea toward the interior), except for the islands closest to the mainland, whose toponyms are oriented in the opposite direction, or, more often, placed outside the islands themselves (or omitted, when they are not the principal sites). In any case, the place names are packed close together along the entire coastal strip. This results (as Magnaghi says) in our "circumnavigation" of the Mediterranean, beginning at Gibraltar and going from left to right, for, in order to read the names, we must continually adjust the chart's position.

The wealth of information about the shoreline (for the coastal areas that were known), its morphology, and its toponymy stand in contrast to the poverty of data regarding the inland: even when mountain chains, rivers, and lakes are portrayed, the representation is sketchy (with gaps in some places) or downright crude.

Embellishments and border decorations with wind roses abound, however, especially in later works, as do town views (much enlarged), images of saints (especially on the *linguetta* or near the Holy Land), drawings of animals and rulers of faraway lands, and references to "legends," either from classical or patristic literature or from the book of Marco Polo. All these elements — as mentioned earlier — would become ever more ornate and numerous with the passage of time, especially in the sixteenth century, but they had little or no practical use whatever, other than filling in for the farthest and least known areas.

This may justify a timely distinction between "real" and "decorative" nautical charts. The real ones were intended for practical use; their decoration, if any existed, was to be austere. The majority of these were probably lost or worn out through actual on-ship usage, exposed as they must have been to salinity, variations in temperature and humidity, and tearing. The decorative ones were instead "library" or "study" editions, so to speak, intended for the learned, the powerful, and the famous. It is obvious that these charts, stored in patrician homes or monasteries, would be preserved in greater numbers. In the sixteenth century, as we shall see, it became a veritable mania of the rich to acquire and possess nautical charts, and certainly not for the purpose of navigation.

When the chart was produced by the head of a school or, better yet, a "master of the laboratory (or office)," one of its various "legends" would report the author's name, and the city and year in which it was made (a chronologically important factor, indicating how up-to-date the chart was). In this case, one was dealing with a meticulous piece of work. But most nautical charts, the result of more or less rapid retracing and copying, perhaps by apprentices or subordinates (Columbus may have been one while he was living in Liguria), are anonymous, bearing no indication whatsoever. In these works it is not uncommon to find bungled names, errors in transcription, and distortions, with captions shifted to places where they have no reason to be.

*   *   *

One last formal issue should be mentioned here, involving terminology. It concerns the use of the terms "nautical chart" and "portolans." In foreign literature, especially German, the terms are often used synonymously. This, as I have at other times had occasion to write, is a serious error, and has created widespread confusion in common parlance even in Italy (I find the French term *"cartes-portolans"* more acceptable, but still unclear and inappropriate). We know, in fact, that the portolan was a book, a literary text — even though it functioned as a sailor's guide — in which landmarks of the coastline were described, usually in minute detail.

Some of the surviving portolans have been published. It may be of interest to cite here a passage from the *Porttolano di Grazia Pauli ...*, dating from the second half of the fourteenth century (though some even older ones have also come down to us). It concerns the central portion of the Ligurian coast:

> And from Noli to Vado is five miles going north and northeast. And on the way there is an island called *Santo Eni*, and there is a port there, and one can put ashore in front of the white house.
>
> . . . . .
>
> And from Vado to Savona is five miles going north and north-east. Savona is a city and has a man-made harbor.
>
> And from Savona to the city of Genoa is 30 miles in a direction between northeast and east.
>
> . . . . .
>
> At Genoa there is a man-made harbor, and to the west a cape called the Capo di Faro, and there is a tall tower there that gives light at night.
>
> And here is how to recognize Genoa: above Genoa there is a forked mountain called *Due Fratti*. And to the east there are other mountains, with a rounded one called *Fara*, and also above Arenzano, to the west of Genoa.
>
> . . . . .
>
> And from Genoa to Capodimonte is 15 miles to the east and southeast.

This example shows, therefore, in a very obvious way, that the portolan was quite distinct from the nautical chart both in its origin and use (more on this later). Nevertheless, both were employed while sailing: the portolan primarily during the *starea* (that is, coastal navigation, in sight of land), and the map especially during the *peleggi* (that is, stretches on the high seas).

Unfortunately, a certain lack of precision in the nomenclature of nautical charts goes back as far as the centuries in which they were first used. The documents published by Revelli, and others preserved in the State Archives of Genoa, speak generally of *charta pro navegando* [chart for navigation]. In other places one finds the term *tabula*, which does not seem accurate. Some authors use *compasso*. In modern times they have also been called *carte a bussola* (*Kompasskarten* in German). To me it seems more apt to call them "medieval nautical charts" (even if they are works from the early centuries of the modern period), in order to distinguish them, by the first adjective, from the works of hydrographers of today or of recent centuries. Moreover, in modern usage the term "map" still refers to any kind of drawing that depicts all or a part of the earth's surface. This happens in other languages also, except in English, where the word "chart" refers generally to a nautical drawing, in opposition to a "map," that is, a drawing of the earth.

In any case, nautical charts and portolans were irreplaceable tools on board ship, and were used conjointly for navigation, as I shall discuss later in greater detail. For now we should emphasize that for several reasons medieval nautical cartography has an important place in the thousand-year history of picturing and measuring the earth: first, because it was a specific product of the Mediterranean basin, that is to say, one of the most intensely sailed and traveled, and hence best known, marine areas of the time. This knowledge was reflected in the various cartographic documents, of which it was the essential part. Moreover, these maps were the products of the daily experience of pilots, ships' captains, and sailors, an experience accumulated with a great sense of realism and concreteness, and one that laid aside, or was even totally unaware of, any preceding speculative theorizing. Finally, they were the work of artisans (all the charts of which we are speaking are handmade), which, by gathering together a great bundle of practical information, represented a radical innovation in the history of cartography, inasmuch as they were based on life on the sea.

4) *From the Mediterranean portolans to representations of the entire known world*

What the scholars of the past, especially Nordic and German ones, called the standard portolan — that is, the nautical chart most commonly used in the late Medieval Ages — was an inclusive depiction of the Mediterranean basin, along with the entire Black Sea and a small section of the Red Sea; the Atlantic coasts of Western Europe were usually shown as far as the English Channel and British Isles and those of West Africa as far as the shoreline opposite the Canary Islands. This was so whether the depiction was divided up among several sections, as was mentioned earlier, or the nautical chart was only a part of the whole.

The Black Sea, the Aegean, and the Eastern Mediterranean in general are shown fairly accurately (sometimes even remarkably so), with a great abundance of place names, even in the earliest charts known to us, for example, those from the beginning of the fourteenth century. This documents how well acquainted the Genoese and Venetian sailors were with these basins, to which they traveled regularly. The representation of the shorelines along the western edge of the known world, on the other hand, would be extended and improved with the passing decades. Indeed, along the coasts of Africa stretches of shoreline are added, and toponyms become more frequent, as knowledge of these coasts and their offshore islands increases. In the earliest charts the coastal outline of Europe along the Atlantic and the North Sea is shown schematically to the northeast only (this is probably evidence of the maritime links that already existed in the thirteenth century between Genoa and the English Channel ports). This outline becomes more realistic, as it is greatly extended and later enriched with many more geographical features. From about 1340 Catalan cartographers depict Scandinavia almost completely, though summarily, and, finally, Andrea Bianco's nautical chart of 1448 (preserved in the Ambrosiana Library, Milan) provides what could be called an adequate drawing of the Atlantic coast from Frisia to Africa.

* * *

In these same centuries there were also attempts, however, to provide overall representations of the world and of the seas then known, by drawing on information from nautical cartography, albeit limited to its confining methods. Thus we have a group of planispheres or *mappaemundi* with characteristics quite distinct from those of nautical charts, but still in some ways connected to them or influenced by them; they attest in a very meaningful way to the progress of geographical knowledge in the last centuries of the Middle Ages. It seems expedient to mention here some of these planispheres that are particularly relevant to the topics this book tries to address. We are dealing here with works of the pre-Columbian era, and in particular with that period of time that extends up to the middle of the fifteenth century or not long thereafter. And the inclusion of a Mediterranean nautical chart into a planisphere (or something like a planisphere) is the closest thing to the transition from practical navigation to geographic theory.

Overview maps, comparable to planispheres by virtue of their comprehensive depiction of all the lands then known, appear as early as the atlases of Pietro Vesconte and other works attributable to him. It would be well to point out here that, for ease of expression and comprehension, I prefer the terms *mappamundi* or "planisphere" to the word *oikumene* (more or less circular) proposed by Baldacci, especially since, for consistency's sake, one would have to say "depiction of the *oikumene*" (from a Eurocentric point of view, obviously). Similarly, because it seems too academic to me, I do not use the word *geomap*, invented by the same author. Throughout my work, I do not differentiate between *mappamundi* and "planisphere," which are traditionally equivalents, after all, in Italy, when in reality the former word, so widespread because of the Vulgar Latin *mappa mundi* (= map of the world), is not entirely appropriate, given the strong reduction scale ratio of these works (in contrast to the modern meaning of *mappa* in Italian), and when, likewise, it would be better to speak of "planispheres" to imply the depiction of the whole world in a single flat drawing. Still, I fear that the distinction Baldacci makes — though relevant — between an *amappamondo*, which gives (or ought to give) the entire picture of the globe, and a "planisphere," which properly shows only a portion of it, will only result in more confusion for the reader.

One of these planispheres, then, is found even among the maps of Marin Sanudo's *Liber secretorum fidelium*; the maps were inserted into the book that the Venetian presented to Pope John XXII in September 1321 in Avignon (the manuscript is now preserved in the Vatican Apostolic Library, Rome), in order to illustrate his plan for a new crusade. Today almost all scholars agree that these maps are the work of Pietro Vesconte, a Genoese, even though he almost certainly executed them in Venice (Plate IV).

The image of the world shown in it, with the east on top, goes well beyond the area usually represented in medieval nautical charts, including as it does a rough depiction of Asia with a single large peninsula and a few islands. But at the margins of the circumference the sixteen wind roses (or rather, parts thereof, since only the rhumb lines aimed toward the middle, eight for each rose, are shown) recall the methods of nautical cartography, as does the wind rose in the middle of the circle right over Jerusalem.

The Holy Land, therefore, is still the center of the earth and thus re-echoes themes from the geographical and cosmographical culture, mentioned earlier. Also, it shows that Vesconte obviously harkened back to the work of the Minorite friar, Fra Paolino, who was a Venetian, author of a treatise *De Mapa Mundi*, apostolic penitentiary, and papal councillor on questions of this sort (the influence of this person on the geography and cartography of the time should, it seems to me, be studied again and reevaluated). But the man who drew this planisphere (that is, Vesconte) must have also taken into account the information about Asia in general that was brought back by Christian missionaries, and that provided by Marco Polo about the "kingdom of Cathay." Moreover, the "legends" reveal affinities with Pierre d'Ailly's work, which, as we have seen, was probably known to Christopher Columbus. Also attributable to the innovations of medieval nautical cartography, in addition to the wind roses, is the precision and care with which the shoreline of the countries bordering the Mediterranean is drawn. The Atlantic coasts of southwestern Europe and the British Isles are also depicted with notable accuracy.

On the other hand, references to the activity of the clergyman from Pavia, Opicino de Canistris, do not seem very pertinent with regard to these works. His representations of short coastal stretches are of high quality and his depictions of cities have undoubted descriptive originality, but they alternate with very inaccurate cartographic drawings of the whole and especially with interpretations inspired by medieval symbolism and musings, sometimes mystical and at other times anatomical and sexual. Moreover, no one has ever been able to demonstrate a sure collaborative link between him and any cartographers, either Genoese or Venetian, even granting that he did learn to "illuminate books" in Genoa, where he stayed from 1316 to 1318. It is certainly to him that we owe anthropomorphic (so to say) depictions of Europe and other areas of the earth, but he himself declared that he was not a cartographer (at least not a professional one, it should be understood) and that he did not know how nautical charts were put together. As Astengo pointed out, he seems to have had to examine them long and hard, as he evidently did when dwelling over an explanation of how to use a scale in calculating distances.

As for Vesconte's techniques in making planispheres, something (though nothing definitive) can be learned from what Revelli called the "diagram for constructing a map," sketched on the back cover plate of Vesconte's volume produced in 1318, perhaps in Venice, and now kept in the Austrian National Library in Vienna. This sketch depicts a circle divided into sixteen equal arcs, each measuring 22 1/2°. The arcs are bound by as many fragments of wind roses of eight rhumb lines (heretofore I use the terms rhumb and wind as synonymous), of which the middle one converges in the center of the drawing, where the complete main rose lies.

The meaning of the horizontal white stripes drawn toward the center and beyond the edge of the circle is uncertain. Among the various hypotheses Revelli formulated in this regard, I think the most likely is that they indicate the boundaries of one or more "climates" on the earth's surface, thereby re-echoing themes from earlier cultural theories. I add only that the smaller circles, possibly representing the stars — upon which variations in climate depended — are drawn on the sides, and are similar to the ones appearing also in the drawings appended to Columbus's *Postille*. Even though I agree, on the whole, with Pagani — who has devoted an excellent work to Pietro Vesconte, in which some of Revelli's hypotheses are judged "a bit strained" — I still believe, on the one hand, that this sketch reiterates the idea of the roundness of the earth as a body independent of cosmological systems, and, on the other, that the wind roses show it to be a work that paved the way for early fourteenth-century nautical cartography.

* * *

The so-called World Map (or planisphere) by Father Giovanni Mauro da Carignano dates from the same period as, or little later than, these world maps of Vesconte (of whom I will speak again later, as the maker of individual nautical charts). Like Vesconte, Giovanni Mauro was a Genoese, but he spent his entire life, we can safely say, in the capital city, where he was the rector of the church of San Marco al Molo, which still exists (although enlarged and remodeled beginning in 1510). Unfortunately his map no longer exists; kept in the State Archives in Florence, whence it was sent to Naples for an exhibition, it was destroyed during the bombardments of the Second World War. Fortunately it may still be studied via the photographs that had been taken before that time (Plate V).

Revelli has inventoried the documents in the Capitular Archives of San Lorenzo and the State Archives of Genoa. These documents indicate that the clergyman took over the church of San Marco in 1291, and that he must have died between September 1, 1329 and May 6, 1330 (Giovanni Mauro and his works had already been studied by Ferretto, who also tracked down information about his father and two brothers, one a *physicus* [scientist], the other a notary and schoolmaster). Still, very little is known about his cartographic activities outside this one map, which Revelli calls a "sea and land" map, and bears the identifying inscription *Presbiter Joannes rector sancti marci de Janua me fecit* [Father John, Rector of St. Mark's in Genoa, made me] in the area of the Baltic.

As it is known, St Mark's church was in the heart of the harbor at that time. In the rectory that Giovanni Mauro had had built one room was reserved for receiving the admirals of the Genoese fleet. Beside it, in a suitable pavilion, the preparatory gatherings before a ship's departures were held. Nearby, therefore, on city property, there were shops belonging to coopers and oarmakers (who came from the Aveto valley). The rector himself kept, in his church, in his houses, and in the adjacent cemetery, a great quantity of sails, spars, rudders, shrouds, and other sailing gear, having rented space to the merchants. In 1314 the archbishop, Porchetto Spinola, would challenge him on this improper use of ecclesiastical property, but the priest appealed to the papal curia and kept up his habitual ways.

The time frame for Giovanni Mauro's cartographic activity is uncertain. Some have wanted to claim that it started in 1303, when a Tatar or Armenian embassy passed through Genoa, or better yet, in 1306, when ambassadors from Prester John, sent to an Iberian king and to the pope in Avignon, stopped over in Genoa for a time before leaving for Rome. Seventeenth century tradition, which tends to confuse the inhabitants of Ethiopia and Asia (as often happened at that time), reports that Giovanni Mauro obtained knowledge from them about their countries and, in particular, about the places and customs of Central Asia. La Roncière, as we shall see, emphasizes the information the priest received "out of the depths of the Sahara" from a Genoese businessman; perhaps these data came from several merchants. The number of Africa-related elements that appear in his planisphere certainly reflects Genoa's intense and frequent links with that world (about which more will have to be said). Much less certain is the assertion, also from the seventeenth century, that Giovanni Mauro wrote a book as well, based on information given by the ambassadors of the king of the Ethiopians — could this book, described as *mappam in quo de huius generis conditione multa conscripsit* [the map in which he wrote about the condition of a lot of these things], be the very planisphere of which we are speaking?

We know for certain of only one journey of his, which he made between April 16 and November 19, 1316, but it seems to have had no connection to any cartographic activity. It turns out, in fact, that he intended to leave for Sicily on some business matters and go on to the Roman curia [still in Avignon] in order to pursue some appeals he had undertaken.

Magnaghi, too, is uncertain about whether to date this planisphere before or after 1325. Works of Bagrow and Skelton place it in the year 1319. Baldacci leans towards 1320-1325, because the Aragonese coat of arms already appears on the island of Sardinia. This issue matters little, however, compared to the fact that the first decades of the fourteenth century saw a work of great technical perfection and high cultural value, worthy of our greatest attention, come out of Genoese circles.

In actuality the "World Map of Father Giovanni Mauro" results clearly divided into two sections. The central part is a nautical chart, comparable in some ways to the *Carta Pisana* of which I shall speak later. At the outer edges the countries of Northern Europe, Asia, and Africa are drawn with much less precision (they are sometimes barely indicated). Only a very tiny portion of the Atlantic is shown, almost as if to demonstrate the dearth of knowledge about this basin at the time the chart was made, not to mention the scarce interest felt in sailing the high seas there (even the depiction of the British Isles is distorted, and the Baltic appears as a long, narrow gulf). This is in contrast to the precision and detail with which the coasts and islands of the Mediterranean are drawn, with a fairly accurate outline of the Italian peninsula (which recalls in some ways the planisphere *de mari et de terra* believed to be by Vesconte as indicated earlier), and a basically correct siting of the three major offshore islands.

Revelli has declared the work of Giovanni Mauro to be the oldest nautical chart "with information about the land's interior" and the first document "in which there appears a phrase concerning the scale of miles (by the left margin)." In point of fact, a scale of distances was already present in the *Carta Pisana* (in the National Library of Paris), but that chart lacks features about the interior of the continents, as does the Carta di Cortona (in the Library of the Etruscan Academy in that city). The scale, as calculated by Revelli (evidently only for the Mediterranean area), is, with the usual approximation, 1:5,500,000. The wind roses, arranged in two crowns of sixteen each (the central one is east of Sicily), are without decoration, and their rhumb lines are colored black, green, and red. There are numerous city coats-of-arms, as well as many cartouches, of which more than a few are in the area of the Sahara Desert. One of these, rather long, provides information obtained from a Genoese merchant who stayed in Sijilmasa; it says that the Tuareg people, who wear veils, engaged in trade between that town and the center of the kingdom of Ghana, south of the Atlas mountains (confirming La Roncière's reference, reported earlier).

If the definition given earlier for this document as "intermediate" between nautical chart and land map is justified, the wealth of information about Africa with its "sandy desert» (this inscription appears four times) stimulates other reflections about the geographical knowledge of this part of the world that was available in Genoa in the early decades of the fourteenth century. In the first place, as previously mentioned, there must have been more than one gold-seeking merchant who traded with Africa beyond the Atlas mountains, and who could provide information. Moreover, the name of *Carena*, foreign to the classical tradition, is used to designate the central and eastern portions of the Atlas range. This word comes from Saracens and would appear in a great many later maps, though some scholars have erroneously declared that it was introduced by Catalan cartographers.

More complicated questions have to do with the Atlantic coast of this continent, where a deeply indented gulf is depicted. On its northern shore are found the words *Gozola* and *regnum Gozolae*. One is immediately reminded of the place, with the same name, in whose waters the ships of the Vivaldi brothers were last seen after they left Genoa in that same year of 1291, right at the time Giovanni Mauro da Carignano was settling in at the church of San Marco. In several fifteenth-century nautical charts, to be sure, the term *Gazolla* would appear in more or less the same location, whereas on the planisphere attributed, with so many arguments and reservations, to the Columbus brothers, *Cazola* is identified with Cape Bojador.

Nonetheless, in Giovanni Mauro's drawing the stretch of African coast familiar to Mediterranean navigators, where the toponym *Saffi* appears, is quite far south, well beyond this locality. Thus it cannot be denied that the Ligurian cartographer knew many facts about the coastline and its morphology, even though I do not share entirely all of Revelli's theses about Genoese sailors being the first to sail along it. How else did Giovanni Mauro know of the existence of a long river in the interior (perhaps the Senegal, or better, the Niger), part of whose course he showed, with an island in it that the cartouche describes *as insula palola ubi aurum colligitur* [the island of Palola, where gold is collected] (note that the expression *aurum de paiola* appears in a notarized Genoese cartulary list of charters from as early as the second half of the twelfth century).

The entire territory south of the Atlas mountains is outside the area covered by the system of wind roses, as are a great part of Northern Europe facing the Baltic and the fringes of Asia beyond the Caucasus (approximately). As regards Northern Europe, this is the first attempt we know of — sketchy as it may be — to draw it in a non-Ptolemaic configuration, with the Baltic Sea vastly elongated from west to east, as stated earlier, and a Scandinavian Peninsula that ends in three fingers of land. The distortions in the depiction of these northern lands (which in this case contrasts with the wealth of elements shown for the inland nations of Central Europe), and of those of other marginal areas — a recurrent factor in medieval cartography — have been explained by the fact that very little space was left on the parchment for showing the lands farther out, once the Mediterranean basin had been accurately drawn.

Perhaps something similar could be said, in this case, for the depiction of Asia as well, which is very incomplete. Apart from the wealth of features concerning the Holy Land, the Eastern Mediterranean, and the Anatolian Peninsula, the innovations in this part of the document include the representation of the Arabian Peninsula and the Persian Gulf, into which the Tigris and Euphrates drain. Coats-of-arms, views of cities, and place names are quite numerous here as well, even in the land's interior, whereas the depiction of territories farther east is reduced to a few elementary indications (some tears in the parchment also lessen our opportunity for observation and discussion).

For Quaini, Giovanni Mauro da Carignano's work is the trunk of a family tree that tended toward a synthesis of medieval world maps and nautical charts, a synthesis "made easier by the fact that the products of nautical cartographers, especially those made for scholars and famous people, had constantly enlarged their depictions to include the interior regions," with "a considerable quantity of elements and geographical features."

No observations or considerations of importance for this study have come out of the essays of other authors, such as Almagià, Baldacci, Caraci, and Pagani. Baldacci, for instance, affirms that the work of Giovanni Mauro da Carignano is "an important geomap," while Pagani stresses its originality among coeval works of nautical cartography, on account of the information it gives "about the interior parts of the regions," the ornamentation, the inscriptions, and the presence of an explanation of the scale (today only partially legible). He also points out, however, its relative lack of toponyms, written on the area depicting the sea, since the interior is loaded with other symbols.

* * *

At this point it would be well to consider how the contribution of nautical cartography, on the one hand, and the general progress of knowledge due to reports of travelers, missionaries, and merchants, on the other, were reflected in the last centuries of the Middle Ages in successive planispheres and documents that aimed at depicting the entire known world of the time. This is how the transition from medieval to renaissance cartography took place, thanks to the diverse contributions from travelers and navigators, whose experiences varied according to time and place.

Over a period of more than a century, in fact (beginning with the work of Father Giovanni Mauro), a number of similar documents, worthy of mention for a variety of reasons, marked the stages of this process. In order not to go beyond the range of this study, however, I shall be able to mention only some of them (especially since they are generally outside the Genoese tradition and only in part — though substantially — influenced by nautical cartography).

For example, it will be sufficient, for now at least, to mention only in passing the map of the known world made in Mallorca in 1339 by Angellino Dulcert and preserved in Paris at the National Library. According to Nordenskiöld and other foreign scholars, this was the prototype, or one of the prototypes, of the so-called "Catalan school." According to Italian scholars who have studied the matter, Dulcert was none other than the Genoese, Angelino (or Angellino) Dalorto, who had moved to the Balearic Islands; I shall have occasion to speak more of him later.

The world map contained in the anonymous work known as the "Medici Atlas" (in the Laurentian-Medicean Library, Florence), dating back to 1351, seems to have very few links with nautical chart-making, except for the fair degree of precision and detail of the coastal outline of the Mediterranean and the Black Sea. I do not, however, share Revelli's opinion (which has not found much of a following) that it could have been made by a Genoese. To prove the contrary it would suffice to point to the summary way in which the Atlantic coasts of Africa are shown, even along the northern stretches (the depiction of the southern part is comparatively better). The evidence is also too feeble to support the thesis of those who see Catalan influences here.

In another group of significant world maps from the second half of the fourteenth century the *mappamundi* in the Catalan Atlas is especially well known (it is preserved in Paris at the National Library); dating from 1375, it is attributed to the Majorcan, Abraham Cresques. It should be compared to the 1339 map mentioned earlier and to the so-called *Catalan mappamundi*, kept respectively in Modena (in the Estense Library) and in Florence (National Library; the latter is attributed to Jafudà Cresques).

These works have in common the adoption and utilization of many features typical of nautical cartography, but with a new and appreciable consideration of the geography of the interior of continents, with particular attention to the Asian and African world. Therefore, in addition to views of cities, they include figures of certain animals and long didactic inscriptions, the outline — albeit sketchy — of mountain chains and rivers, and the representation of numerous tents with the images of rulers, whose varying skin colors attest to the differentiation of the human races. The depiction of the western coasts of Africa stops at the Gulf of Guinea, which is schematized and imperfectly portrayed, and thus shows no progress — indeed represents something of a regression, all considered — compared to Genoese works. The Baltic still appears as a narrow gulf, but its coastal outline is articulated in some places. The lands to the north of it take on an almost triangular shape, which will remain traditional in many later maps.

Mention should also be made of the fragment of a planisphere from about 1380 that is preserved in Istanbul (at the Topkapi Sarayi Kutuphané); it bears the usual system of "rhumb lines" and the depiction (typical of Catalan works) of a caravan crossing Asia (the latter, however, is one of the features that prove the influence of Marco Polo's descriptions). Also, today we have lost track of Albertino de Virga's Venetian world map of 1411-1415, since no one knows where it is preserved; it amounts to a typical "compromise between the classical medieval world map and the nautical chart" (in Wieser's definition; Destombes points out in it the influence of the nautical charts of the Genoese and Catalan schools). The world maps of Giovanni Leardo, dating from the fifth and sixth decades of the fifteenth century, belong to the Adriatic school of cartography (they can be found in the Municipal Library in Verona, the Bertoliana Civic Library in Vicenza, and the American Geographical Society Collection of the University of Wisconsin respectively). They are rich in typical motifs from medieval tradition and echoes of Marco Polo's descriptions, but they also have some similarities to the so-called "Catalan maps." The latter, however, are on the whole among the farthest removed from nautical cartography, because of the schematic nature of their coastal outlines and the space given over to the continents (including areas uninhabited "due to heat" or "due to cold," according to the theory of the "subdivision of climates;" the southern continent is greatly developed south of the Gulf of Guinea and the Horn of Africa). Finally, and still in this context, only a brief mention need be made of Andreas Walsperger's world map, made in Constance in 1448 and preserved in Rome (at the Vatican Apostolic Library); it is expressly written on it that the "geometric description of the orb" is computed according to the "cosmography of Ptolemy, in a proportional way, reflecting longitudes, latitudes and the distinction of climates," but that a "true and complete chart for navigation on the seas" has also been taken into account. According to Destombes, however, "the drawing of the coastlines does not derive from nautical charts" (as proved by the fact, among others, that the Baltic is shown as a closed sea). We may conclude that this, like any other similar work, was only influenced by nautical cartography, indirectly and partially, since there were also other features and models to draw upon.

* * *

Basically, the broadening of knowledge concerning Northern Europe, Africa, and especially Asia was reflected in fuller and more complete representations of the lands then known. But it was impossible to ignore certain elements of medieval theories (such as, for instance, the division of the globe into climatic zones), and attempts were made to align them with the principles of Ptolemaic geography. His works, first translated into Latin in the early decades of the fifteenth century, would circulate with ever increasing frequency around western Europe and, with the passage of time, would become better and better known through printed editions (we shall see that fully formed planispheres inspired by them go back to the last decades of the fifteenth century). At the same time, however, it was impossible not to make use of the products of nautical cartography for the Mediterranean and adjacent waters, as well as for nearby lands. The central portion of many planispheres of the time — as pointed out earlier — was derived, indeed copied, from a nautical chart. To this category belong two great Italian cartographic documents that introduce us, as it were, at a distance, to the Columbian age.

The so-called "anonymous Genoese world map" (preserved in the National Library in Florence) goes back to 1457 (it seems the most reliable figure of all the various readings given for the second to last digit of the date). It is elliptical, or lens-shaped, and became famous when a scholar, fifty years ago, tried to identify it with the well-known "sailing chart" of Paolo dal Pozzo Toscanelli. This was said to have been sent to Portugal in 1474, with a later copy given to Columbus, who would have used it as a guide on his first journey to the New World. This theory triggered a dispute that led to a careful examination of the document and a more thorough critical discussion of its characteristics. I shall take into account the examination and the discussion later, rather than at this point, especially as there still remain strong doubts (in my opinion) about the authenticity of the correspondence between the Genoese navigator and the Florentine sage (doubting even that they ever corresponded) (see Plate VI).

The document's elliptical shape is unusual for the period to which it belongs, but this does not seem significant; in all probability it was adopted simply in order to allow for a better representation of the lands and seas farthest to the west and especially to the east. In the latter direction, that is, for the area depicting Asia, the drawing is still decidedly Ptolemaic in substance, but the mapmaker shows evidence of having set great store by the descriptions brought back by Nicolò de' Conti about the Spice islands in the East, along with information confirming that it was possible to reach them by circumnavigating Africa.

Precisely because Poggio Bracciolini, secretary of Pope Eugene IV, was in Florence when he heard the story of the Venetian traveler's excursions into Asia, it has been supposed, on the one hand, that the world map of which we are speaking was made in the Tuscan capital, and, on the other hand, that its maker was Paolo dal Pozzo Toscanelli, who would have obtained his information about the East from Nicolò de' Conti on that occasion. It is quite true that various sources of the time attest to the Florentine physicist's interest in everything that concerned new geographical knowledge and that we know for sure of a world map that he borrowed for a long period of time, from 1459 to 1484, returning it "quite spoiled and ruined" (it belonged to a patrician family in Florence, the Castellani), but no one has never known anything about his possible work as a cartographer, and there is no proof that the document lent to him was the same anonymous one dated 1457. All we know for sure is that the former was "shown to certain ambassadors of the King of Portugal" in 1459 (or earlier).

Almost all scholars continue to believe that the world map is Genoese, especially since it bears the coat-of-arms (a red cross on a silver field) of Genoa — even though Venice is shown as the most important city in Italy and there is no city view of the Ligurian capital. The other coat-of-arms must be that of the patrician family for whom the map was made; it could have belonged to one of the branches of the Spinola family (the checkerboard band is very frequent in the coats-of-arms of Genoese noble families) — for example to the Spinolas of Luccoli, who had married into another clan. On this paper reproduction, which may be a copy, the drawing of the coat-of-arms seems quite distorted; in any case, it seems difficult to believe, as has sometimes been supposed, that the two ends of this band represent two castle towers, suggesting a coat-of-arms belonging to the Castellani Florentine family.

Various discussions have also arisen over the inscription (or title): *Hec est vera cosmographorum cum marino accordata descricio, quorundam frivolis naracionibus rejectis* ("this is the true description reconciled with *marino*, the frivolous narrations of certain cosmographers having been rejected"). The entire content of the document leads one to exclude the identification of *marino* with Marinus of Tyre, to whom the only truly valid reference here would concern the dimensions of the known world, or rather its proportions, on the north-south and west-east axes). Unacceptable also is the reference to Marin Sanudo, whose work — which in reality was produced by Pietro Vesconte, as stated earlier — differs from this one in a number of significant ways. The remaining possibility is that the name refers to a sailor and maker of nautical charts. If what we have here were a copy rather than an original (a hypothesis that is anything but unlikely, as we have seen), we could theorize that during the copying of the inscription the word *charta* occurring before *marino* was accidentally dropped, and that the original reference was to a nautical chart, as has been ascertained in the case of Andreas Walsperger's world map.

The earth as shown in this document stretches from the western part of the Atlantic Ocean — including the British Isles, the Azores, Madeira, and the Canary Islands — to Africa, shown with a sizeable gulf and extending eastward to the Indian Ocean, which opens to the south; the southern coast of Asia forms three gulfs, with two large islands in front of the easternmost one. Mountains, rivers, and cities are drawn in the land's interior, and the names of countries and regions are reported in red. Moreover, there are numerous cartouches and inscriptions, as well as flags with coats-of-arms.

The north is at the top, and there is no wind rose, but an incomplete system of "rhumb lines" is delineated in red. Outside the frame of the map are two small distance scales, in gradations of 50 and 100 miles respectively. Of the various pictures, the most notable are isolated trees in north-east Asia and images of princes and rulers in Asia and Africa, not to mention animals (an elephant and a camel in Africa, and fish in the Indian Ocean).

Evidently, as Destombes points out, various sources were used: one or more nautical charts for the Mediterranean, the Black Sea, and western Europe; Ptolemy's *Geography* for the Nile and, especially, its springs; a medieval world map for many other features. But the source most used for southern Asia is the one already mentioned, by Nicolò de' Conti, from the waters of India to the islands of Ceylon and 'Taprobane' (Ptolemy's name for either Ceylon or Sumatra), the two 'Javas' (Java and Borneo), and the Moluccas, considered to be the extreme edge of the world, beyond which contrary winds made sailing impossible.

A route for circumnavigating Africa in order to reach the Spice Islands of Asia is also shown (even though it is now difficult in places to make out the line). This shows that the document could have been useful in giving the Portuguese information about their endeavors to sail eastward, but it had nothing to do with the western route across the Atlantic that was supposedly mentioned in Toscanelli's correspondence.

One can, however, dispute the provenance (Genoese or Florentine) of this world map. But first I should note that we are not dealing here with a chart made for practical purposes, for navigation, but with a document intended for learned people, the libraries of noble families, or monasteries. Moreover, as mentioned before, the one that has come down to us is perhaps a copy. In any case, for the redaction of the original Genoese nautical charts may have been used, indeed, they almost certainly were.

Revelli has emphasized some features in it that "bring to mind the map of Giovanni da Carignano" — such as the scrolls containing the cartouches — or other Genoese nautical documents — for example, the flags over the Genoese colonies in the Black Sea and the Sea of Azov, and many place names. The latter are found not only along the coast (among them *Saphi*, that is the Saffi or Safim already mentioned, a Genoese commercial base on the north-west coast of Africa, bathed by the Atlantic), but also in the interior (again by way of example, in the Sahara south of the Atlas range, an area with which the Ligurian merchants had business dealings even before the middle of the fifteenth century). Revelli explains the lack, already mentioned, of a view of Genoa by the fact that the cartographer (or perhaps whoever retraced this work) did not have enough room, since he also wanted to depict the course of the River Po.

Nothing keeps us from supposing (though this is just a conjecture) that Columbus had seen this world map (or a least one like it) in Genoa or in Lisbon, that he had studied it, and that he had made use of it in constructing his own image of the world.

* * *

In Lisbon Columbus must certainly have seen another important cartographic document of almost the same period: the World map of Fra Mauro, a Camaldolese monk from Murano. I shall try to speak of him more succinctly, since his work is totally outside the Genoese tradition and depends only in a small way on the contributions of nautical cartography (Plate VII).

We are dealing almost certainly with a replica — in the shape of a circular planisphere — of a map, now lost, that had been commissioned to the Venetian monk by Alphonse V of Portugal while Henry the Navigator was still living. Thus it was almost certainly meant to satisfy the requirements of the navigational enterprises in which Henry was engaged, designed to reach the East by circumnavigating Africa. Albuquerque reconstructed the events by which the Portuguese ambassadors arrived in Venice while the work was still in progress, but with the drawing well advanced; they thought it mediocre, but paid for it anyway, so as not to lose the money already advanced to the cartographer. The world map was finished in August 1459 (as an inscription on the back side of the Venetian copy states) and sent to Portugal that same year (or in 1460 at the latest, if completed by the students of Fra Mauro, who had died in October 1459). A copy of it, together with other "designs and writings," remained in the monastery (in the last century it was transferred to the place where it is preserved today, the Marciana Library in Venice).

In the preparation of this work the Camaldolese monk must have been helped by Andrea Bianco; it may also have been started a few years before, perhaps in 1457, though a first draft may date to even earlier (Almagià and Caraci have discussed this point). It is oriented with the south on top and totally lacks scales and "rhumb lines," while eight roses of eight winds apiece are arranged around the edges. It belongs to the family of planispheres in which the lands are surrounded by a single sea, and it departs from Ptolemaic ideas in several of its features. The general design is, if anything, traceable to that of the maps of Marin Sanudo (that is, Pietro Vesconte), but with some innovations.

As usual the coastal outline of the Mediterranean, the Black Sea, and Western Europe takes nautical charts into account. For Scandinavia and the Baltic area the model is that of the so-called "Catalan maps." For Africa (or rather for its western coasts) Fra Mauro is generally said to have used maps of Portuguese manufacture; indeed some claim that a number of his mistakes derive from the fact that he was sent falsified maps from Portugal (among other things, he was accused of confusing miles with leagues, which is obviously impossible, since conversion tables were available to everyone). Some of the cartouche contents certainly must have reported information obtained from Portugal, such as the place where it is stated that beyond "Cape Verde the northerly wind is not found." Still on the subject, he writes that he "had frequently heard from many people that there is a column here with a hand pointing to an inscription forbidding anyone to sail beyond it... But it would have pleased me that the Portuguese, who sail this sea, would have said whether such hearsay was true, since I dare not say so myself."

Fra Mauro certainly could have utilized information about countries of Africa and Asia — even those in the interior — that was obtained in Italy from the people who came to the Council of Florence in 1451. He could, moreover, have used Arab models and sources. This last possibility is especially evident for the Indian Ocean and the lands around it, for whose depiction he markedly departed from Ptolemy's ideas. And for central Asia, and even more so for the eastern and south-eastern regions of that continent, it is obvious that, as a Venetian, he profited from the information brought back by Marco Polo (with some innovations in regard to the coastal gulfs and the hydrography) and by Nicolò de' Conti. Finally, if his interest in the Near East is in some sense traditional, it should be noted that for Fra Mauro it extends as far as Mesopotamia and Persia, reaching in his depiction north-eastern Asia on the other side.

For all its natural shortcomings, and certain defects, perhaps inevitable at that time, Fra Mauro's world map has been called "the culmination of medieval cartography." It was certainly the best product that could be provided by the geographical culture of the 1450's (enriched also by the example of nautical charts), before the revival of Ptolemaic representations which again became fashionable and circulated widely, and before the great discoveries began. The depiction of Africa and Asia that it contains shows that the former continent was thought to be circumnavigable (as it was by the maker of the anonymous Genoese *Mappamundi* of 1457), and that in both cases the major focus was on the East.

These two cultural treasures, then, appear not to have any connection with the origins of Columbus's inspiration, for which the time was not yet ripe. That was to come much later. Even if it is true that the correspondence between the Portuguese ruler and Paolo dal Pozzo Toscanelli (about which some doubts remain, as has been said) began in 1474 or slightly earlier, and even if it resulted in a world map like the one of 1457 that we have discussed (or a similar one) being sent to Lisbon; or even if it is true that Fra Mauro's world map was also sent to Portugal (which is certain) in 1459 or 1460, still neither of the two cartographic documents that we have examined can be linked to what Randles calls "Columbus's Asiatic project." Indeed given this fact, the originality of his inspiration is all the more remarkable: after seeing and studying these representations of the earth (and certainly others as well), he nonetheless foresaw the Atlantic route, which, because of a mistaken estimation of distances and of the measurements of the earth, he stubbornly believed to be the shortest way to get to the East from Western Europe.

CHAPTER II

MARITIME CULTURE
AND NAUTICAL CARTOGRAPHY
IN THE MEDITERRANEAN AND IN GENOA
FROM THE THIRTEENTH CENTURY
TO THE TIME OF COLUMBUS

1) *Nautical charts and medieval navigational techniques*

We have already spoken of the significant contribution that medieval nautical charts made to the history of cartography as well as of their originality as products of the actual experience and knowledge of Mediterranean fleets. Similarly we have pointed out that they can also be called "compass charts," inasmuch as their origin and dissemination are closely linked to the use of this instrument, which introduced radical innovations into nautical techniques.

It is well known that various peoples in antiquity were aware of the properties of magnets, or rather of magnetized needles. We know little or nothing, however, about the details, especially as regards their earliest use in nautical technology. What is known is that at the end of the twelfth century Mediterranean navigators turned them into instruments — widely adopted thereafter — that enabled them to cease confining themselves primarily to coastal routes, in sight of land — as had been true earlier — and to engage sailing routes onto the high sea.

This was happening at the very time when Western European contacts with the East had become frequent, when navigation in the Mediterranean had grown also as a result of the Crusades, and when wars for predominance in this basin had caused population migrations; information about Iceland and part of Greenland had come via the Normans, and a better understanding of the shape of Africa and the Indies had been obtained from the Arabs.

It is particularly important to note here the contribution that the use of the compass made to cartography, for it made possible a fairly accurate representation of the shape of the islands, and also the coastlines and promontories of the mainland, as one sailed past, calculating the approximate distance traveled and identifying directions following the magnetized needle. In 1580 Gregorio Giraldi, a native of Ferrara, wrote this about the compass: "using it, together with a table on which there is a drawing of the world, sailors estimate their course and measure very easily how far they have sailed." He said this even though it was possible in the sixteenth century, especially on the Atlantic, to determine distances traveled by using astronomy to establish the differential in latitude between the points of departure and arrival and then to convert the results from degrees into miles.

Some scholars have maintained that works similar to medieval nautical charts must have existed in classical times; the medieval ones, therefore, would represent an improvement over the earlier ones, thanks to the use of the compass and to a broader geographical knowledge. This was the position held by Wagner and Uhden, among others. It was easily refuted, especially by Winter, but also by others, since none of them ever saw or heard speak of any such charts. The *stadiasmi* to which Breusing refers, for example, and the *periploi*, for which we have conclusive evidence, were really only coastal guides, similar to the medieval portolans of which we offered an example earlier. They might very well have been derived from classical prototypes, though expanded over time to include many additional features.

In the case of nautical charts, however, there is no documentary basis for a similar "theory of continuity" with the classical world. On the contrary, everything points to the conclusion that, just as the introduction of the single rudder made it decisively easier to steer boats (the single rudder, which came from the North Sea, pivoted on a fitting that at first could be provided only by a metallurgy more advanced than that of the Mediterranean), so too, the use of the compass was an innovative factor in marine technology that made it possible to draw up and use nautical charts.

More decisive arguments for this last hypothesis could probably be advanced if there were better documentation about the significance of Arab contributions to marine technology in the Mediterranean and, therefore, to the origins and development of medieval nautical cartography (it has been suggested, for example, that one of Idrisi's maps, from the year 1154, was derived from an older one that depicted Sardinia complete with features typical of coastal surveys). Better argumentation would also result if we could resolve the old problem (which we will have to address again later) of whether or not, in the art of cartography, the surveying technique of various coastal stretches originated prior to the adoption of the "rhumb" system whose lines come together to form the wind roses.

I am convinced that the first nautical charts were created by assembling partial coastal surveys (this is only a personal opinion, though it is supported by personal thinking and observations, as well as considerations by previous writers), and that the surveys could be executed only through the "rhumb" system and wind roses (or, at least, that their crossreferencing became accurate enough, and hence suitable for navigation, only after the introduction of such a system to provide a frame of reference, which presupposed the use of the compass). A distinct discussion is to be reserved for charts produced later, since they implied, most of the time, the copying and updating of already complete, coastal outlines, onto which it was possible to superimpose the reticulate "rhumb" system in a separate operation (indeed this must have happened often).

The use of the magnetized needle (the "strange device" with an "iron needle," as this instrument was referred to by a Crusader in 1218) may seem simple to us, but on board a small boat like those of the Middle Ages it could present certain difficulties on rough seas, especially at night. I find the most accurate and effective description to be that of Campodonico, who sums up various pieces of evidence in this way: "At first the needle, made of iron and very thin, is threaded into a reed or straw (*calam* in Arabic) floating in a 'bay,' a wooden vessel partly filled with water... to allow the straw to display its orientation as it follows the magnetic field. But the iron needle remains magnetized for only a few moments. Hence the shipmaster is forced to use a lodestone, or true magnet, bringing it up over the needle and rotating it quickly before removing it. The needle naturally spins, following the rotation of the magnet, but when it stops it points to the North Star."

Everyone knows that the ancient Chinese were familiar with the magnet's directional property; in addition to uncertain legendary information from a very remote period, it is mentioned in sources from the second century B.C. Sailors from Amalfi undoubtedly knew and made use of it toward the end of the twelfth and beginning of the thirteenth century. Out of this came an instrument, which would then undergo successive improvements and widely spread in the fourteenth century (in the Iberian Peninsula it was called "needle for sailing").

The receptacle adopted was a square container made of wood — perhaps preferably boxwood, because it was hard and salt-resistant — with a pane of glass on the top. The word *bussola* (compass), which was used for the first time in 1294, undoubtedly came from *boxum* [boxwood] and *bossolo* (that is, a box or container), though in notarial evidence, even afterwards, we still find *acus* (needle) and *stella maris* (star of the sea). The first description of the instrument's familiar look as a whole dates from 1324. As early as 1269, however, after writing about the properties of lodestones, Petrus Peregrinus (Pierre de Maricourt) described two boxed compasses (or kinds of compasses), one with a floating magnet and the other with a needle on a pivot. In any case, the documents cited by Ferretto and Revelli show that the compass and the nautical chart were always (or almost always) present in inventories of ships' property.

The needle, in turn, came to be made of steel, so as to retain its magnetic properties over a longer period (and, thus, prevent having to repeat too often the procedure for magnetizing it). It was probably in the mid-fourteenth century that the custom spread of fastening it to a pivot, nail, or shaft of iron fixed in the center of the box. In later centuries there would even be two needles and other improvements, concerning the "star," which was drawn on a piece of heavy paper and consisted of a circle divided originally into eight sectors (corresponding to the principal winds) with the needle usually glued on the underside. It was only in the sixteenth century that it became customary to suspend this instrument in gimbals, thus enhancing its use.

In fact various kinds of compasses were assembled over time; the ones with two needles and two wind roses must have been used to compensate for magnetic declination. After the extent of declination in Atlantic waters became known, it was common practice to attach the needle under the rose not in correspondence with the North mark of the instrument but more to the west or east, depending on the angle formed by the direction of the needle and that of the geographical meridian. The Flemish compasses that were so widespread in the sixteenth century were based on this principle, whereas the Genoese and Italian ones were still wedded to the traditional system, perhaps because they were employed mostly in the Mediterranean, where the degree of declination was small. The needle could even be completely loose, that is, not glued onto the underside of the paper bearing the wind rose. This meant that if the pilot knew the value of the magnetic declination he could turn the "star" in the right direction as needed to effect the correction.

Very quickly, in any case, the eight winds originally recorded by the said sectors (each sector, therefore, being of 45°) were joined by as many "half-winds," resulting in the 16-point "rose" (each sector now being 22° 30′ wide). A later stage brought the number of points to 32 (with "quarters" and half-quarters, and sectors of 11° 15′). This, too, is an innovation typical of the Italian naval tradition: in antiquity, in fact, the Greeks used the 12-point rose (with sectors of 30°), and likewise did the Arabs later. The anonymous cosmographer from Ravenna (ca. 700 A.D.), however, had already adopted the 24-point rose. As early as the eleventh century the names of the winds also changed, with those of the classical period giving way to the adoption of the Italian names of *tramontana, levante, ostro [austro], ponente, greco, scirocco, garbino or libeccio, and maestro* (north, east, south, west, north-east, south-east, south-west, and north-west). Some of these names have their roots in Arabic; in any case their use quickly spread among the fleets of the Mediterranean.

Until late in the fifteenth century, when sailors began to observe the stars in order to determine the ship's position by the latitude, the compass was an essential instrument, and almost the only one, during voyages on the high seas, in a type of navigation that remained unchanged for a long time. Hence, nautical charts, in order to be useful to pilots, had to have a complete system of wind roses: a central one (or sometimes two, as we shall see) of sixteen winds, and a ring of as many wind roses, each with 32 winds, spaced along a circle described around the center rose, precisely at the points of intersection between the circumference and the sixteen winds radiating from the central rose. The circle, then, marked the edge, so to speak, of the area one wished to depict.

Not all 32 winds of the roses on the outer ring were recorded, however, only the odd-numbered (usually between nine and 13), those directed toward the central rose or the other outer roses, since these winds were basic in representing the area to be drawn up. Only when this area was particularly large did the chart maker resort to a system of two central roses and two outer rings (ignoring for the moment what the dual system may suggest about the origin of nautical charts, as we shall see).

In general, and especially in the sixteenth and seventeenth centuries, the wind roses were carefully illustrated with particular symbols (the lily and the Greek cross) to indicate the north and east respectively. The different colors of the various sectors of the central wind rose were extended into the lines of the winds (called "rhumb lines") that radiated from it and from the outer roses, intersecting each other so as to form a dense web. Using different hues made it possible to avoid the confusion that could have resulted from the intersection of "rhumbs" (the principal winds were usually in yellow or a dark color, the eight secondary winds — or *mezzanini* — in green or blue, and the quarter winds in red).

The use of the compass and the nautical chart with its rhumb lines system allowed the medieval pilot to solve the problem of which direction to take and follow during the voyage. This obviously presupposed that one was sailing in a straight line (in this regard, no one was then concerned with the effects of the earth's being round; we will have to wait until the sixteenth century to arrive at the concept of loxodromics). But it could happen (and must have occurred fairly often) that a ship deviated from the predetermined route because of side-slipping due to the wind and to wave motion, and also because of drift-inducing currents. Instead of going forward in the direction indicated, the boat was compelled to go wide, at which point a return line was needed to compensate for the forced error.

Knowledge of coastal landmarks helped to make such a correction, whether the shoreline was indeed familiar to the pilot or described in a portolan or *Compass for Sailing* (such as was mentioned earlier; the oldest that has come down to us, kept in the State Library of Berlin, dates from 1296 and is written in thirteen-century Italian). This, too, was an indispensable aid in medieval navigation, especially since it indicated not only the distances between coastal locations, but also the existence offshore of sandbanks or other dangerous places to be avoided, as well as pinpointing to landings where one could find provisions of water and wood or shelter from squalls.

From about the middle of the fourteenth century, a geometric system came into use to compensate for forced deviations, but it was apparently not very widespread. This system was set out in "navigation tables," such as the *raxon* ('calculation') and the *toleta* ('table') of the *martelogio* (or *martelojo* in Venetian dialect). The origin of this system, as also of the word *martelogio*, is uncertain. The fact that the few copies that have come down to us were all drawn up by Venetians makes it likely that this was an invention of cartographers from that lagoon city, but it is certain, as the documents published by Ferretto show, that in 1390 this nautical aid was also in use in Genoa, or at least by Genoese. In fact it is mentioned in a notarial act, and another copy shows up in an inventory of books belonging to a doctor of the law. Sometimes the *martelogio* appears next to the *carta pro navigando*, or the *agogie seu acus pro navigando* (or the *agogie pro timono*), the 'guides or needles for sailing' (or 'guides for the rudder').

In essence, these tables, based on the properties of right-angled triangles, showed by how many degrees to correct one's route in relation to the deviation experienced. A fine example of a "*martelojo* table" can be found in Andrea Bianco's atlas of 1436, kept at the Marciana Library in Venice. Baldacci has written recently, and on several occasions, about the use of this nautical aid; he maintains, among other things, that Columbus used such a table on his transatlantic voyages and that he also knew how to make them (as I discuss later).

Even when the route was determined and eventually corrected, the problem of the precise location of the medieval sailing ships was still not completely solved, except approximately, since no instrument allowed one to compute exactly the distance covered. It meant that one had to be content with empirical observations, such as the greater or lesser billowing of the sails, the direction of the winds, and the foam produced in the ship's wake, all of which needed to be related to the elapsed time, carefully measured by the hour-glasses (the best Genoese ones were made in Altare, in the Savona area), to which one of the sailors on guard duty was assigned (sometimes there were two, one beneath the prow and one beneath the stern). This measurement was not always precise, however, because the device could always be turned over late, or even left unturned if the sailor on duty fell asleep.

The distance thus estimated was entered on the nautical chart, on which a line had earlier been traced, representing the route to follow in reference to the direction of the rhumb lines (the number of leagues traveled in 24 hours, from midday to midday, was called a *singradura* or *singladura*, a word of uncertain origin from the Iberian languages). For this operation a compass was sufficient (indirectly one could also deduce the approximate latitude reached), but one had to know the scale of the chart. Needless to say, the graphic scales given on the charts were always approximate, whether because of the empirical method of their construction, or because their reduction factor was considerable (often up to 1:5,000,000) since the areas depicted were quite large, with variations among the different latitudes (that is, they were what we today call small-scale charts; small reduction factors were exceptional and limited to the Aegean area). Or, finally, the sheep's vellum on which the charts were drawn could have undergone distortions and curling as a result of contact with the salty sea air.

* * *

The reference just made to imperfections and possible distortions in the graphic scale of nautical charts (the reduction ratio varied from one million to five or six million) brings up some long-debated questions, such as that of their projection. I have already pointed out that charts must have originated from the direct observation of individual coastal stretches and from the depiction, detailed but limited to specific features of a particular shore, of whatever the pilot and sailors saw from the sea. The most widely held opinion, which I share, is that the piecing together of such sketches led to the construction of the first nautical charts using rhumb lines to indicate the cardinal directions. Thus, the existence of charts with a dual system of rings of wind roses may confirm the hypothesis that originally separate surveys were joined in one document.

This assumption, together with the fact that no cartographer of the time and no scholar of the art of navigation (even in subsequent periods) has left a single indication about their chosen projection system, leads one to conclude that those who made these sketches and charts nourished no interest either for projection (and therefore in the feasibility of representing on a flat plane portions of a spherical surface, such as that of the earth), or in magnetic declination (as we shall soon see), since the orientation of their drawings was provided by the compass lines, which in turn determined the connecting routes between places were based on them.

This situation compels a scholar to limit his or her research to the issue of which kind of projection, of those known today, could best fit the construction of medieval nautical charts. So I discussed both, flat projection and loxodromics, but in both cases (and in others as well) there are numerous objections and contradictions. Fiorini, who maintained that the projections were azimuthal, seemed closer to the truth, even though his view was opposed by Magnaghi and, more recently, by Baldacci. The latter scholar appropriately underscored the fact that the idea of the earth as a sphere was totally neglected in nautical charts until the late sixteenth century and that the charts were constructed on the basis of polar coordinates, which were referred from the place of origin to the North Pole and to one's destination according to angles that are not azimuthal, and used not geographical, but magnetic meridians.

If we reflect on the fact that the surveys of coastal stretches and partial bodies of water, whether made by sight or with a compass, involved areas of the Mediterranean — a sea with generally excellent visibility and with shores that are almost always elevated (and thus quite easily seen) — then we are likely to conclude that the outline of the original sketch must not have been hard to draw, nor subject to gross errors and distortions. Errors, if anything, occurred when the various sketches, perhaps drawn up on different scales, were assembled in one overview chart, without the opportunity to refer to astronomical data, which observers were not capable of establishing or could not be determined on board except with considerable difficulty. Hence the distortions in distances, angles, and surfaces that are found in all parts of every nautical chart (whereas, if the distortions were due to the type of projection adopted, they would be found to interest only one section, or part of it, and would progressively increase).

In conclusion, the network of rhumb lines has nothing to do with projection — as everyone now agrees. This also explains why the rhumb lines could be drawn onto the outline, as it certainly happened in the cases when the outline was retraced — in the seventeenth century, as Crescenzio attests.

On the other hand, the errors and distortions arising from inaccuracies of scale are extremely numerous, just as the adoption of the cartometric method (as the only one available today) is not without difficulties for calculating true scales. To apply it, one usually measures the distance between locations, whether close or far apart; very often the distance from Marseilles to Bougie (today's Bejaia), or from Savona to Tunis, equals 750 kilometers. But places were marked on nautical charts not by precise dots but by toponyms, written one after the other, so that the reference to their location was always approximate. Parchments, moreover, changed with use and time, acquiring humps and hollows that cannot be appreciated in the photographic reproduction (even someone working with the original cannot reconstruct what the former conditions were). Finally, we are dealing ostensibly with small-scale maps, and a difference of a few millimeters in the measurement of distances can cause noticeable discrepancies in the actual numbers from one chart to another, even within the same atlas.

This is probably the reason why the graphic scale is missing in some (but not many) nautical charts, when the scale on the other hand is generally repeated several times in the margins of the document (in lengths of 50 *miliaria*, each subdivided — but often not very accurately — into five sections). This displacement to the margins of the chart is common from the mid-fourteenth to the mid-fifteenth century. Older charts, however, have scales like ladders with rungs that intersect each other to form a Greek cross with two transverse diameters of a circle. Later the placement of the scales would vary from document to document.

As for the charts that have no scale, Magnaghi does not accept the theory of forgetfulness on the part of the maker, but assumes it was deliberately omitted it; mapmakers preferred that "the pilot adhere without fail to the measurements provided by the portolans," when confronted with significant variations in distances among different parts of the map. It is also conceivable, however, that this omission was limited to copies intended for libraires, princes, and scholars.

Another issue, partly connected to the question of scale, concerns the mile used by cartographers. Neither the nautical charts nor the portolans specify, even approximately, the length of a mile. This led, therefore, to the formulation of the most diverse hypotheses, using data obtained by the cartometric method cited above. The results vary from Nordenskiöld's "portolan mile" of 1166 meters (corresponding to about a fifth of a Catalan league, from which fact he deduced that the Catalans were the first to produce medieval nautical charts) to the Roman mile of 1480 meters. Magnaghi, following Wagner's example, proposes an intermediate value of 1250 meters for the nautical (or "Italic") mile.

The Atlantic coasts, however, especially those of Portugal, were drafted on a smaller scale, so that the distance calculation reflected a larger mile. It has been suggested in this regard that the unit used for these coasts was the Roman mile of 1480 meters, which was approximately a fifth of the so-called "Iberian league" of 5565 meters. According to this theory Mediterranean cartographers would then have confused this mile, which the Portuguese portolans used in reporting distances (although we are not sure they existed), with the one to which they were accustomed, without being aware of the difference. This is a far-fetched and implausible hypothesis, because it is hard to believe that the difference went unnoticed; had the cartographer realized it, he could have remedied the situation by inserting a different graphic scale onto the sea, offshore. Besides, the use of a smaller scale in the representation of western Iberian coasts can be explained in other ways: for example, either by the smaller size of that part of the parchment, which usually corresponded to the animal's neck and was on the outside (and therefore more exposed to humidity and salinity); or by surveys originally figured on a different scale, the cartographers who compiled the overview chart having judged the discrepancy irrelevant enough not to require a correction.

Many arguments have certainly been raised about whether there was an early Portuguese nautical cartography. I shall have to address this later in greater detail, since the oldest extant examples of that country's nautical charts date from the fifteenth century (I, for one, am convinced that there exist no earlier ones). Similalry the perpetuation of errors and distortions in the various subsequent charts, here as elsewhere, may be explained as a result of the retracing process by which (as I showed earlier) errors were passed from one original work to another, and from the each original to any number of copies. A very well-known Portuguese writer, Armando Cortesâo, even while declaring himself convinced that charts "indispensable for Portuguese navigators ... and made in Portugal" existed as early as the thirteenth century, admits that there is no "documentary proof" in this regard. Moreover, in 1335, Opicino de Canistris, whom I mentioned earlier, said, while speaking of a scale of distances, that it is to be found "*in mappa maris navigabilis secundum Januenses et*

Maioricenses," that is, "on the map of the navigable sea according to the Genoese and the Majorcans" — implying therefore that it was not the custom to depict non-navigable seas on charts of that time, and that the chart-making centers were in Genoa (whence the "craft" was exported to Venice) and Majorca, not in Portugal.

* * *

Another much disputed question concerns the effects of magnetic declination, a phenomenon that neither the nautical charts, nor the portolans, nor any medieval author mentions, and one that would undoubtedly complicate the construction and use of such nautical aids. In actuality, magnetic declination must have been known even before Columbus. He, however, discovered during his first voyages across the Atlantic, at about 100 leagues west of the Azores, that the declination varied from east to west (which would complicate further things thereafter). But in Andrea Bianco's atlas of 1436 there is no record of this phenomenon (despite what was formerly believed), nor any trace of an attempt to compensate for its effects. The first precise indications and corrections seem to have appeared in German circles in the second half of the fifteenth century.

Since the declination in the Mediterranean in those centuries was to the east with deviation values in the range of 5 to 7 degrees (but even up to 10° and a little more, depending on local conditions), all the coastal contours in nautical charts — moving from west to east — are shifted northwards and turned from right to left (that is, counterclockwise). As a result Gibraltar and Alexandria of Egypt appear in these charts on about the same parallel, whereas the latter is actually 5° farther south than the former. Similarly the west-east line passes through Lisbon and Saint John of Acre, whereas the difference in latitude between the two cities is almost 6°.

This disorientation of the Mediterranean, which is found in all medieval nautical charts, can be explained by the fact that when the first partial surveys of the Mediterranean coasts were made this magnetic phenomenon was probably — indeed almost certainly — unknown, and so its effects were ignored in cartographic drawing. When pilots and cartographers became aware of declination and came to understand it (perhaps through using the charts) they did not find it helpful to add corrections, because they must have realized simultaneously that it varied from place to place and time to time. This made it impossible, as well as pointless, to make alterations in cartographic documents. Meanwhile, compasses with two needles and two wind roses enabled them to make allowances for the differences in declination. The description given by Petrus Peregrinus in the second half of the thirteenth century may already have assumed that one knew the necessity for correction.

It was thought preferable, therefore, to rely on experienced pilots to correct, from time to time, the errors made in the ship's course as a result of using these disoriented charts and of following the false north shown on the compass. For these corrections, the pilots would rely on observations of the sun (and perhaps also the North Star), but especially on their knowledge of the coastlines — already visited on previous sailing trips — and the indications reported in the portolans.

Unless, that is, — as Magnaghi, among others, assumed — magnetic declination on the high seas was corrected using the small black crosses, that are drawn far off the coastlines on many nautical charts, especially in the open Tyrrhenian Sea and west of Sardinia and Corsica (along the shore it would have been enough to refer to known places and landmarks, as we said earlier). The black-ink crosses always form right angles, but are tilted to the west, though in varying degrees. Thus one can imagine that for some positions on the open sea, for which the size of the magnetic declination was known, they meant to indicate to pilots that true north, at such a point and at that time, was not what was indicated on the compass, but rather corresponded to the vertical axis of this symbol (the crosses could be drawn on any nautical chart, copied from a prototype that had none).

If this hypothesis is not accepted, the meaning of these crosses remains uncertain. Since they are found (as I said) in the open sea, in deep water areas, they would have nothing to do with the lines drawn along the coasts — together with festoons of dots — to indicate cliffs or sandbanks (as is done in modern hydrographic charts). Nor would they correspond to reference points along the route, marked from time to time as one traveled, which, we know, were penciled in and later erased.

In essence, we can conclude that medieval nautical charts — drawn up without any concern for projection or theoretical references to the idea of a round earth, and without taking magnetic declination into account — were useful to pilots on the relatively short routes over the open sea that were customary in the Mediterranean. Here one was never out of sight of the coast for more than two or three (maybe four) days at a stretch. The routes, therefore, were hardly affected by the curvature of the earth's surface, at a time when celestial navigation was little practiced, or not at all.

Thanks to these charts, the ship would arrive in the stretch of sea opposite its port of destination. Only then could one determine the ship's position — this being impossible on the open sea without astronomical references — and establish the remaining course of travel to reach one's target, using the knowledge one had of the coast and the advise of the portolan. In the last phase one might also use a sounding line (another instrument that was always part of a ship's gear at that time).

This is how one sailed in the Mediterranean and along the coastlines of adjacent bodies of water, including the Atlantic, during the Middle Ages. But the situation changed in the fifteenth century, when sailors were faced with longer routes on the high seas of that ocean. This made it necessary to refer to the North Star and other astronomical points. Matters became even more complicated when one entered the waters near the equator (or beyond it), and saw stars of a heaven different from that of our own hemisphere.

Columbus made his voyages during just this delicate phase of transition, as a result of which nautical charts, also, underwent changes that continued throughout the sixteenth century, before beginning a subsequent, slow decline.

2) *Genoa, center of seamanship, commerce, and nautical culture in the Middle Ages*

To speak of Genoa's prominence as a maritime center in the Middle Ages would go beyond the limits of this book and would be quite useless, since I would end up repeating information and facts that are already well known. If anything, it is worth recalling, for the purposes of this work, the many commercial channels through which elements of geographical and cartographical learning may have found their way into the city, and similarly all the other channels that possibly originated out of it in more than one direction.

In this regard it is obvious that the Genoese commercial settlements established early on in the Aegean, the Eastern Mediterranean, and the Black Sea had a positive influence on the acquisition of knowledge about the East. Information, including geographical information, about vast regions of Asia, both the interior of the continent and its southern portion, naturally converged in those areas and sites where for centuries Genoa had had stable and very active colonies. It is no accident, for example, that at the time of Benedetto Zaccaria the Genoese were considered to be the best experts of the West in Chinese matters.

Similarly, the unabated contacts and trade with the Muslim shores of Africa, from Alexandria to the Maghreb, must have favored the dissemination among the Genoese and Ligurians of information about not only the coastal stretches, but also the territories lying even quite far inland from them.

On more than one occasion Revelli has laid emphasis on narrative accounts, of which a good example is the case of Antonio Malfante, a Genoese merchant-explorer who arrived in the oasis of Tuat, in the Western Sudan, in 1447. Such relations certainly existed before the fifteenth century, since it was known in all the maritime and commercial circles of the Mediterranean that at least a portion of the products traded along the coasts of the Maghreb during the Middle Ages came from the regions beyond the Atlas range — so much so that a traditional image, shown on more than one nautical chart, was that of a caravan of merchants and camels crossing the North African mountain chain. We have seen that the fluvial island of *Palola*, or *Paiola*, whose gold-bearing resources were important for Genoa's single-metal monetary policy, was depicted south of the Sahara on Father Giovanni Mauro da Carignano's world map.

Hence from these traditional sources, as well as from his reading and especially from his experiences with the Portuguese in the Gulf of Guinea, Columbus may have taken the elements that made up his image of Africa, prompting these comments among his *Annotations*: "It is twice the size of Europe, and even though there are sandy lands in the middle, they are inhabited in some places; countless people live in the southern and northern parts and the very great heat does not prevent it."

Another matter to be discussed concerns the geographical information about the western part of Europe, and the Iberian Peninsula in particular, that came to Genoa (or was already there) in the Middle Ages and which must have ended up in nautical charts. In this regard the colonial policy practiced by the Genoese is well known, even for the part of Iberia that was subject to the Muslims for the period that their rule lasted, as well as in its later development after the *reconquista*. Granada, Seville, and Lisbon were the main centers; from there this policy spread to the Atlantic islands (with the latter, in the fifteenth century, came the establishment of the sugar trade, which seems to have been the "business of the century" for Ligurian merchants).

Lisbon, in turn, was for them an important forward base along the northbound routes. It is known that Genoa imported, among many other goods, even grain from Northern Germany, via Flanders. As early as the end of the thirteenth century Ligurian ships made regular stops not only at that Tagus River port, but also at the harbors of the Algarve and the northern Portuguese coasts, as well as at other smaller ones, now silted up, such as Salir and Atonquia. In the fourteenth century Genoa's sailors and merchants would arrive in this country in great numbers (they would become even more numerous after the discovery and occupation of Madeira), and the routes that followed that coastline, heading for Sluis (the forward port of Bruges), Southampton, London, and other English ports would become more heavily traveled.

The British Isles were already quite familiar, therefore (except for the mistake, repeated in all, or almost all, nautical charts, of separating England and Scotland by a long channel; this is one of many examples of cartographers' "conservatism" and of the long-term persistence of traditional models, even if they were in error). From Britain came information about lands and islands farther north, as well (from Iceland to Thule, if they are not the same geographical entity). Other facts concerned Denmark, Scandinavia, and the Baltic, even though the Hanseatic league's policies tended to shut foreigners out of the harbors of this area.

Moreover, Genoese sailors and merchants certainly traveled the Atlantic coasts of northwest Africa and, later, the offshore islands. As mentioned earlier, Revelli contends at length that the Genoese discovered them before the Portuguese. He uses arguments that seem quite reasonable and to the point (even if they are rejected by Portuguese scholars), especially when one considers the detailed depiction, with related toponyms, of those coastal stretches in Genoese and Italian cartographic documents well before the period in which Henry the Navigator encouraged explorations departing from his country. And, as I said before, no one has ever seen drawings and coastal surveys made by the Portuguese before the fifteenth century. Even if one could not claim that the Genoese were the first to discover these coasts, there is no doubt that Ligurian sailors and merchants traveled there regularly.

It is certain that in the case of the Canary Islands (reached by a Portuguese-Italian expedition in 1341) a long-standing tradition depicted the *Insula de lanzarotus Marocelus*, or Lanzarote Malocello's Island, with Genoa's coat-of-arms (in memory of the discoverer's homeland). It is certain that the first map to represent the Atlantic islands was that of Angelino Dalorto, in 1325, and that the Medici Atlas of 1351 already includes depictions of four islands that are reasonably assumed to belong to the Azores. Naturally, the location of these islands was approximate or totally unrealistic, especially in the older maps. The island or islands called '*Brazil*' in various spellings were placed west of Ireland, but ended up in the position of the Madeiras. '*Antilia*' — which appears for the first time in 1435 in the planisphere of Battista Beccario, a Genoese (it is kept in the Palatina Library in Parma) — has a schematic, almost geometrical, shape that would be repeated for some time; it seems to be located in the middle of the ocean, almost as if to fill up empty space.

In any case, this completes the picture of Genoese geographical knowledge concerning western Europe, which went into nautical cartography (we have already spoken of how information about African countries south of the Sahara progressively expanded as the Portuguese advanced along the coast in the fifteenth century).

* * *

Genoa in these centuries was not just a "caravan city," as Heers calls her, inhabited by a people that, from Idrisi's time, was described as mistress of the seas and expert in trade and navigation, a city that gave overwhelming importance to money and was inspired by excessive individualism, with the result that wealth and the circulation of currency was accompanied by internal strife and political instability. Genoa was also, in fact, a highly respected financial center, blessed with a technical knowledge that had evolved over time so as to become, in Heers' words, one of the most advanced of the districts and cities of Western Europe.

All the tools on which the development of modern capitalism would be based were present there from the middle of the fifteenth century: paper money, letters of credit from banks, exchange markets and their related trade, including *ricarico*, or markup. Thanks to the practice of the *moltiplico*, or compound interest, the bond market was quite widespread there and organized according to rational criteria. Hence the famous prosperity and influence of the "Purchases of Saint George" and the Bank associated with it.

Finally, Genoa was a center of culture, with its own peculiarities; using modern terminology, one could say it was primarily an "applied" culture. Indeed, the age of troubadors and poets ended very early in the Ligurian capital, there being no stable center of power around which they could gather to form a coherent body. In the second half of the thirteenth century, moreover, the local culture, which until then had been primarily lay, began to revolve around the monasteries, especially those of the mendicant orders, as Petti Balbi observes, listing a group of scholars belonging to religious congregations. It was for this very reason, however, that this culture later became detached from the more active life of the city.

The *gramatica ad usum mercatorum Januensium*, or "grammar for the use of Genoese merchants" would continue to develop, however, even into later times; this was a technical and practical course of instruction that emerged in the thirteenth century for the purpose of introducing young men rapidly into the world of business and production. Judges, notaries, *fisici* (natural scientists), and also merchants acquired these books, studied them, and bequeathed them to their heirs with a provision against alienating them. The capital city undoubtedly had a *scriptorium*, but secretarial work, which was not congenial to the Ligurians, was left by preference to foreigners.

Thus mercantile culture held sway. Notaries engaged in intense commerce even for themselves. Petti Balbi keenly observes that the Genoese Dominican, Giovanni Balbi, used to describe the incarnation of Christ as a commercial operation (*fuit commercium, quasi commutatio mercium, scilicet divinitatis et humanitatis*, "there was a trade, almost an exchange of goods, between divinity and humanity, that is"). Jacopo da Varagine often represents Christ as a merchant. Galvano da Levanto, also a Dominican, uses the word *passagium*, typical of bequests left to the Crusades. Jacopo da Cessole (not a Genoese, but another Dominican, who had received his training in Genoa) considers the merchants to be the financiers and holders of power.

In the second half of the thirteenth century the same Giovanni Balbi cited earlier, who was already the author of a table for calculating the date of Easter as well as of a theological work, wrote, in the Ligurian capital, his *Catholicon seu Summa prosodie*, a long treatise on orthography, etymology, syntax, prosody, and especially lexicography. Galvano da Levanto, already mentioned, in addition to being chief physician to the pope, was also the author of didactic-allegorical works, such as the *Liber Sancti passagii*, or "Book of the Holy passage" (to the Holy Land). Andalò di Negro, born no later than 1260, devoted himself to what passed at the time as scientific literature. He was Boccaccio's teacher in Naples, where he died before June of 1334; he was the author of a *Treatise on the Astrolabe*, a synthesis of the astrological and astronomical science of the time (his successor as *fisico stipendiato* [salaried scientist] at the court of Robert of Anjou was one "Nicolinus de Sancto Prospero," also a Genoese).

In these same years and decades Genoa hosted a handful of *fisici* interested in medical and scientific learning based not only on the current theories, but also on actual observation of the natural world; in order to test its natural phenomena they undertook long voyages, in the typical, pragmatic spirit of the Genoese. Thus Simone Cordo, better known as Simone da Genova, almost certainly composed his *Sinonima medicinae* in this city (he also had been chief physician to the pope, but had retired; he died, apparently, in the monastery at Paverano). A certain Ruffino wrote a well-known *Herbarium* in Genoa. Among those who received their education in Genoa were Guglielmo da Varignana, a philosopher and physician, as well as the author of a treatise on the *Secreta sublimia*, and Giovanni d'Incisa, who wrote a treatise on eclipses of the sun and moon in the early decades of the fourteenth century. Jacopo Doria, the probable author of *De pratica equorum* [On Managing Horses] was also Genoese.

On the ladder of social hierarchies doctors and natural scientists were at one of the highest rungs, somewhat above the notaries (who were often considered mere scribes, but were not detested as in Florence). Among the latter were some who devoted their efforts to drawing up nautical charts and planispheres, including Pietro Vesconte, of whom I have spoken and will need to speak again. But clergymen could also be cartographers, including Giovanni Mauro da Carignano, as mentioned earlier; a brother of professionals in the liberal arts, he perhaps did not have his own *bottega*, or workshop, but made charts purely as a hobby and for his own cultural satisfaction. The fifteenth-century cartographer Bartolomeo de Pareto was also a clergyman.

The case of learned men from Genoa moving to other cities was part of a continuing process throughout the fourteenth century, a diaspora of men of letters who left the Ligurian capital for other cities in Italy, where princes and lords offered them stability of employment; examples include Andalò di Negro, various jurists — among them Francesco da Saliceto, who went to Bologna to teach at the University (Genoa did not then have one) — and other men of culture. Professionals in the field of grammar and specialists in law (as Petti Balbi notes), being linked to the merchant milieu, remained in Genoa (where the second half of the century would see the flourishing of the *maone*, or trading companies, which directly engaged entire families and groups of families in commerce and navigation).

Things did not change much in the fifteenth century, as Genoa's cultural model continued to be that of the merchants. Their field of activity widened from east to west (by now there were non-stop routes), but interest in Egypt, as a trading center that attracted middlemen from far and wide, remained stable. Nor did the *devetum Alexandrie*, or "Interdiction of Alexandria," decrease trade with Africa and Islamic lands; it was not hard to get papal dispensations, and bequests *pro passagio ultramarino* (that is, for the Crusades) made it possible to soothe one's conscience, as did legacies left for harbor works (which was considered as a way to give to God, therefore counting as much as religious works).

For this reason, too, as Airaldi writes, Genoa was always ready to welcome a *scriba littere saracenice*, or scribe of "Saracen," and there is evidence of documents composed in the city in Arabic. In any case, the

Genoese "studied reading and writing out of necessity:" in the schools they were taught especially "to speak Latin and to make calculations... for the use of merchants." This immediately brings to mind the poor and ungrammatical Latin that Columbus would prove to know.

Airaldi refers to Genoa's traditional place in the period of Humanism, quoting the well known opinions of Flavio Biondo (that "Genoa has few educated men") and Andrea Silvio Piccolomini (according to whom the Genoese are "scarcely interested in knowledge," except for the little reading and writing needed for business, and "few are engaged in other kinds of studies"). In fact, even though recent studies have partly modified and filled in this picture, a persistent lack of political stability (indeed, local history proved to be a succession of feuds among families, with no princely court or center to stimulate and promote cultural interests) further aggravated the problem of the absence of a university. Hence, even though all the merchants knew how to read and write and some members of the most important families devoted themselves to letters, Genoese public life remained outside Humanism, which for the city was reduced to a series of isolated cases, finding expression and leaving a trace only in certain external features, such as architectural ones (never frequent, in fact).

Native Genoese men of culture continued continued their diaspora, dispersing now not only throughout Italy, but all over Europe. Musso has compiled a long list of them, men of letters, philosophers, and scholars in other fields. Among them, as also among the few who stayed in the city, there seem to have been not many interested in scientific studies during the entire fifteenth and the beginning of the sixteenth century.

Substantially then, Genoa's interest in the cultural movement of renewal and rediscovery of classical values that signals the transition from the Middle Ages to the Modern Age seems to have been overestimated, and what little development there was took place late, though Heers, inspired perhaps by excessive affection and immoderate esteem for the city, claims to have discerned it. Nor did the arrival in the capital of some Jews and Byzantine scholars toward the end of the fifteenth century offset this and undeniably, Greek books can be found in the inventories of monastery libraries of the time. In the second half of the century, there was a lively cultural life in Savona, another city linked to the history of Christopher Columbus; she, too, was home to more than one humanist and some learned men of Greco-Byzantine origin.

If this was the picture of humanistic studies in fifteenth-century Genoa, one that caused the rediscovery of classical authors and enthusiasm for their values to spread at a much slower pace, compared to other regions (there were, for instance, no Ligurian editions of Ptolemy, as elsewhere), nonetheless the applied sciences, including cartography, continued to flourish in the city and the region. As we shall see, there was an intense production of fourteenth-century Ligurian cartographic documents (always nautical), attesting to the existence of a number of laboratories and artisans' workshops. Probably, this cartographic tool became increasingly necessary as navigational horizons expanded, as was indeed happening; this is supported by the words that often appeared in the notarial acts of limited partnerships, in reference to ships' destinations: "or wherever God shall direct me...", an allusion, as Airaldi rightly pointed out, to the uncertainty of the routes, as well as to the whims of human history.

This, then, was the cultural milieu in which Christopher Columbus was raised before he moved to Savona in 1470 or soon thereafter. This was the learning that he absorbed in the city's schools, since he belonged to a family of modest artisans and working class people. He must have read the classical authors and the great learned works of the time in Andalusia and Castille, in order to convince the scholars to accept a plan that was already well defined and precise in his own mind.

3) *Nautical charts of the fourteenth century*

We have positive information about the use of nautical charts on board ships that traveled the Mediterranean in the second half of the thirteenth century. Whereas in 1269 Petrus Peregrinus (of whom I spoke earlier), a contemporary, friend, and teacher of Roger Bacon, confined himself to explaining the properties of magnets, as we have seen, without mentioning the use of maps, shortly thereafter, instead, Guillaume de Nangis reported, in his account of the voyage of King Louis XII of France to the East to participate in the Crusade, that when the ships of the fleet on which the king was traveling were caught in a storm, in 1270, the pilots brought out *leur mappemonde* [their own world map] and showed him the position of their company near shore off of Cagliari in order to dispel his apprehensions. This rather well known episode in itself never properly credited the fact that the ships had been hired by the French king from Genoese shipmasters; they belonged to the Ligurian capital at a time in history when the latter had close relations with France (among other things, earlier the Genoese had taken an active part in the construction of the harbor of Aigues-Mortes, which had been promoted by King Louis IX himself in 1226).

In 1286 Ramón Lull, a Catalan philosopher and theologian, wrote, "how do sailors measure miles travelled on the sea? ... and to this purpose they have a chart, a compass, a needle, and the star of the sea." The ordinance issued by the king of Aragon, moreover, requiring all ships and armed galleys in his ports to have on board not one, but *dos cartas da marear* [two charts for sailing], goes back to the thirteenth century.

Of course, no chart from those decades is extant. The oldest ones to survive can be dated between the end of the thirteenth and the beginning of the fourteenth century, though there have been some scholars who thought they could be placed definitively as far back as the second half (or end) of the earlier of the two centuries. But the criteria by which one establishes the time period to which a chart belongs, when it is not dated, are often only approximate. Heuristic clues may include the presence, among the places marked, of a city founded in those years, or a port likewise destroyed at that same point in time, the depiction of a ruler's coat-of-arms, and so forth. Often, however, these indications are not certain. We need, in fact, to take into account what has already been defined as the "conservatism" of cartographers, in the sense that they often copied earlier documents, even retracing the name of a place that had gone out of existence in the meantime. Martinez, in a map from 1571, was still placing Genoa's flag in Galata, which the Ligurians had lost more than a century earlier.

Whether the oldest medieval nautical chart (if one may speak this way, after all that has been said about the origin of these documents) is to be dated back to 1250 or 1275 or 1300, no one will ever be able to prove it, and it is absolutely pointless to argue about it. In the second half of the thirteenth century, of course, as has been shown, this tool, already in a highly evolved form, was used for navigation in the Mediterranean, since the first dated charts (the ones by the Genoese Pietro Vesconte, of whom we spoke earlier, from 1311 and 1318) are of such high quality as to make it certain that the related science was already far advanced. This is so even though it is impossible to discern in these charts any connection with similar works from classical antiquity, which must never have existed (despite those who have believed them to be numerous, the last of such believers, in chronological order, being Armando Cortesâo).

It is impossible to say how many nautical charts are still extant today. Some time ago the estimate was a little fewer than 200, while Baldacci, who has carefully kept track of more recent finds and discusses all the documents through the seventeenth century, speaks of a thousand (of which two thirds are anonymous). Not counting studies made in the last century, Guarnieri, several decades ago, provided a partial but fairly exhaustive list of at least the principal works, including some descriptions. In the following pages I shall, of course, be speaking only of Genoese works or works influenced by Genoese prototypes, and in particular only of the most important ones. I shall also illustrate the appropriate links with planispheres (or *world maps*) of the period, of which I have spoken before and shall have to speak again, especially since in the fourteenth century it became common practice to insert a Mediterranean nautical chart into a 'map of the world,' as seen earlier; some planispheres are nothing but the reproduction of a nautical chart, rich in detail, in the center, but with a sketchy representation of barely known territories at the periphery.

Probably the oldest nautical chart known to us today is the so-called *Carta Pisana*, mentioned earlier and so named because it was rediscovered in Pisa, in the possession of a family from that city. It was almost certainly by a Genoese hand, however, as all scholars recognize, even though it is anonymous. We need to insist on its title, because a very long essay in *The History of Technology*, the work of very famous English-speaking scholars but translated into Italian, speaks several times of *Carte Pisane*, in the plural, as if to imply dependence on a prototype, a cartographic model, "outside" the Genoese tradition (the book includes a reproduction of a section of the document we are discussing) (see Table VIII).

The chart was certainly made after 1256, because it bears the toponym of Manfredonia, a city founded, as is well known, by King Manfred in that year. It may also have been made before the battle of Meloria (1282), because immediately south of the mouth of the Arno river one still finds the denomination 'Pisan Harbor,' which the Genoese destroyed after their victory. Yet, Baldacci is right to consider this a slender indication, because the destruction, occurring a few years after the battle, was not total, and, since some of the towers survived, the place name could have been kept. Nevertheless a whole series of other elements relating to historical and political situations in the second half of the thirteenth century lead one to believe that this document was undoubtedly drawn up in these years, perhaps (though this is only a hypothesis) around 1290.

It certainly exhibits archaic or "primitive" traits, as Baldacci writes, pointing out the contrast between the wealth of information about the coasts of the Mediterranean and the dearth of documentation and place names for the Atlantic coasts of Europe and Africa. This incompleteness, which led Revelli to believe that the chart was "probably unfinished," must instead be ascribed to the lack of information about peripheral and remote areas at a moment (or period) when detailed nautical knowledge was available only for the Mediterranean, the body of water in which this type of cartography originated.

The chart has two systems, or rings, of wind roses placed, in fact, over the Mediterranean, which is elongated from west to east. The roses are not embellished, as is true of many other documents of the thirteenth century, including the Cortona chart. This twofold feature may be an indication, as Baldacci suggested, that the network of the winds drawn here was derived from two originally separate surveys (one for the western part and one for the eastern), which were later brought together but which reflected considerable differences in latitude, on account of ignorance of magnetic declination, as I mentioned earlier. In the peripheral areas a discontinuous graticule of squares, corresponding to the eight principal wind directions, constitutes a geometrical supplement, a useful checkerboard design that provided an orientation for those portions not covered by the pattern of rhumb lines (this does not happen without some awkwardness in the fit between the two systems).

All this leads one to believe that the *Carta Pisana* is an original, not a copy, and indeed a cultural treasure from a period in which nautical cartography had only recently begun to develop. Hence, even the contours of the mainland are often rudimentary and unrealistic. Therefore, if this chart is to be likened to other similar documents from the same period, the only term of comparison is the so-called *Carta di Cortona*, which too exhibits archaic traits and two systems of wind roses. The latter dates perhaps from the beginning of the fourteenth century and (as Baldacci hypothesizes) was subject to corrections and tampering in the area representing Tuscany. These alterations may have resulted from the fact — as Capacci shows in a work in progress — that the chart was probably used for a pilgrimage itinerary to the Holy Land.

* * *

Other cultural treasures of great interest in the Ligurian tradition are those by Pietro Vesconte. Here we have a cartographer who was also a doctor and surgeon and belonged to a family of note, almost certainly of consular rank. He was certainly from Genoa, as is shown by his signature ('Petrus Vesconte de Janua'), even though no document concerning him has been found in the local State Archives, but only a rather late annotation regarding a credit claim. This is easily explained, since he moved (probably fairly quickly) to Venice, where he must have spent all (or almost all) of his professional life. Of course, his large nautical chart of 1311, which was drawn up in that city and shows the central and eastern Mediterranean and the Black Sea, is the first one known to us that bears a date (Plate IX).

The quantity of his works and the highly specialized level they represent (the quality of his cartographic documents is greatly superior to that of the *Carta Pisana*) lead one to agree completely with Pagani, whose important and very fine contribution to our knowledge of this map maker has already been pointed out: Vesconte must have been a professional cartographer, who professionally organized a fully equipped laboratory in Venice. As far as we know, he was the first to put together the collections of maps that would later be called 'atlases.'

In addition to the just mentioned chart of 1311 (preserved in the State Archives in Florence), of which I shall speak in a moment, Pietro Vesconte is known also for the five atlases, containing a varying number of maps, that have come down to us. Sometimes they also contain a calendar, and sometimes a planisphere. I spoke earlier of one of these planispheres, just as I mentioned that the authorship of the maps appended to the codices of Marin Sanudo's *Liber secretorum fidelium Crucis* is almost surely attributable to him. Finally, the maps appended to four other codices may also be credited to him, although this is not certain; these codices, however, do not really concern the purposes of this work. I will mention only for curiosity's sake that on one plate of the 1318 atlas, under the inscription bearing the signature and date, there is a painted miniature of a cartographer (himself?) seated at his work table. This is one of the few decorative elements shown in Pietro Vesconte's works (the others are usually pictures of the Madonna and saints, and are found only on the margins of the maps included in the atlases).

The area depicted in the 1311 nautical chart — the central and eastern Mediterranean including the Black Sea — provides further confirmation of the thesis that the contours of the coastal outlines (begun as surveys for flat maps, based on adjacent horizons) were made separately for the two main sections, eastern and western, of this body of water, using two different systems of wind roses. The fact that place names in the Tyrrhenian Sea are particularly abundant can be explained by the Ligurian origin of the map maker. The drawing and the place names of the Black Sea — a traditional destination of Genoese trade, with numerous and important commercial colonies along the various coastal stretches — are very precise in this, as in other nautical charts. Similarly, the wealth of documentation about the Atlantic coasts in Pietro Vesconte's work, from Mogador (western Morocco) in Africa to Scotland and Ireland in Europe (that is, the areas that were "appendices" of the Mediterranean for purposes of Ligurian trade at that time), leads to a quite accurate and faithful representation of the coastal stretches, compared to the vague and summary renditions of the *Carta Pisana*.

The frame drawn around the 1311 chart shows clear affinities with the world map of Father Giovanni Mauro da Carignano, as Pagani has already shown. Any possible relationship between the two cartographers is yet to be documented and studied, however, since I do not wish to indulge here in the facile suppositions and inferences to which other writers have succumbed. In this 1311 chart by Vesconte there are two graphic scales, each in the form of a cross enclosed in a circle, as in the *Carta Pisana*. The central rose has sixteen winds. The detail in the depiction of the charts and the islands contrasts with the void that characterizes the interior of the dry lands, except in a portion of the Balkans, where certain symbols serve to mark geographical features.

This is certainly the first extant nautical document to be labeled *carta*; the word is found in the Latin inscription that bears the signature and the date. On the other hand, Pietro Vesconte used the word *tabullam* to indicate the tables in the atlases; in the case of the latter (or rather, of the planispheres), as I said before, he surely also had in mind the world map of Fra Paolino, the Minorite friar, Venetian ambassador and, later, papal ambassador. From this we can conclude that the Genoese cartographer, after being educated in the Ligurian capital, brought his initial experience to Venice, where he improved his learning and probably adapted his work to the requirements of that mercantile milieu (it has, in fact, been suggested that the 1311 chart was intended to highlight the routes between the city on the lagoon and the East).

We cannot reject a priori the theory advanced by Revelli, and then supported by Piersantelli, that the *Tammar Luxoro Atlas*, of which we will speak in a moment, is the work of Pietro Vesconte. But in this regard also, since we lack any documentary basis, I am in agreement with Pagani that, "this does not go beyond conjecture" (Plates X-XI).

Similarly, it is uncertain whether *Perrino Vesconte de Janua*, who drew up, dated, and signed a nautical chart of the entire Mediterranean, was a son or kinsman of Pietro; the chart, now kept in the Central Library, Zurich, repeats many features of the *Carta Pisana*. Some have suggested that "Perrino" was the diminutive for Pietro, but it seems more reasonable to me to think of him as a descendent who continued the family profession and passed on to posterity the work and fame of the head of the school. Another nautical chart by the same Perrino was drawn up in Venice in 1327 and is now in the Medicea Laurentian

Library in Florence. It is interesting to note that this map maker, of Ligurian ancestry but working in Venice, used a Genoese prototype, carefully omitting Genoa's flags and coat-of-arms from all the republic's traditional possessions.

Pietro Vesconte's atlases, therefore, are the first example known to us of a type of work that would become widespread thereafter. Perhaps, indeed, it would be more appropriate to speak of collections of charts, since, as I said before, the word "atlas" would come into use much later. In any case, it was a matter of subdividing the areas to be depicted (excluding a possible overall planisphere and the tables reserved for the calendar, zodiac, and solar declinations) among a certain number of partial charts (usually from six to nine of them) sharing the same format. These charts, or at least the ones belonging to the period we are examining, have often come down to us either glued or nailed onto wooden boards.

Revelli maintains that these were "office" editions, that is, intended for scholars, monastery libraries, and princes, since they include all those pieces of information that were later depicted with greater breadth in charts suited to the needs of navigators. An equal but opposite conjecture could assert, to the contrary, that precisely because they were attached to wood (their final arrangement certainly done after completion of the drawing) to prevent creases and curling, these tables may have had a practical purpose, namely, to provide an overall picture to navigators, who then would consult more specialized and detailed charts as needed.

Such is the case of the *Tammar Luxoro Atlas* in the Berio Civic Library in Genoa (also known simply as the *Luxoro Atlas*; its name goes back to the scholar of the last century who discovered it among family belongings and brought it to light). It is divided into eight charts, devoted respectively to the Black Sea, the eastern Mediterranean, the Aegean and the Sea of the Levant, the Adriatic, the central Mediterranean (using two tables), the western Mediterranean including the neighboring Atlantic waters, and the Bay of Biscay and English Channel as far as Ireland.

The work, in a fairly good state of preservation, bears neither date nor name of maker, but is certainly by a Genoese hand and is not without relatively archaic traits here and there. The technical structure is the usual one, with wind roses and "rhumb lines." The place names, very abundant in the best known Mediterranean areas, are mainly in Italian, though we also find expressions in other languages and even dialects. The drawing of the coasts and islands is carefully done (each chart has its own graphic scale), and the depiction of the seas and lands is quite precise and rather far advanced, so as to deserve the respect it has received from Kretschmer and Caraci, among others, while Almagià has made the observation that this is a work that must have been produced by "consummate cartographers or specialists in drafting."

Various debates have arisen over the order of the charts in the atlas (the present order, as listed above, is apparently not the original one), the date of its compilation, and the identity of the maker. We have already spoken of this last issue. As for the question of dating, the theory that this work goes back to the end of the thirteenth century, when nautical cartography was certainly less advanced, does not seem very acceptable, whereas any date in the first three decades (or the first quarter) of the 1300's is admissible. With this I return to the issue, insoluble in our present state of documentary evidence, of the relationship Father Giovanni Mauro da Carignano must have had with other cartographers, and not only Genoese ones.

* * *

The example of Pietro Vesconte, who moved from Genoa to Venice, proves that among these dynasties of cartographers there were often people who relocated from one port to another, from one coastal city to another — perhaps a rival or competing one (we will see other instances later). This can serve as an introduction to the thesis of those Italian scholars (the first being Caraci) who believed that Angelino de Dalorto — a Genoese and maker of the nautical chart dated 1325 that was formerly kept in the Library of the Prince Corsini in Florence (today, as a result of legacies being split up, we have lost track of this document) — was the same as Angellino Dulcert, the maker of a nautical chart "in the nation of the Majorcans" in 1339 (mentioned earlier).

Rivers of ink have been spilt over this question, and yet, with the present state of documentation, it seems insoluble. Whereas Pietro Vesconte, for example, always signed his name *de Janua*, even when he was working in Venice, scholars have found no indication of Dulcert's country of origin. To me, the question seems badly posed in any case, tied as it is to the argument — often even the furious controversy — over whether Italian or Catalan cartography came first (Paolo Emilio Taviani has recently alluded to this, with a review of the principal writings). In fact, even if it were proved that Dalorto moved from Genoa to Majorca around the year 1330, or shortly after, and that he devoted himself to redacting and drawing up nautical charts (which is quite possible and even probable), it still would not answer our question, since that fact would not exclude the possibility that the techniques of nautical cartography had spread to Catalonia and the Balearics even earlier at the hands of experts of both local and foreign origin (which is also likely).

I shall have to address again before long the links between Italian and Catalan cartography and related arguments, but for now it is enough to say something about the characteristics of the two charts of which we are speaking. Magnaghi, who has carefully studied Dalorto's 1325 chart, first shows the reasons for which it is thought to be undoubtedly from a Ligurian hand (the Mediterranean is depicted looking just as it does in Genoese works, as cited earlier; the shape of the Italian Peninsula is very similar to that of Pietro Vesconte; the place names are more abundant along the Tyrrhenian coast, and especially on the major islands, than they are on the Adriatic). Then Magnaghi draws attention to the relatively accurate and detailed representation of the coasts of northwestern and northern Europe. This is something new, introduced by this chart maker, when compared to the shorelines of Scandinavia and the Baltic, for example, on earlier charts, where they are shown with gaps in some places and are drawn schematically and with distortions in others. Hence he declares this chart to be "a true prototype from which other Italian and foreign cartographers will later take inspiration." One can also argue, therefore, that it served as a model for the world map in the *Catalan Atlas* of 1375, of which we have already spoken (Table XII).

Dulcert's chart of 1339, when superimposed on the preceding chart, matches it almost perfectly, even with respect to the northwestern and northern coasts of Europe. The outline of the shore, sharp, sure, and elegant, shows a knowledge of landings and coastal features, which are more numerous and detailed than in the previous charts or in the world map of the *Catalan Atlas* of 1375. Hence Magnaghi concludes that this chart, still with a double system of wind roses and very few decorative elements, "represents that type of world map — land map and sea chart at the same time — that was later copied" by various map makers.

What we have said so far allows us to draw two conclusions. The first is general in character and useful in an effort to draw up a typological classification; it derives from the realization that advances in nautical and geographical knowledge had already led, by this time, to the use of overview maps, which Capacci defines as "nautical-geographical," alongside medieval world maps and the planispheres mentioned earlier. Overview maps, in turn, were derived from, or included, true nautical charts. The latter, as is suggested by the archival documents published by Ferretto and Revelli, were subsequently (though not always) differentiated into two types: the *carta una* (that is, a single section for the entire Mediterranean basin and adjacent waters), and the *carta media* (that is, the depiction of a half, and later on of an even smaller body of water). A specification of the purpose for which they were to be used — *pro navigando* — often followed in both instances.

Naturally, it is not always easy to distinguish among the various types; indeed it is often well nigh impossible. Some documents, including some of the planispheres and world maps discussed earlier, could more properly, perhaps, be called "nautico-geographical maps," but I prefer to avoid the use of such a term, even though it is a good one, for simplicity's sake and for ease of comprehension on the part of the non-specialist. Moreover, we have seen that chart collections, which we usually call "atlases," using the modern word, became current during the fourteenth century; over time these collections were destined to enjoy an ever growing success.

The second conclusion concerns the issue I have already met of whether Genoese or Catalan charts came first. In this dispute we have looked to the study of place names, or rather, the language in which they are written in the various documents. While waiting for the results of Capacci's systematic research, which compares, by computer, the place names in a whole series of important cartographic documents, it seems helpful to recall that cartographers frequently moved from one part of the Mediterranean to another, and even beyond it (as we have seen and will see again), just as sailors and merchants obviously traveled with their maps and charts.

A continuous and lasting osmosis had established itself among the various coastal areas, resulting in a common nautical (as well as maritime-commercial) culture, a sort of *koine* among the various "nations" (there were nation-states in only a part, and not the larger part, of the Mediterranean). This interaction was reflected in exchanges of vocabulary and loan words, if not exactly in the use of a kind of *lingua franca*, thanks to which people could understand each other in the ports and on the ships. Place names on nautical charts must also have been affected by this state of affairs, so that the language and the form in which individual toponyms are reported may even be barely significant (becoming perhaps only clues at best) — not to mention the fact that place names, or at least some of them, could have been taken from earlier documents. It has even been suggested that the copyists of charts could have been illiterate (though this may have been true only of those given the tasks of retracing the coastal outlines, carrying out the initial preparation, or painting the illuminations and decorations).

Among various authors, Mollat has written a very fine account of economic life in the Mediterranean and of the maritime and mercantile social class that animated it, citing numerous examples from the sixteenth century especially, but also including references to structures that had been present for centuries. He emphasizes a variety of aspects, since the sailors and navigators were also businessmen, and people of all types embarked on ships of the time, from the artisan looking for raw materials or markets in which to sell his products to the gentleman from a noble family, like Vasco da Gama, who would be asked to head an expedition of discovery by virtue of his organizational capabilities, and possibly also his political and military qualifications.

Nautical and cartographic methods certainly played an important role in the practical and applied culture of this maritime and mercantile class (if there is a piece missing in this overall picture — with regard to the Arab and Byzantine contribution, for example, which was certainly not insignificant — this is due to a lack of documentation and research). I must insist on the practical and applied aspect of this kind of culture in order to account for certain characteristics of nautical charts and the importance acquired by semiological and symbolic elements in them. At a certain point these went so far as to make the nautical chart understandable even to the illiterate, including the sailors on Columbus's voyages, who, as we know, could neither read nor write but knew how to *marear* using nautical charts (the number of illiterate sailors aboard ships in earlier centuries was certainly not smaller, but rather, if anything, greater).

Actually, once the ability to use the compass had spread, together with the custom of navigating according to its indications, then the practice of noting the details of the coastal stretches along which one was sailing and depicting them in sketches (instead of describing them in portolans) also may well have developed in various places and in different areas, followed by the technique of assembling the sketches into more or less extensive tables, until one arrived at the true nautical chart. This is to say, therefore, that in the thirteenth century nautical charts may have arisen independently in various territories, be it in Genoa, Venice, Catalonia, or the Balearics (but certainly not in Portugal, for the reasons mentioned earlier, regardless of what is said by scholars of that country, who forget that in 1317 their ruler had to resort constantly to Genoese *sabedores de mar* [experts of the sea]). Very soon, however, such works became known outside their original environment; they were improved through mutual contacts and borrowings, often by copying and even through instances of espionage (otherwise there would be no sense in the demand for "exclusivity" attested by the archival documents and submitted to rulers and government officials by certain cartographers, in order to protect "copyrights" over their work, as we would say today).

In conclusion, nautical cartography, developing in various ways over the centuries, was a product of the marine civilization of the Mediterranean in the Middle Ages. In the face of this established claim, the age-old debate over whether Italian or Catalan charts came first loses much of its significance.

Nevertheless I must speak of the innovations introduced into nautical charts, probably in the third and fourth decades of the fourteenth century (judging from the examples that have come down to us); and note that it was then that elements appeared that would become traditional and characteristic of Catalan, but not only Catalan, works. Above all, as I said earlier, we observe a more accurate and detailed depiction of the northwestern and northern coasts of Europe — in the Baltic, for instance. It is possible that Catalan sailors were better informed about these shorelines and the adjacent areas than the Genoese (who left from a port located farther to the east), or, even more, the Venetians. Hence Genoese cartographers may have gotten information from the Catalans in order to improve the representation of northern Europe on their charts. Thus pictures (of cities, mountain chains, rivers, etc.) concerning the interior of the continents made their appearance, perhaps because they were useful to merchants, who, upon reaching the seaports, needed contacts and information about the respective hinterlands. Thus decorative elements began to crowd these charts.

In Europe the Alps are represented by a strange cross-shaped design, which is basically confined, however, to the northwestern part of Italy. The Elbe flows in the center of Europe down from a circular mountain chain and into the North Sea, following a course that bears little resemblance to reality. The Rhine and the Danube, on the contrary, run latitudinally. No other mountain systems are depicted, but the peaks of Scandinavia, looming over the neighboring lands and seas and populated by griffins, are represented schematically by two triangles (as early as Dalorto's charts).

In Africa a prominent chain rises north of the Sahara, stretching from the Atlantic to the Libyan desert; this is the previously mentioned *Carena* (a word of uncertain derivation, perhaps Arabic), which in the east forks into two branches of peaks, according to Dalorto, or three, according to Dulcert. In the western part, the chain is interrupted by a valley running from north to south (in margin Dulcert includes the annotation *hoc est via per ire ad terra nigrorum*, or "this is the way to the land of the black people"); toward the center a semicircular mountain system rises up and looms over a city. It should be noted that these mountain elements would disappear from nautical charts between the mid-sixteenth and the mid-seventeenth century. As for the *Carena*, only in 1508 would the synonym 'Atlas mountains' appear for the first time, on a map by Andrea Benincasa.

Elephants, rhinoceroses, lions, ostriches, birds, and trees of various kinds appear among the decorative elements on the continents, especially in exotic countries. Caravans of merchants heading toward then unknown or little known lands are shown. Everywhere flags and coats-of-arms serve to introduce elements of political geography which migh have served a practical purpose, after all, indicating how various lands belonged to particular nations or sovereigns, who, in turn, were represented by more or less fanciful figures. Images of saints, however, do not appear in this century, as they will in later times.

One could almost claim that when depicting the land's interior, especially if unknown or little known, Christian cartographers, even of a later time, nourished a kind of *horror vacui*, so that they filled up such areas with the most varied drawings and symbols. This was in contrast to the Jewish tradition, which, as is well-known, greatly appreciated the expressive value of blank spaces.

Certain elements would thus become traditional for centuries, such as the red cross on a white (or silver) field — Genoa's coat-of-arms — on Chios or the island of Lanzarote, and the white cross on a red field (the coat-of-arms of the Knights of St. John) on Rhodes and later (on a gold field) on Malta in the sixteenth century. This relative semiological uniformity is derived, in essence, from the *koine* of maritime culture I referred to earlier (in the charts of Catalan map makers the decorations are generally more abundant and prominent).

The fourteenth century witnessed the full delineation of that proto-typical representation of the Mediterranean and adjacent bodies of water that has been called the "standard portolan," especially by non-Italian scholars, and using an inappropriate term. The area depicted essentially covers the same as the one whose coasts are described in the *Compasso da navigare* studied by Motzo, corresponding to the economic sphere of Genoese commerce, but also to that of other Western European cities facing this sea.

In such representations the system of a double ring of wind roses remained, and would for a long time, well into the fourteenth century (it is found in the Medici Atlas and the Catalan Atlas, already cited, and, for example, in the nautical chart of Guillermo Soler, dating from 1385 and kept in the State Archives in Florence). This system was progressively replaced, however, by one based on a single ring and one central rose, which gives greater unity to the network of winds and allows the chart to be better utilized (as Baldacci notes) — even in those cases where the networks of the western and eastern portions reflected asymmetrical values (they would become totally symmetrical only later, as navigational practice demanded).

In the cartographic works of this century there was, understandably, no application of Ptolemaic theories about latitude. Later, when references to longitude appear, they will be found only along the equator, since there is no concept of converging meridians farther north. It is equally understandable that nautical charts of the Mediterranean, even at a later time, would carry no indication of the height of the tides, which was of little concern to sailors in this body of water, even though they were already traveling (and regularly) along the coasts of the Atlantic. Graphic scales, on the other hand, continue to appear and will be located in different places with the passage of time.

In the so-called atlases, lastly, the areas to be represented were divided up differently according to the number of tables, assuming that the overall boundaries of the material stayed the same. The plan of the *Tammar Luxoro Atlas* was often repeated, but with numerous variations, attesting to the cartographer's flexibility with respect to the demands of the person who commissioned his work and the use for which it was intended.

* * *

Few nautical charts from the second half of the fourteenth century have come down to us, and none of Genoese production. This does not at all mean that none were produced, since the archival research done in Genoa by Ferretto and Revelli has yielded documents in which charts *pro navigando* are mentioned ever more frequently as we approach the end of the century and pass beyond it. Obviously the perishable material on which they were drawn and the unremitting use to which they were subjected on board ship have led to their destruction.

4) *Nautical charts of the fifteenth century and the first globes*

As the new century was beginning, therefore, and the Middle Ages headed for its epilogue, nautical cartography had achieved a rather well-defined character. Its most widespread product was the representation, on a single parchment, of the Mediterranean, together with the adjacent lands and seas, and with the boundaries cited above. The atlases, or rather, the chart collections (with six to ten tables), which were destined to keep on multiplying thereafter, became more detailed and began to include decorative elements, as did individual cartographic documents. Planispheres began to take on a look of their own, independent of medieval cosmological and legendary motifs; they also ceased to be based on the reproduction of a central nautical chart, as had been the case earlier, resulting in new delineations of known lands (for which the elements furnished by nautical charts, selected and elaborated from time to time, were very valuable).

The new century had not yet begun when a Genoese living in Barcelona, Francesco Beccario, together with a Catalan cartographer of Jewish origin, received an order from a Florentine merchant on a business trip to the Iberian Peninsula for four large maps, which perhaps were meant to be true planispheres (they were intended for four monarchs). This story has been reconstructed by Skelton based on archival documents, even though the maps have been lost. The documents refer first to Jaime Ribes (the name adopted by the Jew Jafudà Cresques when he became a Christian) with "Francesco Beccha" given only as the name of the decorator of the maps. Later, only *Franciscus Becharius, magister cartarum navigandi* is cited, with the specification that he was a Genoese citizen residing temporarily in Barcelona.

Two of the maps had been completed in May of 1400; the other two, for which a price increase had been requested, were then in an advanced state of production. Becharius must have returned to Liguria not long after, since he made a nautical chart (now at the Yale University Library) in February 1403 in Savona (Astengo suggests that he stopped there on his return home). This chart deserves attention, and not only for the quite realistic depiction of the harbor and city of Genoa, with a perspective view of the houses along the wharves (Savona, in contrast, is marked by a flag with the city's coat-of-arms, as is Paris).

A very long cartouche on the chart affords us some interesting observations. It mentions of "Catalans, Venetians, Genoese as well as other chart masters, who made charts for sailing in times past," proving that the craft of nautical cartography had spread, with three principal centers in Catalonia, Venice, and Genoa.

In the same cartouche the cartographer claims to have corrected mistakes from previous charts as to the location of Sardinia and to have lengthened the coastlines of Western Europe from Cape St. Vincent to the "coast of Britain and the island of Anglia." A notification ascribed to the very sure experience of many great patrons of shipmasters and pilots in the Sea of Spain and those parts . . . ." In other words, since the depiction of the Atlantic coasts of Western Europe in previous nautical charts was based on distances shorter than the actual ones, Becharius claims to have corrected these linear measurements so as to equalize the scales. The results, however, show that he did this (or was successful) only in part.

We know almost nothing more of Francesco Beccario. Among other things, we know that copies of his charts are included in a collection of nautical documents from the end of the fifteenth century; they are now held in the British Museum in London. It is likely (though we have no certain proof) that Battista Beccario, a Genoese and maker of nautical charts in the third and fourth decades of the fifteenth century, was descended from him, though the place where they were drawn up has not been determined.

These charts deserve special attention because of the interest they show in the Atlantic and, in particular, in the islands recently discovered (or rediscovered). The 1435 chart, kept in the Palatine Library in Parma, is the first to bear the name *Antilia* (or *Satanasso*), as well as *Royllo*, *Tanmar*, *de mam*, and *Brazil*. References to island groups in the Atlantic had already appeared, however, in his 1426 chart, now preserved in the Bavarian State Library in Munich. With respect to the Atlantic Ocean it is obvious that the earliest information about the discoveries the Portuguese were making there in those years entered into this cartographer's work. He proves to have been very careful about the accurate depiction of the Italian coasts (insofar as this was possible), and especially the Ligurian ones (including a fine view of Genoa, which recalls the one already mentioned on Francesco Beccario's chart); he also makes much use of Genoese toponyms.

This has a bearing on the age-old question of the links between Italian, especially Genoese, cartographers and Iberian ones, as well as of the relationship between the discovery and the depiction of the geographical sites explored (in this case, of islands in particular). In this regard I do not believe we can accept the answer given in the past by Italian scholars, who, in a fully nationalistic climate (between the two world wars) claimed not only that Italian cartography came first, but also — according to what was for them the natural consequence thereof — that at least the greater part, if not all, of the discoveries of the Atlantic islands should be attributed to Italian navigators, known and unknown.

If it is true, in fact, as stated earlier, that the Portuguese fleet in the early decades of the fourteenth century was just coming into existence, a hundred years later it was, on the contrary, capable of undertaking impressive enterprises of discovery and exploration. In addition to the earlier expeditions to the Canaries (which also continued into later times) incontrovertible achievements attributable to the Portuguese in the fifteenth century include: the discovery (or rediscovery) of Madeira and its neighboring islands beginning in 1419 (or 1418); the reconnoitering and initial colonization of the Azores between 1427 and 1439, as they progressively distinguished among the various islands (which lasted into later periods); and systematic sailing trips along the western coast of Africa (where the Genoese presence, more or less episodic, goes back to the end of the thirteenth century, as I pointed out before), pushing ever farther to the south until they arrived at Cape Verde and its islands after the middle of the century (with Italian seamen also participating in some voyages).

All of these discoveries were destined to be transferred meticulously onto cartographic representations that were more or less approximate, or (on the contrary) more or less faithful. It is possible that Majorcan cartographers (or more generically, Catalan ones) were informed of the results of Portuguese discoveries before the Genoese given their geographical proximity (one of the Catalans, Jafudà Cresques, mentioned earlier, had been summoned by Prince Henry of Portugal to become part of his court of experts on the seas). But the Genoese, too, had contacts with Lisbon and with maritime circles in Portugal, where a cartographic tradition must have developed, or rather, been in the process of developing, even though the first nautical charts by Portuguese makers that have come down to us are from the second half of the fifteenth century, and are also rather behind the times.

Mythic islands, derived from medieval features if not from classical reminiscences, appeared alongside the *ilhas hachadas*, or "discovered isles." It is not surprising, therefore, that some of the Azores, depicted relatively accurately in the 1413 chart by the Catalan, Mecia de Viladestes, are "in ambiguous proximity to entirely imaginary traditional islands in the ocean," as Baldacci writes. It is only with Andrea Bianco's work of 1436 that these Atlantic islands would be given a definite location, later repeated by other cartographers. It would be arbitrary to conclude, from the fact that one or more islands were depicted on a dated chart, that they had been actually reached in that year (one could have heard of them, even indirectly); still less can one infer, from the fact that the cartographer used a particular language or dialect to refer to place names on that island, that it must have been discovered by navigators from the country in which that language was spoken.

Among the Atlantic islands that always (or almost always) appear on fifteenth century nautical charts is the well known island of *Antilia*. From time to time scholars have wanted to see in this an indication or foreshadowing of American lands, especially as it would not seem to correspond to the "true" Azores, since both it and these islands are shown in many charts (for example, in the one by Battista Beccario, dating from 1435). So the island must have been an imaginary one, a geographical myth, like *Saint Brendan's Isle*, or like the medieval *Hesperia*, which, like its classical antecedent, always receded westward in the face of efforts by explorers and travelers to reach it. Indeed, *Antilia* would disappear from maps once the New World was discovered, even though Peter Martyr of Anghiera and Amerigo Vespucci mentioned it (the term "Antilles" would return to life in the seventeenth century, in Ortelius's maps, for example, to designate the Caribbean Islands).

Battista Beccario was certainly practicing the craft of nautical cartography in Genoa in 1427, when he accepted as his "pupil and servant" (as a document published and studied by Petti Balbi says) a nine-year-old boy, one Raffaelino, the son of a Genoese citizen by the name of Simone da Sarzana, *navigator*. The boy would have had eight years to learn "the art of making charts and signs for sailing." Hence it can be presumed that the master was also in Genoa the year before this, and that the chart of 1426, cited above, must have been made in this city, whereas some uncertainty remains for the chart of 1435, since it is possible that Beccario moved elsewhere.

In 1438, in fact, Agostino da Noli asked the Republic of Genoa to exempt him from all personal taxes and assessments on food and clothing for him and his family for as long as he lived, on the grounds that he was the only master of the craft of nautical cartography left in the city; this had already been granted to a master "who... makes guides for sailing" (that is, a manufacturer of compasses; for this craft, too, it seems that only one specialist had remained in Genoa). After calling himself "very poor," Agostino alludes to the traditional importance of nautical cartography in the Ligurian capital, since "without these charts no one can sail anywhere, because it is they that furnish the sailors themselves with safe routes and point out the ports." The Doge acknowledged the charts' importance and the fact that Agostino was poor, since he was unable to "accumulate much money by the very laborious craft mentioned;" he therefore granted the requested exemptions, except for the consumption tax. The municipal offices then limited the exemptions to ten years and added a provision that he should teach the craft to his brother.

Of Agostino da Noli's nautical charts not a trace is left. His brother has been identified by a number of scholars, including Revelli (though it is only a hypothesis), as Antonio da Noli, who later discovered some of the islands in the Cape Verde archipelago. This story tells us, however, that Battista Beccario was no longer in Genoa in 1438; he was either dead or had moved elsewhere, perhaps to Majorca, where Pietro Roselli in 1447 signed a chart, now held in a private collection in New York, declaring himself to be a disciple *de arte Baptiste Becarii*.

This last hypothesis is not unlikely. The question remains, however, of the possible reasons for the decline in Genoa at this point in time of the craft of nautical cartography, whose recent development Agostino da Noli had reported in the same document. Without assigning too much importance to the complaints of a man who was trying to avoid his taxes, it is still clear from the episode mentioned that it was not a comfortable state of affairs, as a consequence, perhaps, of the monopoly previously established in this field, or because of competition from other cities, even smaller ones, to which cartography had spread. One reason was surely the diaspora caused by local political conditions, which, as stated before, encouraged the Genoese, in this sector as in others, to look for better employment elsewhere.

We know little or nothing else about Pietro Roselli. There seems to be no foundation to the theory that he was one of the many converted Jews living in the Balearics and Catalonia under an adopted Latin surname. The form of the latter has made some think he was of Italian origin, and many have maintained that his birthplace should be sought in Venice. But we may recall that surnames like "Rossello" or "Rosselli" were quite widespread in Liguria, too (as they still are). In the 1447 chart, moreover, there is a coat-of-arms that has been identified as belonging to the Genoese family of Usodimare.

However that may be, this, too, is further evidence of the mobility of cartographers at that time, just as in previous and subsequent periods. Such professionals were armed with privileges that protected their craft and especially their abilities given the real risk of illicit copying and the not rare forms of espionage from one port city to another. Armed also with the professional experience they had developed, they carried with them the prototypes of their charts and their store of ideas. These ideas were constantly enriched as they gathered information from the ships' crews as they disembarked onto the piers and wharves and then, reaching the ground, headed for the cities' public baths. The latter were places not only for hygiene, but also for pleasure, after the trials of sailing (some Catalan cartographers would be members of a family that managed such establishments).

Within the context of a common Mediterranean culture this explains the frequency with which certain motifs are repeated in the various charts, no matter who the maker was or in what city they were made. Certain pictures and images would in time become almost obligatory, especially when the charts began carrying information about the land's interior, as happened in the course of the fifteenth century, and when decorative elements — destined to become ever more prominent over the decades — appeared among them. There are, for instance, crosses (or a single crucifix) in the Holy Land, figures of the rulers of distant and exotic countries together with their tents, symbols — coats-of-arms and flags — of political sovereignty on islands and territories (even those where that rule had ended some time before), not to mention the embellishment of wind roses, the city views (more or less in perspective or stylized), the repetitive (or almost repetitive) delineation of certain geographical features such as mountain chains or groups and large rivers, etc., as well as the cartouches, sometimes very lengthy, which reflected the master cartographer's culture, of whatever varied origin that might be.

Another Genoese map maker of whom little is known (in 1461 he was provost of the church of San Giorgio in the Ligurian capital) was Bartolomeo de Pareto, who authored a cartographic document of considerable interest; made in Genoa in 1455, and now kept in the National Library in Rome, it reads, "the priest Bartolomeo de Pareto of the city of Genoa, an acolyte of our most holy lord the pope, made this chart in 1455 in Genoa." In some ways it would be better to speak of a planisphere than of a nautical chart, since it depicts (or tries to depict) the entire known world of that time; the representation of the seacoasts and of the islands is predominent in it, however, especially in the case of the Mediterranean and the neighboring bodies of water, as is usual.

To the west, in the Atlantic Ocean, are depicted the customary *Antilia*, the Azores, and Madeira with its small neighboring islands, in the midst of which is written "Saint Brendan's Fortunate Isles." The island of *Allegrancia* in the Canaries repeats the name of one of the Vivaldi brothers' ships; as usual, the Genoese flag, with the inscription *Lansaroto Maroxello Januensis*, flies over Lanzarote. Along the African coasts opposite them are numerous place names, such as *Mogador, Caput finis Gozole* [the cape at the end of Gozola] and so forth.

The coastal outline of Northern Europe is incorrect and full of gaps, especially as regards Norway. Between Norway and Great Britain stands an island, *Archania* (obviously the Orkneys), to which a "legend" attributes a phenomenon that, as everybody knows, is to be found, on the contrary, only beyond the Arctic Circle: "here constantly, day and night for six months, it is light, and constantly for another six months, day and night, it is dark and not light." On the opposite, southern, side of the chart, in Africa, beyond a large mountain chain is the "Land of the Blacks," with a reference to Guinea and its king, "a black ruler... Musamelidus... who is nobler and more famous than all the others because of the great abundance of gold that he has in his land." An effigy of this ruler is shown, as is the place name of the city of "Melly;" the city and its kingdom are mentioned by the Italians Alvise da Cadamosto and Antoniotto Usodimare, as well as by other writers of the late Middle Ages, in the same years that this chart was made.

Not many areas of Asia are represented apart from the Holy Land and the regions facing the Mediterranean and the Black Sea, and there are only two or three cities in the interior. For every country, however, views of the main cities and figures of every great nation's rulers (with the national banner beside them) are generally very conspicuous features of the chart.

The abundance of these and other similar decorative features leads one to believe that this is undoubtedly a "study edition" (one such feature consists, for instance, of black birds swimming in the blue waters of the Nile-likely swans, the current color being probably the result of oxidation of the silver tint used originally). The chart was intended for some important person or institution, perhaps an ecclesiastical one, as additional details might seem to justify. Beneath the cartouche with the signature and date once stood another inscription, almost entirely effaced, of which only the first word, *Camara*, survives. Moreover, under a coat-of-arms bearing a checkerboard band on a shield are the letters N and V. Could these be allusions to the Reverenda Camera Apostolica (the Reverend Apostolic Chamber) and to Pope Nicholas V, born in Savona apparently, but not of Ligurian stock?

This chart certainly has many elements similar to, or derived from, those of the 1435 chart, already mentioned, by Battista Beccario, and it should be compared to the anonymous Genoese world map of 1457, of which I spoke earlier. Still the work of Ligurian hands, it could perhaps be the connecting link between those two documents.

* * *

In the 1450's the previously cited chart by Bartolomeo de Pareto, as well as the anonymous Genoese world map that has given rise to so many discussions because of its untenable attribution to Paolo dal Pozzo Toscanelli, show that Mediterranean nautical cartography still followed almost traditional patterns, even if the latter were enriched with new elements and expanded outward to a greater or lesser extent into the

Atlantic (which began to appear no longer as an insuperable barrier to knowledge, like the Earthly Paradise on the other side, but as a navigable sea, especially after the Portuguese experiences, and a sea in which one expected to find new lands, whether islands or not). Nor could this be otherwise, since, even though Ptolemy's *Geography* was already circulating in the west, it was still in Latin manuscript versions without maps, and the maps were even omitted from the first printed edition, which was published in the next decade; they would be reproduced in printed works beginning in the 1470's.

In the second half of the century, judging from the examples that have come down to us, only a small number of nautical charts was produced in Genoa and Liguria. This can perhaps be attributed to those states of crisis and to the dispersal throughout the Mediterranean of Genoese masters that we mentioned earlier and of which the episode of Agostino da Noli is a revealing example. In addition to these tendencies, cartographers from other parts of Italy came to learn the craft in Genoa, as we shall see, but left again after a certain number of years to open workshops and laboratories elsewhere; these would flourish and become quite active, which undoubtedly must have facilitated the relative decline (if there was one) of the Ligurian cartographic tradition.

This is especially true because these were the decades in which the activity of cartographic centers like the Catalan and Adriatic ones continued and intensified in the Mediterranean, while Portuguese production, as I mentioned earlier, was developing along the Atlantic seaboard. For instance, after the successful conclusion of the experiment of Gil Eanes, who had succeeded in going beyond Cape Nâo (considered impassible, or at least risky for navigation: *quem for ao Cabo Nâo, ou virá ou nâo,* "whoever goes to Cape No either capsizes or does not") and then the equally mythical Cape Bojador, Prince Henry gave orders that the results be shown cartographically (*manda fazer uma carta de marear,* or "he ordered that a sailing chart be made"). Portuguese cartographic workshops undeniably made contributions of singular importance to the knowledge and depiction of the Atlantic beginning in this period and even more in the sixteenth century.

For the purposes of Columbus's history and the origins of his great discovery it is worth reiterating and emphasizing this expansion of geographical knowledge toward the west, which occurred precisely in the fifteenth century. In essence, as Randles has written, the Pillars of Hercules had been moved from now on into the middle of the Atlantic — into the "immeasurable and untraversable" ocean, in the words of Isidore of Seville, into "the sea... that was closed for so many hundreds of years" — as far as Cape Verde, the Azores, and Iceland. Even though only a portion of the islands marked on nautical charts had been explored (and some were in the process of being colonized), while the depiction of others was derived instead from traditional information in mythical and legendary sources of the past, yet their existence, in the final decades of the fifteenth century, was integrated henceforth into the geographical learning of the time. They were no longer "disconnected corners of the earth, outside the orb...," but actual part of the known world, and justifying, therefore, their inclusion on the maps, even if somewhat inaccurately, as Columbus himself attests in the Journal of his first voyage. This is all far beyond Ptolemaic geography, which was beginning to spread in these same last decades of the century by way of the engravings mentioned earlier. A Portuguese chronicler could state, with justifiable pride, that discoveries made by their sailors had occurred despite the opinions of classical authors.

Navigation in the Atlantic and at lower latitudes, if not at or beyond the equator, also presented problems of technology and instrumentation. Here another age-old question arises (one that is badly posed, in my opinion), namely, whether or not the Portuguese were the first to adopt so-called "heavenly-science" navigation (the term is used by those Portuguese scholars who claim that their country was first in this field). The reference is to the use of heavenly bodies in order to determine latitude (and, therefore, to locate places and the position of the ship along its route more accurately).

It is still to be proved that the Portuguese "invented" navigation using the height of stars above the horizon (as Italian scholars like Caraci pointed out some time ago). It is very likely, indeed almost certain, that this method was also employed in the Mediterranean in earlier times, but not systematically. The use of instruments in making such calculations spread slowly. Columbus does not mention making any during his first trip across the Atlantic; he did make them, however, once he arrived in the islands of the Americas, but kept the results hidden, giving out erroneous information, for reasons of political geography. In fact, the employment of such an instrument, which was often heavy and not very manageable, was difficult on board the small ships of the time; Vasco da Gama would make mistakes in determining the latitude of the southern tip of Africa. Other instruments that the Portuguese claim to have invented, such as the *balestilha*, or sextant, which is still useful for observing the stars, would spread quite a bit later.

The true merits of Portuguese seamanship are to be found elsewhere, starting with the identification of the stars of the southern hemisphere and of their position. Columbus would not have been able to sail at a latitude so close to the equator on his third trip to America if he had not been to Guinea many years earlier on Portuguese ships. Moreover the Portuguese made decisive contributions to our knowledge of the wind system and the currents of intertropical Atlantic waters. By repeated attempts they learned the easy routes for returning home — by taking advantage of prevailing winds — from the waters off the western shores of Africa, where the Vivaldi brothers, by contrast, had been lost. The usual route came to be that of the *volta do largo*, or veering out onto the high seas, which often (indeed always or nearly so) must have carried their ships to the area of the Azores, that is, to the band in which they found the prevailing winds to be from the west. Thus Taviani is correct in writing that if Columbus had made his first attempt to cross the Atlantic in the service of the Portuguese king, he would have left from Madeira and certainly not from the Azores. Undoubtedly he obtained his knowledge of meteorological and oceanographic conditions in the Atlantic while in a Portuguese environment and from the experiences he had while living there.

The *toleta del martelogio* mentioned before also belongs in the inventory of instruments; the finest and clearest example is perhaps the one found in a fifteenth century chart collection, namely the 1436 atlas by the Venetian Andrea Bianco. From this we must conclude that sailors in the Mediterranean were using it during the first half of the fifteenth century and that they therefore knew how to solve elementary problems in trigonometry, applied to navigation. I would be cautious, however, about stating that it was used in the Atlantic, since Portuguese sources do not mention it. Probably the use of the *toleta* declined or was gradually abandoned as the practice spread of correcting deviations along the route by determining the ship's position through observation of the altitude of heavenly bodies over the horizon with the help of a quadrant, sextant, or astrolabe.

Venetian cartographers in particular kept in touch with the Portuguese, while Genoa was perhaps more interested in the commercial exploitation of their discoveries. According to Albuquerque the echo of Portuguese findings was quickly received in Catalan map making, but very soon passed on into Italian cartography, where it had much greater resonance. Examples of this, in addition to others from the period 1460-1490, include the charts of Grazioso Benincasa and Cristoforo Soligo; the atlas made by the latter (or attributed to him, and kept in the British Library in London) contains information about the African coast from *Mina* to *Cabo de Lobo* (that is, the shoreline explored by Diogo Cão in 1483) and about three of the four islands in the Gulf of Guinea. Particular prominence is also given to the Atlantic archipelagoes.

The idea that they, however, like Andrea Bianco at an earlier time, copied Portuguese nautical charts must be considered apocryphal. Rather, it is likely that these men (some of whom were sailors and others, like Grazioso Benincasa, the authors of portolans) used information obtained from the *roteiros*, the guidebooks of Portuguese seamen. Similarly, it seems logical that Fra Mauro, the Camaldolese friar, had heard of the discoveries that came out of the Portuguese voyages, as later would Henricus Germanus Martellus, who did his work in Italy and, in fact, depicted quite accurately the results of Bartolomeo Diaz's journey one year after it was made.

It should be emphasized, in any case, that Portuguese nautical cartography, according to Verlinden, began not earlier than 1445 (approximately), whereas the inferences made by scholars like Armando Cortesâo, once again, are to be decisively rejected; these scholars suggested that the depiction on Italian (especially Venetian) charts, even before this period, of Atlantic islands with apparently Portuguese names was evidence of presumed discoveries in that ocean by sailors from that nation. In actuality, as I claimed, the islands in question were imaginary ones that people expected to find in the Atlantic but that had no relationship to geographical reality; this is true, for example, in the case of the well known *ixola otinticha* (perhaps meaning "authentic island").

* * *

I have hinted about the work of Grazioso Benincasa, the best known representative of a dynasty of Adriatic cartographers. A member of a noble family from Ancona, he was also a man of the sea who made many voyages in the Mediterranean and authored portolans. His prolific works (we know of more than 25 maps) do not belong to the strand we are discussing here, but it is certain that he was in Genoa from 1461 to 1466; it was very likely here that he learned his craft (which, therefore, must have been very much alive in the Ligurian capital) and that he made a nautical chart (in 1461, to be exact) that is now in the State Archives in Florence. He then moved to Venice in 1463 and to Rome in 1466, and from the following year divided his time between Venice and Ancona, cities in which he established flourishing workshops that continued even after his death. Decorative elements are not lacking in his charts, but signs concerning the morphology of the coast (such as dots in front of the shorelines to indicate sand banks and shallows) and marine symbols show that they were intended for practical use, for navigation (or derived from prototypes designed for such purposes).

Toward the end of the century but before Columbus's discovery (and maybe also afterward) there was another cartographer living in Genoa who completes our review of this century (we have deliberately excluded "learned" cartography, such as the Ptolemaic tradition). This was Albino de Canepa, of whom we also know little. In the Ligurian capital in 1480 he signed a nautical chart (today held by the Società Geografica Italiana in Rome), adding the qualification *civis Janue*, or "citizen of Genoa." This chart can be considered a full-fledged expression of marine and geographical learning as it had matured in the Mediterranean world of the Middle Ages and which was destined to be thrown into confusion by the results of Columbus's enterprise (Plate XIII).

A second chart by the same cartographer, drawn and signed in Genoa in 1489, was kept in Italy until the end of the last century (it was shown in an exhibition at that time). After some rather obscure incidents it apparently ended up in recent years in an overseas collection. The descriptions made of it indicate that it was very similar (almost identical) to the first one. No other documents from this cartographer's workshop have come down to us, so we are justified in believing that his works (at least the basic prototypes) were intended for eminently practical purposes and were almost all lost as a consequence of deterioration caused by use.

The land area depicted in De Canepa's charts is that part of the ancient world described in the so-called "standard portolan" of the fourteenth century, expanded to include what was known at the end of Middle Ages. The extent of the land, compared to the surface of the waters, reflects current theories that Columbus also shared, to the effect that the continents were larger than the oceans. However, the large blank space on the left side of the parchment, to the west, is significant, being reserved for the Atlantic and dotted with the usual islands, as I mentioned several times before. As in all nautical charts of the period, the greatest care has been devoted to the coastal outline, but in the land's interior appear representations of mountain and river systems (both of them with gaps and often formless and erroneous), perspective views of cities, figures of people and animals, symbols, and cartouches with geographical information. Thus the habit of some of today's Italian scholars (Capacci, for instance, as we have seen) of assigning these charts to the "nautico-geographical type" is not inappropriate.

Various elements of diverse origin converged in the cultural heritage of geographical learning reflected in these charts. Some must have been derived from Holy Writ and classical authors, as is shown by the fairly long cartouches placed in various parts of the charts. Here is an example: "The River Nile which has its source in the Mountains of the Moon which are on the shore of the ocean..." (statements that show how the makers must have had a fair knowledge of biblical and classical learning).

The derivation of other elements, present as well in earlier, even much earlier, cartographic works, is obvious and is connected to the greater or lesser frequency with which fleets visited various coastal stretches. An annotation next to a rock on the Dalmatian coast actually records a current event, the shipwreck of a Genoese vessel, although we do not know when it occurred. The depiction of African cities and other geographical features (the perspective views of Alexandria and *Tlemcen* are prominent) confirms that relations with that part of the world were never interrupted, even though it was under Islamic rule. In the case of Genoa, however, the traditional image seen in Beccario's charts is repeated.

The pictures and symbols that appear on the land can be explained either by the earlier conjectured *horror vacui* — characteristic of all cartographers (who sought breathlessly, one would say, to fill somehow all the map's empty spaces) — or by a need to provide informational and cultural features useful to merchants who wanted to know about the hinterland beyond the coasts along which they traveled. Esthetic and ornamental influences (which would be particularly felt in the sixteenth century) as well as distortions due to the persistence of traditional myths and legends probably also had an effect. It would certainly be worthwhile to deepen our understanding of the relationship between geographical features and decorative images in the various maps, including their relative proportions and their roles, and how these varied both qualitatively and quantitatively. But we would have to be able to distinguish between examples intended for practical use and "study" editions.

In De Canepa's charts the mountain systems are represented using quite different methods for the Alps — of which only the western part is shown with the Jura and the Vosges branching off (this almost schematic design is very similar to that found in various maps by Catalan cartographers, in those by Grazioso Benincasa, and in that of Jehuda Ben Zara) — and for the other mountains, where mound and dome shapes are used. The depiction of the European river system really repeats Dulcert's and Benincasa's plan, which is quite distant from reality, with an obvious latitudinal alignment of watercourses in the heart of Europe.

Other features of these charts do not lend themselves to any special consideration, except to mention that there is no indication of latitude (nor, obviously, of longitude). These features include the network of "rhumb lines" of winds branching out from roses (not embellished here, and less obvious than in other documents; the central one is in southern Corsica, the ring around it has sixteen roses, and there are two auxiliary ones, placed outside and laterally on a west-east axis, plus a rose with eight winds superimposed between Sicily and Libya) as well as the usual graphic scales (we can estimate the numerical scale, very approximately, to be 1:5,500,000).

In conclusion, these charts by De Canepa show that cartographers of the time borrowed mutually from pertinent works the motifs that were very soon to become common to all. For instance, the perspective views of many cities in these maps are very similar to the ones that appear in the nautical chart (in the Vatican Library in Rome) made by Ben Zara, whom we just mentioned, in 1497 (this observation was suggested to me by Capacci). Thus we must believe that Ben Zara had Canepa's work in mind and that such views were derived from a single earlier source.

As for the history of Columbus, it is very likely, and almost certain (even though none of our sources bears witness to this), that the navigator knew Albino de Canepa in Genoa before the latter made the first of his maps that has come down to us. Columbus must have navigated in the Mediterranean using aids and instruments like these charts. Perhaps he took them to Lisbon and compared them to Portuguese ones. The geographical frame of reference reflected in Canepa's maps was, in essence, the store of cultural information that Columbus had when he passed through the Straits of Gibraltar. Even the gaps, the uncertainties, and the mistakes — with regard to the depiction of Northern Europe and the Baltic, for example, and to the location of islands in the Atlantic — show the deficits and limitations of his knowledge (here I need to rectify an oversight that escaped me in an earlier writing, intended to explain the Genoese map of 1480, when I suggested that these distortions in Northern Europe could have arisen from an "azimuthal system of projection," whereas I should have said a "system of the azimuthal type"). Columbus filled in just these deficits and limitations and overcame them while living along the coast of the Atlantic.

* * *

Toward the end of the fifteenth century the reflowering of the science of geography in a climate of full-fledged humanism led to the construction of globes with updated drawings of the *oikumene*. The best known of these — although it is entirely outside the Genoese cartographic tradition — and the one that could be most directly linked to Columbus's cultural knowledge (albeit without the slightest basis, as we shall see) was the one Martin Behaim built in Nuremberg, almost certainly in the same year as the discovery of America. Behaim, also born in Nuremberg, was employed by a cloth firm based in Antwerp; he later devoted himself to cosmography and acquired great fame in that field — which modern criticism has shown to be unjustified. In 1484 he went to Lisbon on business, whence he moved to the Azores two years later. In 1490 he returned to Nuremberg and remained there until 1493, when he relocated to Lisbon once again. He died there in poverty in 1506 (or 1507, thus at about the same time as Columbus; even his date of birth, 1459, almost matches).

His globe is 507 millimeters in diameter and consists of a hollow wooden frame covered with a layer of plaster on which strips of paper were laid bearing the drawing, probably printed, of the world then known (obviously without any depiction of the New World). This artefact, which he gave to the city council of Nuremberg, where it is preserved today in the German National Museum, was almost certainly Behaim's inspiration, but someone else drew the planisphere, and two others did the actual material construction of the globe. The areas representing the seas, the land, the mountains, and the forests are painted different colors, with place names and cartouches in black. There are depictions of cities, images of rulers with their tents and banners, animals, and fish (in the waters beside ships).

The representation of the world thus outlined takes into account classical sources, recollections (partly distorted and incorrect) from the account of the Polo family's travels, and the results of Portuguese discoveries along the Atlantic coasts of Africa (though in a very defective and incomplete fashion). The most immediate source, however, was probably a planisphere by Henricus Germanus Martellus, but with some features taken from the anonymous Genoese world map of 1457 and the work of Fra Mauro, together with a series of revisions based on secondhand information received from Portuguese expeditions in the Atlantic Ocean.

The notion that Behaim took part in one of Diogo Câo's voyages (perhaps the second one) is, in fact, nothing but a supposition, unsupported by any evidence and maybe the result of his boasting. Various elements lead one to believe the contrary. Even though Bartolomeo Diaz had rounded the southern tip of Africa years before, Behaim places it at a location, "Monte Negro," corresponding to 38° south latitude, whereas in reality it is only at 15° south (and he gives the entire southern part of the continent a very distorted shape). This latitude was as far as Câo got in 1483, which is also approximately where the African coastline ends in the 1489 map of the Venetian Cristoforo Soligo. The depiction of the coastal outline on the Nuremberg globe represents, in fact, a retreat and a deterioration in knowledge compared to the planisphere made by Henricus Germanus Martellus.

In this regard Portuguese scholars maintain that Behaim used the account of the old navigator, Diogo Gomes, which abounds in obscurities and errors attributable to his advanced age — though it remains a useful source, given the lack of other documents. These scholars have also reassessed Behaim's other presumed merits. It is doubtful that he was a physician to King John II. We know he did not invent the *balestilha*, or sextant, which was in use only after his death. It was certainly not he who introduced celestial navigation into Portugal, since, even if it is true that he brought a copy of Regiomontanus's *Ephemerides* into Portuguese territory, that work does not contain solar declination tables. For this kind of navigation sailors from that country used the tables in Zacuto's *Almanach Perpetuum*, an edition of which is known to us at Leiria as early as 1446.

Finally, it is not true that Behaim took part in the Council of Mathematicians — which, on the king's orders, was said to have examined Columbus's project and recommended that the ruler reject it — for the simple reason, as Albuquerque writes, that this council never existed. From time to time the king asked astrologers and astronomers, cosmologists and cosmographers, especially Jewish ones, for advice on similar questions. As for Columbus, he may have known Martin Behaim in Lisbon and may have talked with him during the very last part of his stay in that capital city. He certainly did not see his globe, however, which was built in Germany between 1490 and 1493.

The globe has been said to bear many similarities to the map of the world that Wagner reconstructed on the basis of the presumed correspondence of Paolo dal Pozzo Toscanelli. Indeed, Eurasia spans 236° of longitude on the globe, so that the navigable extent of the Atlantic is much reduced ("there is little sea"). But even if Behaim, like the Florentine physician, had before his eyes a copy of the anonymous Genoese world map of 1457, would it not be simpler to go back directly to that undeniable and already mentioned source, rather than to yield to tempting theories built around more or less imaginary cultural intermediaries?

CHAPTER III

CHRISTOPHER AND BARTOLOMEO COLUMBUS, CARTOGRAPHERS

1) *Documentary evidence, reliable reports and clues*

It seems appropriate at this point to interrupt the chronological survey of nautical cartography linked to Genoese circles that I have described up to now, so that we may directly address Christopher Columbus and his brother Bartolomeo as "masters" of this craft, and thus attempt to trace, through cartography, their geographical conception concerning the shape and size of the earth. This is obviously a consequence of their education, which first took shape, as regards the basic elements, within the Ligurian and Mediterranean culture, only to reach maturity and its enriched status in Iberian lands, as indicated earlier.

There are many facts and various pieces of evidence to document the claim that Columbus was also a cartographer and had a good grasp of general geography and cosmography. Nor, indeed, could it be otherwise, when one considers the enormous goals of the transoceanic enterprise that he conceived and the maritime and nautical adventures that he was able to bring to a successful conclusion. In addition to these considerations and to the tradition that speaks of Christopher and his brother Bartolomeo as makers and producers of nautical charts, certain other data also emerge from accounts of the Admiral's life and undertakings, as well as from certain passages in his writings.

A first piece of evidence is mirrored in an excerpt of a letter to the Catholic Sovereigns, written by Christopher Columbus himself from Cadiz or Seville in 1501. Although the autograph text has not come down to us, but only a partial transcription by Bartolomé de las Casas, the fact that it appears also in the *Libro de las Profecias* (in folio four) and that it bears corrections and additions in the Admiral's hand in a number of places (as Varela also concurs) leads one to believe that it is entirely authentic. In any case, it recalls facts and experiences from Columbus's life and training that only he could have known well at that time and that would be attributed to him by various people as early as the first half of the sixteenth century (facts, therefore, that could not have been at odds with the truth). Finally, it should be added that — still according to Las Casas — a *figura redonda o esfera* [round figure or sphere] was sent to the King and Queen together with the letter.

In this letter's quite famous account about his cosmographical education and cartographic abilities is the following passage (somewhat freely translated): "at a very young age I went to sea and I have continued to sail up until now. This profession encourages whoever practices it to want to know the secrets of this world. It has been forty years since I became involved in this pursuit. I have traveled everywhere that one could sail to up to now. I have had contacts and friendly relations with learned people, clergy and lay, Latin and Greek, Jewish and Moorish, and with many others of other religions. I have found Our Lord to be very gracious in satisfying this desire of mine and have had from Him for this purpose an inquisitive intellect. In seamanship He made me rich in endowments, in astrology He gave me as much as I needed, and the same with geometry and arithmetic, and in this He gave me a mind and soul and hands able to draw spheres and show on them the cities, rivers, and mountains, islands and harbors, all in their true location. At this time I have read and undertaken to scour all the writings about cosmography, history, chronicles, philosophy, and other arts, for which Our Lord manifestly opened my intellect to understand that it was easy to sail from here to the Indies, and He aroused my will to carry out this intention..."

The letter, which aims to show "the reason for advocating the return to the Holy Church militant of the Holy House" (in Palestine), goes on to claim that it was urgent to carry this project forward to completion, because, according to Holy Writ and the Prophecies, the end time was near. At a time when Pierre d'Ailly was predicting the approaching collapse of Islam, and Joachim of Fiore was declaring that the one destined to "rebuild the house on Mount Zion" would embark from Spain.

Apart from these prophetic, maybe even visionary, accents, and apart from affirmations that could be the Admiral's own rhetorical inflation as to his preparedness and the efforts he had exerted, three other statements of great interest for the purposes of this essay emerge clearly from the passage cited. First he claims extensive nautical and marine experience inside and outside the Mediterranean. Then he reminds his readers that this was accompanied by the search for knowledge of the *segretos d'este mondo*, that is, by theoretical preparation in the field of what today would be called general geography, but which then extended also to cosmography and cosmology. Finally, he states that, thanks to his knowledge of geometry and arithmetic and the inclination of his intelligence, will, and manual dexterity, he is able to make not only spheres, but also charts and world map; the word *esfera*, in fact, should be understood in the last sense, as the equivalent of "planisphere." Las Casas suggests this when he speaks of *cierta figura redondo o esfera*, as we have seen, and Columbus himself clarifies this when he points to a series of particular geographical features in their exact location that he was in the habit of depicting, and that would have been hard to place on a globe, whereas they were customarily found in cartographic works.

But a more specific indication is given in a cartouche placed next to a small world map surrounded by the heavenly spheres; it was drawn on the neck of the Parisian map called that of the Columbus brothers (we shall speak of it at length later on). It states: "ABOUT THE SHAPE OF THE SKY. First of all it is to be assumed that the sky is a spherical or round shape. Hence the image or map of the world may be represented on a flat plane, though it must be imagined as spherical..." These are the exact same words that Pierre d'Ailly — a cardinal, philosopher, cosmologist, geographer and astronomer — wrote in a chapter of his *Epilogus Mappe Mundi* that is entitled, precisely, *De figura celi*. And in the copy of the 1483 Louvain edition of D'Ailly's *Treatises* that Columbus owned and annotated he repeated: "The sky is spherical, its image or map of the world may be drawn on a flat plane, yet it must be thought of as spherical" (*Celum est figure sperice ymago seu mapemundi, licet figuretur in plano, tamen debet imaginari esse in sperico*).

Sfera, therefore, also meant a plane figure, with a circular outline, that represented a spherical body. *Debujar* (the verb used by Las Casas in transcribing the Admiral's letter) means "to draw," and so *debujar sferas* should be translated as "to draw planispheres." This does not at all exclude the possibility that Columbus used globes and perhaps knew how to construct them as well. In this regard it is instructive to look at his supposed correspondence with Toscanelli, in particular the second letter (in whose authenticity few people believe today). In it the Florentine scientist says that he was sending *una forma de espera redonda* in addition to the *carta da marear* already dispatched, in order to show better the possibility of sailing from the east to the west. Don Fernando later wrote that his father in turn sent Toscanelli "a small sphere, telling him of his intentions" (Las Casas mentions an *esferilla*).

Other testimonies of the cartographic abilities of the Columbus brothers come from passages written by their biographers (or other writers who provide information about their life and undertakings). A prime source is provided by Antonio Gallo, a notary, banker, and merchant, and above all a friend of the Columbus brothers. His evidence should be considered reliable because it was based on letters from the people involved — letters Gallo claims to have seen (in Genoa, obviously) but which have been lost — and also because Gallo was detached from the power plays and current events in Spain. At the beginning of his *Commentariolum* of 1506 he refers to Bartolomeo, who "at a young age had settled at last in Lisbon, Portugal, where he worked hard in the business of painting charts [*tabellis pingendis*], on which the seas, ports, coasts, inlets, and islands are depicted in drawings suited to nautical use, the proportions being observed." He goes on to say that, since ships came and went every year from Lisbon, heading across the Ocean to the land of the Western Ethiops, Bartolomeo gathered information from those coming home as if from another world. Stimulated by his care for painting, he communicated these matters to his brother, as to one "more experienced in nautical affairs," along with his own thoughts, "showing that if anyone leaving behind the southern shores of the Ethiops, and direct his course to the west with the open sea on his right it was altogether inevitable that he would doubtless at some point find the continent in his way."

It is obvious that "painting charts" means making (or painting) nautical charts. Besides, the same Gallo, while telling of Christopher's second voyage, writes that on his way back, after giving the name of *Evangelista* to the last landing place, "he marked on the map [*tabula*], to the extent possible, the inlets, promontories, harbors, and the entire shoreline passed." Even in the previous centuries of the Middle Ages, as we have seen, the word *tabula* was used in the sense of "map."

Some time later Bartolomeo Senarega reiterated this information from Gallo, repeating it in the same words, but in his reference to the second voyage we find the term *tabella* in place of *tabula*. To complete the list of Genoese writers, Agostino Giustiniani, in his *Psalterium*, attributes Christopher Columbus's learning of cosmographical ideas to the Portuguese period.

In the first part of his *Histories* — the part about which we should have major reservations, especially after the incisive coinclusions by Luzzana Caraci — Don Ferdinand tells us about his father's penmanship, which was so good that he could have earned his living even by it alone (Las Casas, in turn, says "his handwriting, which I saw many times, was so fine and legible that he would be able to support himself by it"). Immediately afterwards, he reports that Christopher had devoted himself to studying cosmography, astrology, and geometry, because these sciences were interconnected, and, moreover, Ptolemy said that "no one can be a good cosmographer if he is not also an artist. He also knew how to make drawings in order to paint lands (*piantare*, "to plant," is evidently an error in translation from the Spanish word *pintar*, "to paint") and shape cosmographical bodies both flat and round" (which means to make globes and to construct plane representations of both the heavenly and the earthly sphere).

Ferdinand goes on to report that Bartolomeo left Lisbon for England, where he gained "a bit of a reputation by the maps he was making" and was able to wait upon King Henry VII, to whom he presented a world map with the well known cartouche in verse that bears his signature as "Bartolomeo *de Terra Rubra*" (and the date of February 10, 1488).

Much of Don Ferdinand's information is repeated, of course, in Las Casas's *History*. This includes references to Christopher's ability to "draw and paint," his knowledge of geometry, geography, cosmography, astrology, and astronomy, and his "great expertise, practice, and experience... and the fundamentals and principles and theory... to be very learned in *alturas* (the height of stars above the horizon) and in everything concerning the art of navigation." Las Casas also repeats the information that "during certain periods he lived off the diligent use of his intelligence and the work of his hands, constructing or painting nautical charts, which he knew very well how to make, and selling them to sailors." It was also this Dominican bishop who tells us that Bartolomeo Perestrelo must have owned instruments and writings and *pinturas* (that is, maps) relating to navigation, which his widow gave to her son-in-law, Christopher.

Here is what he tells us concerning Bartolomeo. He went to live in England and was in contact with the king, to whom he showed a world map he had made and signed. Here it is made more explicit (the whole story is told in more detail by Las Casas than by Don Ferdinand) that while he was displaying the document he wanted to point out to the king "the lands that he thought to discover with his brother." Las Casas claims, moreover, to have seen the text of the map's Latin cartouche with the signature and date, but with letters "written in a very bad and incorrect hand, with misspellings, and some of them I could not read" (he does not say where he saw it, however; in any case the text is given here, as it is in Don Ferdinand's *Histories*).

Luzzana Caraci, who is usually very careful and attentive, maintains that both Columbus's son and the Dominican bishop could have examined this world map or a copy of it (the latter seems more likely to me, especially as the handwriting, according to Las Casas, was not good). At any rate this would confirm that Bartolomeo's work continued over time, since neither of the two writers was ever in England. Both Don Ferdinand and Las Casas then tell us that this brother of Christopher, the second-born, "even though he did not know Latin, was nonetheless a practical man and an expert in matters of the sea" (the Dominican adds that he was "more uninhibited and clever and less innocent than Christopher"), and that he was very adept at making nautical charts, spheres, and other instruments used in the profession in which his brother instructed him (it was therefore a family business). Las Casas also gives us a physical description of him ("rather tall in stature, he was an authoritative figure, one that evoked a sense of honor, though less so than the Admiral"), and thinks it only hypothetical that he had learned the art of cartography from his brother; indeed, "he outdid him in some of these matters" and was not much less learned in cosmography.

Next we should cite excerpts from Andrés Bernáldez, a near contemporary, who, as is well known, hosted Columbus in his home after the ill-fated and unhappy conclusion of the second voyage: "a man from the region of Genoa, a merchant of printed books... who was called Christopher Columbus, a man of great intelligence, but who was not highly educated, very skilled in the art of cosmography." Another passage is from Gonzalo Fernandez de Oviedo, who, in reality, gives only indirect evidence of Columbus's cartographical interests; he called him "a very learned cosmographer" and gathered together the legend of the "prediscovery" by an anonymous pilot, who was asked by Columbus, then still a young man, to draw a map of the unknown land that he had seen.

References by Francisco López de Gómara (mid-sixteenth century) are more extensive. According to him Columbus "was a master at making sailing charts" and went to Portugal for the purpose of acquiring information about Portuguese discoveries along the coasts of Africa "so as to make and sell his charts more effectively." On Madeira he is said to have hosted in his house the anonymous pilot, who told him of his discoveries "so that he would put them on a sailing chart to verify them." But the project undertaken by Columbus, "a good Latin speaker and cosmographer," came to maturity not only through such experiences, but also through reading the classical authors (since he was not only learned, but *bien entendido*).

Still to be mentioned are the statements of Esteban de Garibây y Çamallao, the author of the *Compendio Historial*, according to whom "a man of Italian nationality named Christopher Columbus... came to the royal court claiming that it was better to discover unknown lands and great wealth on the western Ocean side. Since Christopher Columbus was an experienced man, skilled in the art of navigation, who made his living by constructing nautical charts..." A brief allusion is also found in the work of Gaspar Fructuoso, who says, in connection with Madeira, that "a man of Italian nationality, Christopher Columbus, trained and skilled in the art of navigation, came... to the island and married, living there off his profession of making nautical charts." As we see, all the authors cited and already studied by Revelli provide essentially the same evidence concerning the cartographic involvement of the Columbus brothers and of Christopher in particular (very few other minor items could perhaps be added).

* * *

To these statements we should add related items taken from the reports and narrations of his voyages (Revelli's work, of which I will omit only a few items of slight importance, is helpful in this case, as well). Everyone knows that in the *Preamble* of his *Journal* Columbus expressly mentions a *nueva carta de navegar* and a book (a portolan chart perhaps?) that the future Admiral intended to compose, putting into it "everything as in a picture, according to the latitude from the equator and longitude west."

Under the date of September 25 is recounted the famous episode of a map that Columbus had sent three days earlier to Martin Alonso Pinzón on the *Pinta*. On it were marked certain islands that they should have encountered on that stretch of sailing but which had not been sighted. When the map was returned, Columbus began to *cartear con ella con su pilota y marineros*. It is clear, therefore, that this was a nautical chart — one, however, that had not been made by Columbus himself (as someone has written). His diary reads, in fact, that *tenia pintadas el Almirante algumas islas...* (which means that the Admiral found certain islands depicted, not that he had drawn them himself). Las Casas is still clearer (*en la qual parece que tenia pintadas algumas islas...* Don Ferdinand does not mention this episode). This same Las Casas states immediately afterwards, however, that this was the very map that Paolo dal Pozzo Toscanelli had sent to Columbus.

Before speaking of the map's contents, the Dominican bishop adds that this document, of Florentine origin, was the one that *yo tengo en mi poder con otras cosas del Almirante mismo..., y escrituras de su sisma mano*, [one that I have in my possession along with other belongings of the same Admiral... and writings in his hand]. This point is precisely what arouses our suspicion. It very hard to believe that a small-scale *mappamundi* (one, therefore, with a large reduction factor for distances) like the one sent by Toscanelli was used for practical navigational purposes and that the depiction of small islands like those in the Atlantic was accurate enough to justify the expectation, on the part of expert seamen, of identifying them on the basis of the map. Hence it seems possible that this reference, which does not appear in the *Journal*, was inserted in order to lend substance and credibility to the legend of a correspondence with Toscanelli.

Both the *Journal* and the *History* by Las Casas speak of this chart again under the date of October 3, still with reference to the Atlantic islands marked on it and the ensuing discussions. Columbus extricated himself by saying that his goal was to reach the Indies, not to search for those islands. On October 6 there is an allusion to the depiction of Cipango (which was shown on the chart); to get there Martin Alonso Pinzón suggested a change of course toward the southwest (which Columbus would choose to do the next day, but on the basis of other considerations).

While speaking of the sail along the coast of Cuba on November 12, Las Casas mentions the surveys of the shorelines that the Admiral sketched (*el padrón y padrones que entonce pintaba el Almirante por sus manos, que tengo en mi poder...* [the drawing and drawings that the Admiral was then making by hand, which I have in my possession]). In this same author's work, as well as in the *Journal*, under the date of November 14, there is a reference to those world maps that show innumerable islands "at the end of the Orient." Finally, on February 10, 1493, there was an attempt on board the Admiral's caravel to establish the ship's position in relation to the Azores, and the pilots made use of *sus cartas* (hence there was more than one; the plural form is found in the work of Las Casas as well as in the *Journal*).

After that there is no further mention of cartography in the sources that relate most immediately to the first voyage. But it was certainly part of the cultural stockpile of sciences and experimental aptitudes that Columbus exhibited during his voyages (occasionally he is, indeed, rightfully called a' storyteller and dreamer by Oviedo; barros uses even less complimentary words) — and which he energetically and proudly defended at the end of his *Letter to Luis de Santángel*, where he gave thanks to God for having allowed him to see in person *estas tierras* of which others had written and spoken, but "entirely by conjecture, without direct proof... so that those who heard and listened, judged more by fables than by anything else."

While living in the Iberian Peninsula, during the short period in 1493 between the end of the first and the beginning of the second voyage, Columbus also must have occupied himself with cartography, in the midst of seeing to many other matters. On September 5 of that year, in fact, the King and Queen requested that he send them an actual map depicting the lands discovered in their precise locations — as had already been asked of him on August 4. Much has been written about the reasons that might have led such an expert cartographer to delay so long in fulfilling such an obvious commission. Since he was quite convinced he had reached Asian territory, it is likely that he had doubts about the proper identification, shape, and location of the islands discovered. What especially made him cautious, however, must have been the political implications connected with the rights that Spain (and he himself, thanks to the Capitulations of Santa Fe) had acquired with the discovery of the new territories.

In the beginning of May, 1493, in fact, Alexander VI's well known Bull had established the boundary between Spanish and Portuguese domains; it was based on longitude, but it traced a line that, if it is not considered a mistake, appears designed deliberately to provoke controversy in its application. Indeed the *raya* was placed one hundred leagues west of any island belonging to the Azores or the Cape Verde archipelago. Now the two island groups are not on the same meridian; the westernmost island of Cape Verde is quite a bit farther east than the westernmost one of the Azores (which must have been pointed out rather quickly, if it is true that a year later the famous and more rational standard of 370 leagues from the western edge of the Cape Verde archipelago was adopted as the boundary).

In view of the Bull's being enforced, the King and Queen requested of Columbus that the map include latitude and longitude markings and that it be sent to them before he left on his second voyage: "We need to know at what degrees the Islands and land you found are located, and the degrees of the route you were on..." The map was also to be "very complete, with the names written on it." But Columbus hesitated, and with reason; he had altered or concealed his data about the latitude of the new territories as long as the rule that the Ocean be divided on that basis was in force. But how could he have provided precise indications about degrees of longitude using the instruments of that time? Even calculations of distances traveled, as he knew very well, varied according to the estimates of different pilots. In any case it took time to convert these data into degrees, without any guarantee that the results were close to the truth.

Columbus was perhaps also constrained by his concern not to reveal his routes to other possible Spanish competitors. The Sovereigns reassured him on this point, guaranteeing secrecy: "If you think that we should not show it, write us to that effect..." In any case they advised the Admiral to take with him on the second voyage a "good astrologer" like Father Antonio de Marchena. Is it possible that the King and Queen, who obviously could have had no doubts about Columbus's nautical abilities, including his cartographic ones, nevertheless suspected that he hadn't told the whole truth (perhaps with a view to the commercial exploitation of his success)?

As we know, little first-hand documentation about Columbus's second voyage has come down to us. As far as cartography is concerned, we have had to make do until recently with the excerpt from Antonio Gallo — mentioned earlier — which tells us that the Admiral, *a man of the sea and very experienced in ships' routes*, sketched a coastal survey of Cuba's shoreline, along which he sailed for 71 days beginning at the end of April, 1494. Today, however, the *Libro Copiador*, published not long ago by Rumeu de Armas, lets us know, through a copy of a letter from Columbus to the Sovereigns, of the construction of what must have been the second map of the American territories reached. Indeed, in January, 1494 he reported to the King and Queen that he had sent a map that showed the newly discovered islands, "together with the others from last year," with the coordinates and distances marked in color "after a lot of hard work."

There are various testimonies concerning the third voyage, during which Columbus, who was already suffering from ophthalmia, may have delegated the task of mapping the lands they were discovering to others, such as Juan de la Cosa. On October 18, 1498 there are two mentions of a map to be sent to the King and Queen showing the land of *Pária*, which had been explored during the first part of the voyage. At the beginning of the letter about it to the two Monarchs there is a reference to the immediate and simultaneous dispatching of the two documents ("the depiction of it that I am sending you with this"), but toward the end it turns out that the map and an account of the voyage would be sent after the letter instead ("In the meantime I will send the report and the depiction of the land to Your Highnesses, and they will reinforce what ought to be done in this matter...").

Las Casas confirms this, writing that Columbus sent to "the King and Queen the whole voyage, and the image and depiction of the land." These documents were seen in Castille, perhaps clandestinely, by Alonso de Hojeda, who, in turn, would testify to this fact in a sworn declaration made in Santo Domingo in 1513 ("he saw the image that the said Admiral at the said time sent to the King and Queen in Castille..."). This cartographic representation — which is important because it refers not to an island, but to a portion of the mainland of the South American continent — is mentioned in other sources as well, sources that also allude, almost certainly, to a nautical chart constructed by Columbus, or under his direction, for the purpose of navigating in the waters offshore (hence, there was probably more than one cartographic document, which makes sense).

Indeed, when the issue of who landed first on these territories was being disputed — in the course of the suit brought by Don Diego Columbus to have his father recognized as the first discoverer of the South American continent (and therefore to have the associated rights of his descendents acknowledged) — a number of testimonies would be given, along with cartographic references. Thus Alonso de Hojeda would be forced to admit that Columbus deserved the credit for "the mainland he had discovered," as Las Casas would also confirm. On the other side, it would be stated that Hojeda had pushed 200 leagues farther south than Columbus, but by using the map and portolan Columbus had made ("notwithstanding the fact that he had before his eyes the map and route that the Admiral had made concerning his discovery of the gulf of *Pária*"). In 1512 we have the testimony of Bernardo (or Pietro) de Ibarra, who had been Columbus's secretary on this voyage ("...having marked... on a sailing chart the rhumb lines and the winds by which he reached *Pária*..."). In 1514 Francisco Morales stated that "he saw a sailing chart that the said Admiral composed in *Pária*, and he believes that everyone steered by it...," that is, all the other Spaniards who came into these waters after him navigated by it. Others state that Cristobal Guerra also "...took with him... the drawing the Admiral had made when he discovered the mainland..." and that "...all who have sailed on the Ocean sea have done so using the maps and drawings of the said Admiral and have followed the routes he discovered; and, had he not been the first, no one would have ventured to sail in those parts because they had no information about those lands, nor did they know the way nor have charts or drawings of them."

The events surrounding the land of *Pária* and its cartographic survey are also confirmed by the testimony of Pedro de Soria, when he tells of the Spanish expedition of 1499 ("...while exploring with Alonso de Hojeda, they used the same point on the sailing chart that the Admiral had made..."). To this we can add Revelli's contention — which I believe to be quite unproven, however — that Columbus's chart of these regions is the one that inspired the famous Turkish map by Piri Re'is in

1513. Indeed, Almagià denies this, thinking it more prudent to speak of Columbian impressions on a Turkish map of 1513. Whatever the case, the writings and cartouches on it confirm what we already knew, that at the end of his third voyage Columbus sent to the King and Queen an account of his journey and a detailed map of the newly discovered lands. Whether or not it, or more likely a copy, later ended up in the hands of the Spaniard who was the Admiral's companion on that sailing trip, or in the hands of someone else who was then taken prisoner by Kemal Re'is, Piri's uncle (which is how the chart would have found its way to Turkey), is only of minor importance for the purposes of this essay.

A letter from Angelo Trevisan, a Venetian, dates from 1501, that is, from the year in which Columbus wrote the Sovereigns the letter mentioned earlier, in which we read not only an enumeration of his abilities (which he considered a gift from God) but also a reference to the possibility — related to the recent discoveries of Vespucci and the Portuguese in the South American continent — of his returning to Iberia by going beyond the New World and reaching the true Indies (that is, by circumnavigating the earth). Trevisan's letter contains information about the cartography of the recent discoveries and about a chart made by the Admiral.

Trevisan, to whom we owe the *Trattato De Tutta la navigatione* wrote from Granada in the second half of August to his patrician countryman Domenico Malipiero, assuring him that he had ordered to be made in Palos, "which is a place where no one lives except sailors and practical men from Columbus's voyage, a chart, at the request of Your Magnificence, one that is to be very well made and full of information and detailed about what has been discovered." In fact, he adds, "here there are none, except the one of the said Columbus, nor is there anyone who knows how to make them..." He would have to wait a few days, because Palos is 700 miles from Granada and then there would be the problem of sending it to Venice, "because I have had it made large, so as to be more beautiful..."

I think it interesting to note the fact that a chart made by Columbus of the discoveries of the new territories existed in that year in a city in the interior of Andalusia, even though it was one as important as Granada. It remains only to imagine (since we cannot do otherwise) whether it referred only to the discoveries of the third voyage or, as seems more likely to me, to all those made thus far by Columbus. Since the chart was quite large, making it difficult to send to Venice, we may suppose that it was a planisphere, like those that were produced by various makers in the years that followed.

There is little or nothing about cartography in the documentation that has come down to us concerning the fourth voyage. In a combined letter and report sent to the Sovereigns from Jamaica on July 7, 1503, which has come down to us in a late copy, Columbus says only that after reaching Cape *Gracias a Dio* he followed the shoreline of the mainland, and that it was surveyed *con compás y arte*. A few other references have to do with Marinus of Tyre's and Ptolemy's concept of the earth and the longitudinal extent of the dry land, including the famous words, "... the world is small: six parts of it are dry land and only the seventh is covered with water..."

But the sketches formerly attributed to Bartolomeo Columbus — which Almagià believes to be the work of Alessandro Zorzi instead, and of which I will speak later — are derived from the experiences of this voyage (or are certainly linked to it). We know nothing of the cartographic work of Columbus's brother over this entire long period, probably because it, like all his activity, was eclipsed by the fame of the Admiral's enterprise. The attempt to credit him with some charts made in the early years or decades of the 1500's fell very quickly into oblivion because there was no scientific (other than documentary) basis for it.

2) *Drawings, sketches, and maps by the Columbus brothers or attributed to them*

If cartographic works seem to have come rather abundantly from the hands of Christopher and Bartolomeo Columbus, according to the testimonies and information we have recounted, very little, unfortunately — indeed extremely little — has been preserved until now. Hence it seems appropriate to mention also attributions made to them that were much disputed later or proven unfounded.

As is common knowledge, the Columbian Capitular Library in Seville, which can be traced back to Don Ferdinand, still holds today some of the works read, studied, and annotated by his father, Christopher. Of the numerous *Annotations* only a few are tables, sketches, or drawings — not cartographic works, strictly speaking, but certainly technical and applied in nature, concerned with navigation, or else referring to cosmographical knowledge. Thus at the end of one of the blank pages of the *Historia rerum ubique gestarum* of Pius II there is a drawing of our globe viewed, one could say, from a polar perspective (from the North Pole), with the words, *orizontem in partibus. X. circulus equinoxialis. occidens rectum in Ispania. occidens obliqum, ubi Sinum Sinarum. circulus Articus. circulus equinoxialis. orizonte in partibus. X. (Annotation* B 859 of de Lollis). As is evident, this document has very little significance (not to say none at all) for the history of cartography (according to Revelli the central elliptical shape recalls the anonymous Genoese world map of 1457) or for the study of Columbus's cultural preparation.

The *Treatises* of the well known French cosmographer, Pierre d'Ailly, whom we have already mentioned several times, are prefaced by two tables from the hand of Columbus (or his brother) before beginning of the text of *Ymago mundi*. One concerns the length of the day, and the other the height of the sun, at various latitudes (*Annotation* C1). These were certainly useful for navigation, especially over long distances in familiar waters, and Columbus, like all ships' commanders and pilots, must have carried a copy (maybe several copies) on board. But these do not concern cartography, except very indirectly. Finally, on a page of a booklet bound together with this work, we find the famous geometric drawing, without any writing (hence it is not included among the *Annotations* published by De Lollis) that continues on the adjacent page with the simple outline of a circle. Revelli interprets this as a "plan (quadrant of a circle) for the construction of a nautical chart," while Baldacci thinks it is a graphic representation of the *toleta del martelogio*, a representation peculiar to Columbus "because it is based on ninety instead of a hundred, as is common usage" (Plates XIV a-d and XV a-c).

The theory proposed by Baldacci, who has returned to this subject a number of times, opens up a discussion of at least two points: the nature and purpose of this drawing; and the possible use of the *toleta del martelogio* by Columbus in the Atlantic. On the first point it should be said that even if Revelli's interpretation seems a little simplistic it can be supported by a comparison with the drawing that appears on the upper plate of the 1318 atlas by Pietro Vesconte that was mentioned earlier. From this it becomes apparent, in essence, that the makers of nautical charts and atlases also used to make drawings of this sort, perhaps — indeed almost certainly — as a preliminary step to their actual work.

But Baldacci seems to have found a valid argument when he points to the three horizontal lines on Columbus's drawing, which ought to have nothing to do with the preliminary drawing of a network of lines on nautical charts. Yet (and this fact escaped him) three similar horizontal lines appear also in Vesconte's drawing, though they are less closely spaced than in Columbus's work. The explanation of their presence given by Revelli — speaking of the lines as corresponding to the Tropics and perhaps to the imagined southern boundary of the habitable earth — seems somewhat labored (in this I agree with Pagani, as I said earlier). The latitudes at which these lines are placed in Columbus's drawing are such as to refute completely Revelli's reasoning. Neither he nor others have noted, however, that in Vesconte's work it is obvious that these lines have a relationship to the heavenly bodies (actually two rather small circles of different sizes) that are probably depicted farther to the right. If this is so, and if we take into account the fact that Columbus's drawing is missing the right-hand portion — which should have been depicted on the adjacent page (where, instead, as we have already stated, there is only the perimeter of the outside circle) — then Baldacci's argument collapses. This document could also be less closely related to cartography.

I do not believe, however, that we can say anything definitive for now. Nothing excludes the possibility that Columbus was familiar with and used the *toleta del martelogio*; indeed, he must have been familiar with it, since this nautical aid had been part of the technical and cultural store of information possessed by Mediterranean seamen for some time. On the contrary, if we follow Baldacci's thinking, he knew it well enough to attempt to present it graphically (but why on a base of ninety? Do not ninety degrees bring us back to a quarter of the earth's full circle, that is, precisely to the quadrant, as Revelli was saying?). Whether Columbus used it, especially on his Atlantic voyages, is another question.

At the end of the fifteenth century, when sailing out onto the open sea, even within the Mediterranean, one navigated at times by taking one's bearings from the stars. Once the ship's position was determined in this manner, it was possible to correct one's route in case the vessel had been pushed off the predetermined course during the preceding sail by winds and currents. In essence, the *toleta del martelogio* had lost much of its utility (especially since its use always presupposed an estimate of the angle of drift and side-slipping). But another observation seems pertinent to me. Celestial navigation must have been even more frequently used when sailing in the Atlantic and on long routes in remote and unfamiliar waters; in such cases measuring the difference in latitude could also serve to determine the distance traveled (or to contribute to this calculation, as we said earlier). Columbus had become accustomed to these sailing trips while living among the Portuguese, and not a single Portuguese source has been found that mentions the use of the *toleta*.

Intellectual honesty also requires that we point out that there is no reference in the *Journal* to any astronomical determination of the ship's position (or rather, there is mention only of one such operation, which could not be executed with the astrolabe because of the condition of the sea, during the return trip, on February 3). Apparently the ship's position was determined only on the chart, based on an estimate of the distances traveled. To establish how far his ships had side-slipped from the course set, did Columbus rely on his ability to assess the force of the winds and currents (and the degree of their interaction), as I am inclined to believe, or did he also use the *toleta*, as Baldacci believes (although it is not even mentioned in the *Journal*)? Here we have a small question mark concerning Columbus's story, one to which we can give no answer at this time.

* * *

The only cartographic work that can be certainly (or almost certainly) attributed to Christopher Columbus is the one usually referred to as the "Haiti sketch," which belongs to the collection of the House of the Duke of Alba in Madrid. It arrived there at about the beginning of this century as a result of the acquisition by the duchess of the time of a folder or notebook of manuscript documents concerning Columbus's first voyage (among which was this very drawing); on the page on which it was drawn the duchess wrote *de mano de Colón* and the date 1492 (in actuality it could also be from 1493, and indeed the latter may be the more appropriate) (See Plate XVI).

Since then all (or almost all) scholars have held, and still hold, that it was the undoubted work of Christopher Columbus, even though recently a few voices in Spain — referring to the means of acquisition, which are recounted — have raised doubts also as to whether the group of documents to which it belongs is original or authentic, but without bringing forth any creditable argument concerning this drawing. Also known as the *Mapa de la isla Española,* it is quite small in size: ten centimeters wide by seven high. It is drawn by pen, in black ink (oxidized today, of course), and is confined to the coastal stretch of the far northwest portion of the island, which belongs today to the Republic of Haiti.

We must be dealing here with one of those partial coastal surveys, made on board ship, that commanders and pilots were in the habit of producing with a view to constructing nautical charts; in the latter, because of the reduction in scale, many details of the coastline were stylized and schematized. Its geographical content is modest for the same reason. Only the place names of *San Nicolas, nativida(d),* and *monte Cristi* (going from west to east) appear along the shore, where the drawing is fairly detailed, with sure and precise coastal stretches. Offshore are the island of "tortuga" with its place name and some groups of rocks or small islands. In the interior there are no geographical features, but only two inscriptions: *la (e)spañola,* and in smaller letters to the east, *civao.*

Plate XIV *a*

ymago mundi Jncipit. Prima figura.

Jgure sequêtes ad declarationê z intelligêtiam yma
ginis mûdi ptinêt. Que licet i plano sint: meliꝰ tñ des
criberêtur in sperico. Eñ secûdum figuras perfecte spericas
seu rotûdas eas ymaginari côuenit. Vec aût prima figura
ad primû capitulû spectat. Jn qua soluꝫ nouê spere celestes
describûtur secûdum opinionê astrologorû. Ma aristotiles
solû octo posuit.   Saturnus naturaliter frigiꝰ est z siccꝰ
i effectu: pallidus z malignus.   Jupiter caliꝰ z humiꝰ:
clarus z câdidus: maliciâ saturni temperâs.   Mars cali
dꝰ z siccus: ignitꝰ z radiosꝰ. Jdeo nociuꝰ z ad bella ꝓuocâs

Sol caliꝰ z luminosꝰ: têpora distinguês: stellas illumi
nâs: z qualibet eaꝗ maior.   Elenus caliꝰ z humiꝰ: inter
sydera splêdidissimꝰ: semper solê côitatur: ꝓcedês lucifer di
cit̄: sequês vero vesperus.   Mercurius radiosus: cum sole
sp graditꝰ. nûcꝗ ab eo. xxvii. gradibꝰ distâs. Jdeo raro cernit̄

Luna frigida z hûida: mater ê aquaꝗ: a sole illuminata
noctê illuminat.

Celum nõ ê de natura quattuor elemêtoꝛ: nec habet qua
litates eoꝛ: quia nõ ê generabile aut corruptibile. Mec dicit̄
calidû nisi virtualiter: qa sua virtute calefacit: nec ê ꝓprie co
loratû: nisi quia lucidû. nec ꝓprie leue aut ponderosû: mol
le vel durû: rarû vel spissû. Tñ iproprie dicit̄ durû: quia in
frâgibile z ipenetrabile. Et iproprie densum vel spissû: quia
stella dicit̄ densior pars sue spere. Mec ꝑt naturaliter moueri
tardiꝰ aut velociꝰ cꝗ mouet̄. Spere aût celi sunt iequales in
latitudine. Mõ tñ proporcionaliter scõm eaꝗ magnitudinê
Sed scõm quod stelle vel planete i eis maiores sût l' miores

The front page and the cosmographic illustrations of the *Imago Mundi* by Pierre d'Ailly (Columbian Capitular Library, Seville). This is the edition annotated by Columbus.

Plate XIV*b*

Secunda figura.

Hec figura feruit duobus primis capitulis fpecialiter. In ea tñ nõ defcribútur orizõ
meridianus ⁊ coluri: fed fequés figura fupplet. Etiã quinta figura huic feruit quafi ei
dem fubalterna.   Zodiacus habet figna.12: fex feptétrionalia que funt Aries Taurus
Gemini Cancer Leo Virgo. Et fex auftralia ḡ funt Libra Scorpius Architenés caper
amphora Pifcis. Quodlibet fignũ habet.30. gradus in lõgitudine ⁊.12. in latitudine.
Sol centro fuo defcribit lineã eclipticã: quolibet méfe vnum fignũ fere pertranfiens:
    Oppofitio fignoᵣ per hunc verfum habetur.
Sunt li. ari. fcor. tau. fa: gemi . cap. can. a. le. pifc. vir.

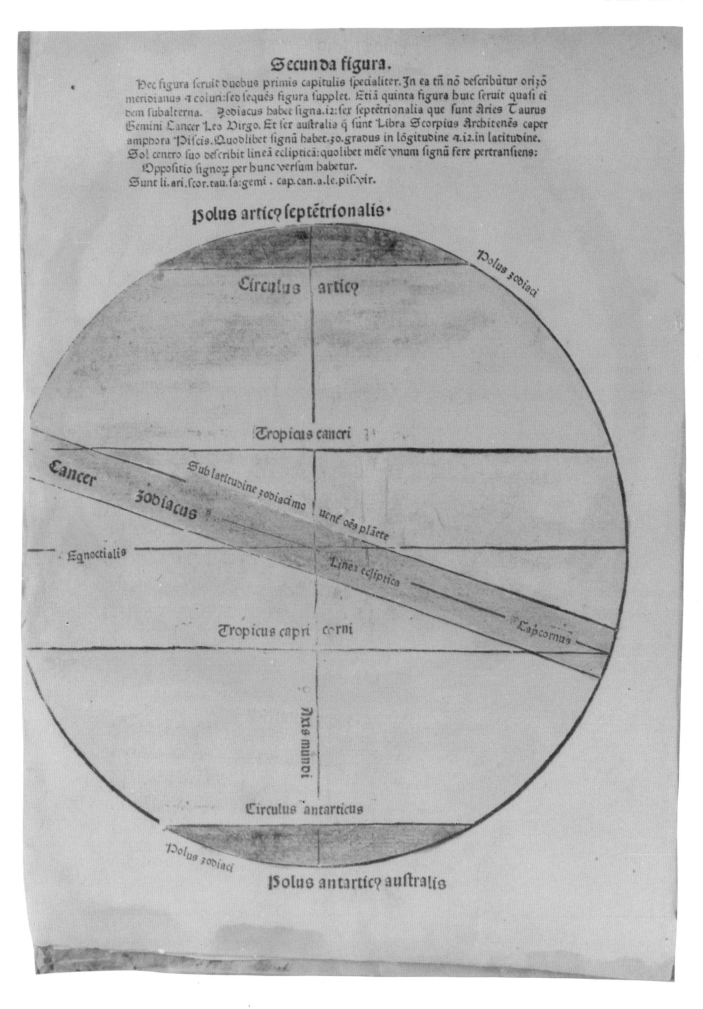

Polus articᵒ feptétrionalis·

Polus zodiaci

Circulus   articᵒ

Tropicus cancri

Cancer

zodiacus

Sub latitudine zodiaci mo   uent oés plãete

Eqnoctialis

Linea ecliptica

Tropicus capri   corni

Capcornus

Axis mundi

Circulus antarticus

Polus zodiaci

Polus antarticᵒ auftralis

Plate XIV*c*

Quarta figura.

Hec figura feruit qrto capitulo: In qua circulus principalis repfentat orbe lune : in
fra que funt quattuor elemeta 7 onia generabilia 7 corruptibilia. Ignis e calidus 7
ficcus immediate post fpera lune situat9: ibi tam pur9 7 clar9 q e inuifibilis. Aer est
calid9 7 humidus in tres regiones diuif9. Quar9 fupma fpere ignis iungitur 7 vtraq
cu celo de oriente in occidete mouet. Aqua e frigida 7 humida q inter aerem 7 terra
naturaliter fituatur. Sed tn vna pars terre q e minus graui; q alia fupeminet 7 pro
magna portione difcooperit aquis vt fit habitabilis. Maxima at pfunditas oceani
e. xiiii. miliariu vt quidā a marinariis inuentū ee afferūt. Dicetes etiā q eade profundi
tas minor e q dupla ad diftantiā centri mūdi 7 cetri terre. Terra e frigida 7 ficca q
figurā habet quafi rotundā. Cuius circuit9 cōtinet. CCC.lx. portiones totide gradib9 ce
li correfpōdentes: 7 cuilibet gradui correfpōdent in terra feptingēta ftadia : quor9 octo
valēt miliare: 7 duo miliaria leucā. Vnde cōcludunt aliqui totū circuitū terre continere
quindecim millia feptingenta 7 quinquaginta leucas.

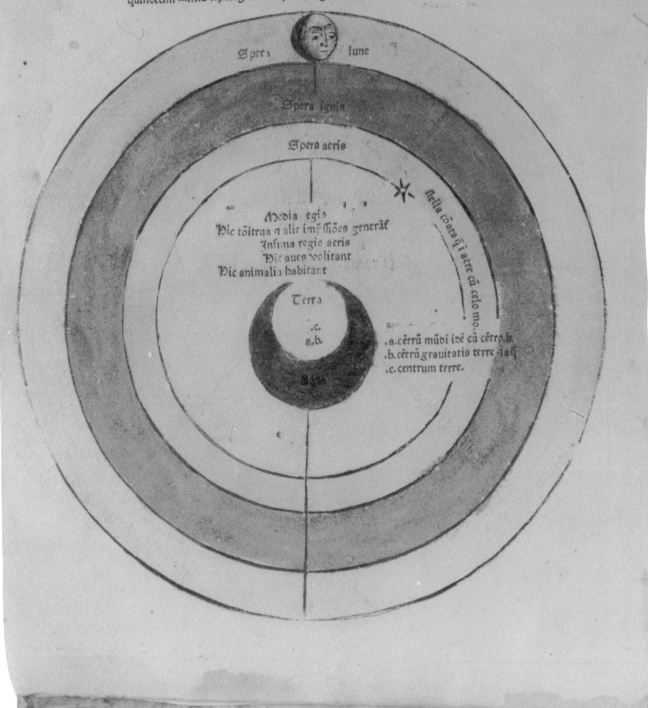

Plate XIV d

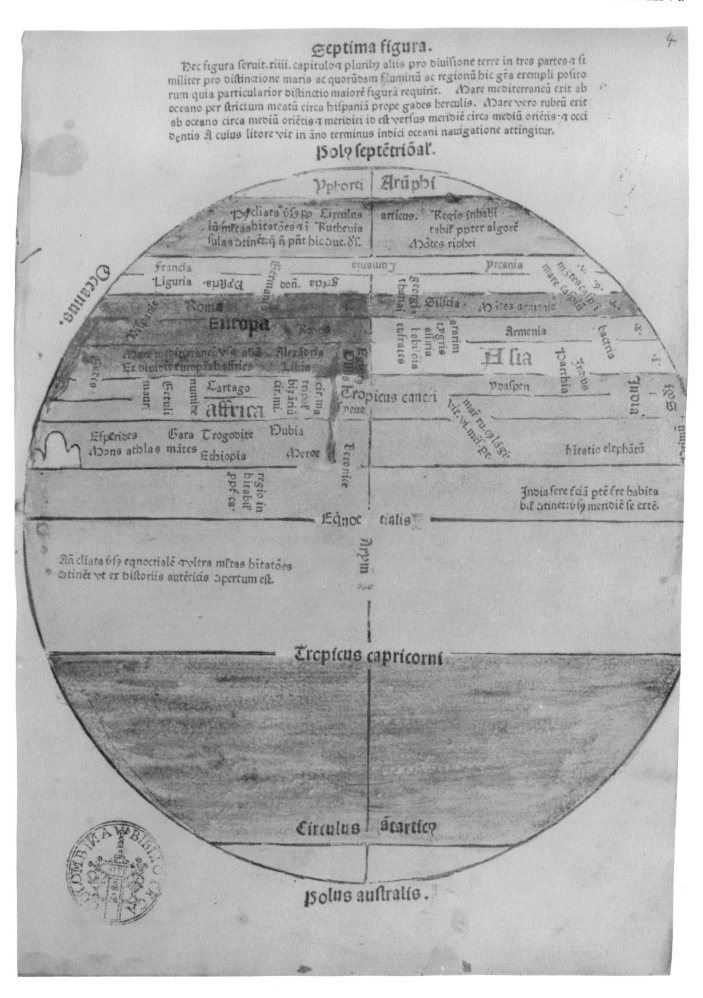

Plate XV*a*

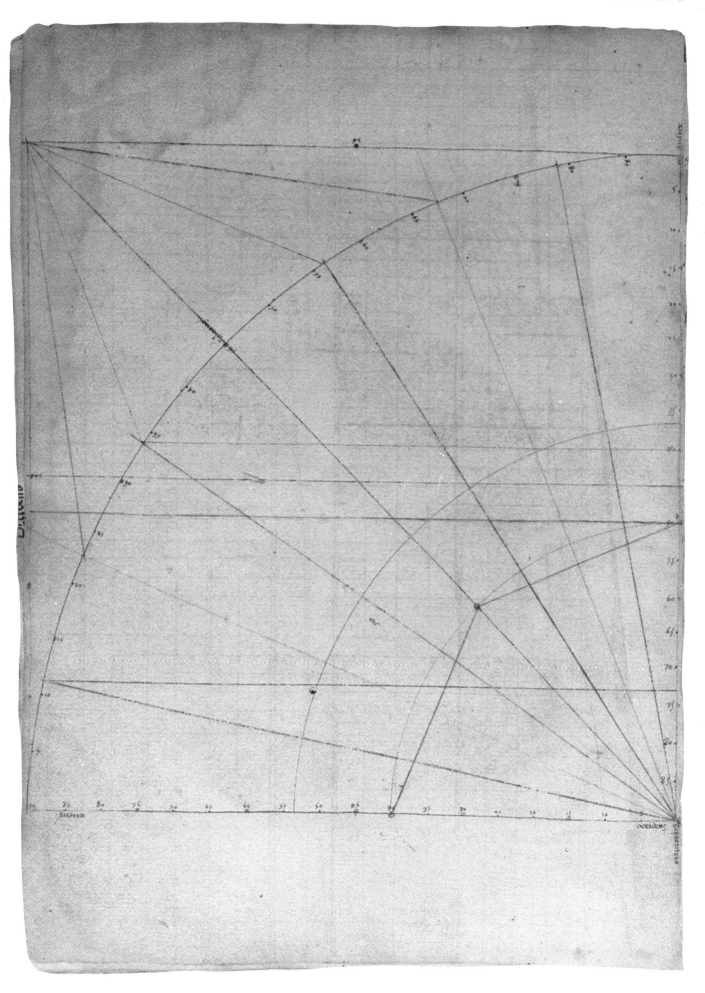

Plates and geometrical figures, by Columbus's hand, in his books preserved at the Columbian Capitular Library in Seville.

Plate XV*b*

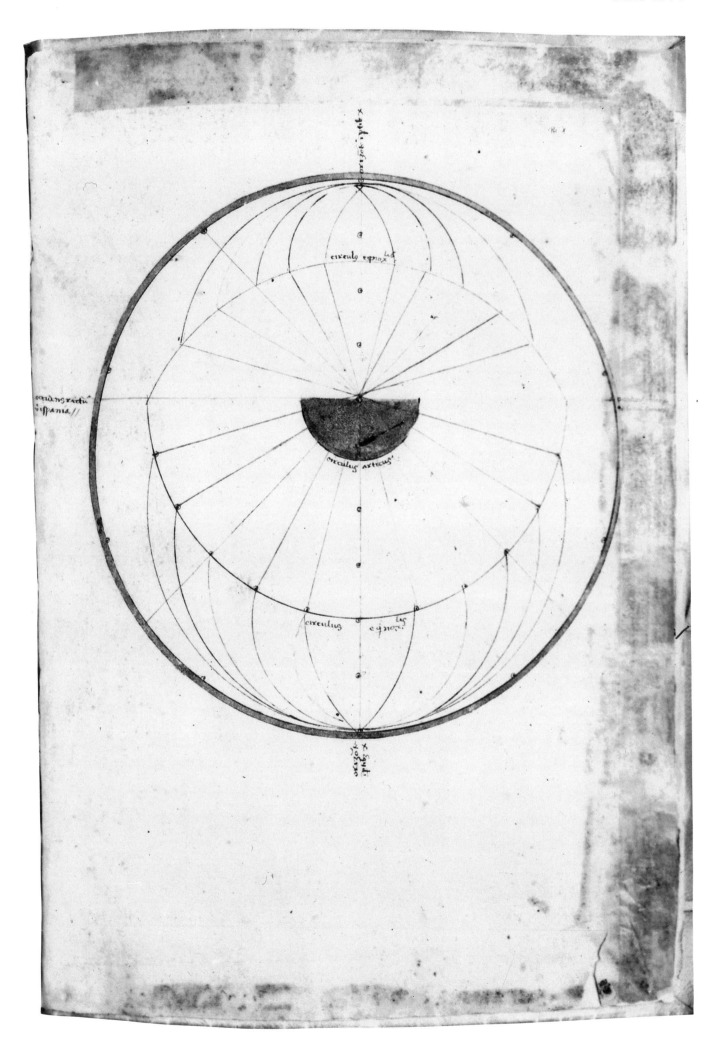

Plate XV c

5

Grad9	Hore	Min te		Grad9	Hore	Min te	Dies
1	12	3	46			35	
2		7	47			43	
3		10	48			54	
4		14	49	16		1	
5		17	50			10	
6		21	51			21	
7		25	52			31	
8		28	53			43	
9		32	54			55	
10		35	55	17	8		
11		39	56		22		
12		43	57		37		
13		46	58		54		
14		50	59	18	12		
15		54	60		32		
16		57	61		55		
17	13	1	62	19	21		
18		5	63		51		
19		9	64	20	27		
20		13	65	21	14	Dies	
21		17	66	22	27	0	
22		21	67	15	18	29	
23		25	68	9	24	41	
24		30	69	8	36	53	
25		34	70	5	22	63	
26		38	71	22	32	71	
27		43	72	20	50	79	
28		47	73	5	23	87	
29		51	74	19	26	93	
30		57	75	17	26	100	
31	14	1	76	0	51	107	
32		6	77	2	52	113	
33		12	78	0	24	119	
34		17	79	18	12	124	
35		22	80	8	50	130	
36		28	81	20	47	135	
37		33	82	6	30	141	
38		39	83	14	21	146	
39		44	84	20	34	151	
40		52	85	1	32	157	
41		58	86	5	24	162	
42	15	5	87	8	30	167	
43		12	88	8	54	171	
44		19	89	13	2	177	
45		27	90	14	55	182	

Left margin note:
hac t.. ostendit dies
pla i qlibg. icipi
endi egnos v dicit'
i. et hor 12 v 9 i
polo v dicit 90 et
hor 19 m 55 et
dies 182 //

Tabula3 Signor iscrius 9cpta ostendit
qituum sol ascendit qlibz diei i qhz Sig
icipieb i i q q arus pco quid iu
ordine hic inposita //

	0. 6.		1. 7.		2. 8.	
	G9	M	G9	M	G9	M	Grad9 suau9
1	0	29	11	52	20	27	29
2	1	47	12	13	20	39	28
3	1	11	12	34	20	5	27
4	1	35	12	54	21	3	26
5	2	59	13	14	21	19	25
6	2	23	13	35	21	24	24
7	2	47	13	54	21	34	23
8	3	11	14	15	21	44	22
9	3	35	14	33	21	54	21
10	3	58	14	43	22	3	20
11	4	21	15	12	22	11	19
12	4	45	15	30	22	20	18
13	5	9	15	48	22	28	17
14	5	33	16	6	22	35	16
15	5	57	16	24	22	42	15
16	6	19	16	42	22	48	14
17	6	42	16	59	22	55	13
18	7	5	17	16	23	0	12
19	7	28	17	33	23	5	11
20	7	51	17	49	23	10	10
21	8	13	18	5	23	14	9
22	8	36	18	21	23	18	8
23	8	58	18	36	23	22	7
24	9	21	18	51	23	25	6
25	9	43	19	6	23	27	5
26	10	6	19	20	23	29	4
27	10	27	19	34	23	30	3
28	10	48	19	49	23	32	2
29	11	10	20	1	23	33	1
30	11	31	20	14	23	33	0

| | 5 11 | | 4 10 | | 3 9 | |

It cannot be said, as Vignaud asserts, that the drawing is "coarse and insignificant." Though few place names are marked on it compared to those that appear in greater numbers in the *Journal*, this can easily be explained by the purpose of the drawing; it was meant to be used in compiling an overall nautical chart of this and other islands (and nearby seas), in which the smaller places would of necessity have had to be omitted. In any case, the part of the coastline depicted corresponds to the entire stretch along which Columbus sailed from December 6, 1492, the Feast of St. Nicholas, to the middle of January 1493, when he began the journey back across the open Atlantic to return to the Iberian Peninsula. It is possible that the drawing was sketched in the last days of his stay in the New World when the Admiral's ideas about the nature and characteristics of Hispaniola were quite clear.

According to Thacher, the unusual shape of the letter "r" in the place name *monte Cristi* is positive proof of the authenticity of the drawing, and Revelli also, on the basis of a comparison of the calligraphy with other writings by Columbus, claims that it is undoubtedly from his hand. The form *natividad* (instead of *navidad*, as is usual in Castilian) also shows the undeniable Italian origin of the person who drew this sketch. .

It is true, of course, as Vignaud says, that this drawing is not a great cartographic work, nor does it show any particular talent or special competence in that field on the part of its maker (in essence, any pilot on Columbus's expedition could have drawn it). But it is the Admiral's only undoubted cartographic legacy to have come down to us, and the only document to show the location of what was the first European settlement in the central and southern part of the New World (even though it was fated not to last long). Indeed, the presence of the place name *natividad* — which appears in the *Journal* in the form of *Villa de la Navidad* only on January 4, whereas the sighting of this place and the wreck of the Santa Maria, as we know, occurred between the 24th and 25th of December — is further evidence that the drawing was probably made in the early days of 1493 rather than at the end of 1492.

* * *

A very fine and interesting cartographic document of the late Middle Ages, dating perhaps from the very year of the discovery of America and now held in the National Library in Paris, has been attributed to Christopher Columbus (or to him and his brother Bartolomeo, or to the latter alone); it is known as "Columbus's Map" or "*Mappamundi*". We have here the usual illuminated manuscript parchment, on which two maps are juxtaposed with a gold strip separating them (this last feature is absolutely new). On the left hand side, on or toward the neck, is a depiction of the world then known (without the Americas, therefore), surrounded by the heavenly spheres in accordance with the geocentric system. On the right is what one can, in essence, call a nautical chart of the Mediterranean and a part of the Atlantic; to the east it is bounded by the Black Sea (included in its entirety) and the Red Sea, and to the west by the coast of the Atlantic, from southern Norway to a land south of the mouth of the Congo (reached in 1484 by Diogo Cão, as we know). A number of the usual islands, both real and legendary, are shown in the middle of the Ocean (Plate XVII).

On the left, in the small depiction of the Old World standing at the center of the spheres, Africa is shown as far as the Cape of Good Hope, which was discovered (as is also well known) by Bartolomeo Diaz in 1488 (hence this representation is more "up to date" than that of the nautical chart). The eastern portion of the known land masses, on the other hand, seems to be drawn according to the Ptolemaic model, with perhaps some distant reminiscences of the data provided by the Polo family. In the sea off "Cathay" the Earthly Paradise looms over a circle of mountains. North of Eurasia a series of islands refer to Saint Brendan and his legendary voyages in the northern seas. Thirty or so perspectival city views on the nautical chart represent the major cities and lend themselves to some useful observations for dating and for providing an attribution of this document.

In the first place, the depiction of Genoa is not more conspicuous than that of Venice and other urban centers — as was claimed by La Roncière, who drew from it a reason for believing the map to be Genoese and saw in it one of the features on which he based his attribution of the map to Columbus. The flag of Ferdinand and Isabella's kingdom flies over the site of a perspectival view of an Iberian city that some have wanted to identify as Granada, while others have claimed to see in this depiction a view of Santa Fe; the latter, as we know, was founded in June of 1491 to house the army of the Catholic Kings, before whom the great Genoese delivered once again a plea to carry out his project (it has been written that he did so while displaying this map or another very similar one). The presence of this banner is interpreted as proof that the cartographer was aware of the victorious conclusion to the siege of the Muslim capital in the early days of 1492. But the city view almost certainly represents nearby Almeria instead, which had been returned to the Christians three years earlier.

In addition to pointing out the inscriptions that indicate the various kinds of exports from exotic countries, especially in Africa, and other pictures that are at times mostly decorative, it is worth mentioning here the long Latin cartouches scattered here and there over the map. La Roncière and others who support the attribution of this chart to Christopher Columbus or his brother Bartolomeo (others believe it to be the work of both of them) referred to these cartouches, or rather to some of them. The attribution dates back to 1924, when, amidst other discussions and arguments by French scholars and those of other countries (even during the International Geographic Conference in Cairo) it elicited a decidedly negative reaction from Almagià, Caraci, and De Lollis.

La Roncière's attention was drawn in particular to three of these long legends, the great majority of which are derived from passages in the *Treatises* of the previously mentioned cardinal and famous scholar Pierre d'Ailly (whose works, we know, were carefully studied and annotated by Columbus and his brother). The one near Iceland states that in Latin it was called *Thile*; it adds some geographical information — about trade with England in particular — using words and phrases very similar to those used by Don Ferdinand, presumably, in his *Histories* and by Las Casas in his *History*, and it repeats what could be an authentic excerpt from Columbus himself about his supposed voyage to the island in 1477 (though the excerpt has not come down to us directly).

Beside the Cape Verde Islands it is reported that they were discovered "by a Genoese, Antonio da Noli." This could be an indication of the Genoese origin of the chart maker, who wanted thereby to highlight the merit of one of his compatriots (along the coast of Guinea, the existence of the place name *Rio del Genoves*, which does not appear on other maps, would have a similar value). Finally, near the Red Sea the inscription states that it takes six months to sail it and that an *annum integrum*, a whole year, is required to reach India from there. The expression "from there" is rendered by a grammatical error (*de ibi*), the same one that appears in one of the *Annotations* made by Columbus (or his brother) to the copy of d'Ailly's *Treatises* that he owned and studied (as we know, paleographic examination does not allow us to ascertain which annotations were made by which brother, nor do we know when the majority of them were written). From all this one would deduce a sure link between this cartographic document and the Columbus brothers as its authors; the *de ibi*, La Roncière writes, is like Christopher's signature.

To try to move closer to a solution to the question we need to start with a more thorough examination of the text of the cartouches so as to ascertain to what extent they correspond to the text of d'Ailly's *Treatises*

— which anyone could consult — or to that of the Columbus brothers' *Annotations* (the latter, in fact, are often mere repetitions or abbreviations of passages from those same *Treatises*). But once this has been done, there still remains a doubt: the author of the *Annotations* could have had the map in front of him and taken the annotations from it (in this case the map would not be the work of the Columbus brothers and would date to before their reading and annotation of the *Treatises*) or the cartouches on the map (at least the relevant ones) could have been taken from the *Annotations*, in which case the map had to be the subsequent work of Christopher or Bartolomeo or someone in their circle who could consult their books.

The attribution to Columbus would then be reinforced by the fact that on the map there are sites marked along the coast of Guinea and southern Africa to which Columbus elsewhere claims to have been and which he gives evidence of knowing (though they could also have been familiar to many others). Furthermore, in another *Annotation* he refers to "our four maps, which also include a sphere" (which, as Pelletier says, was unusual for those times); "our maps," however, could mean "belonging to us" rather than "made by us."

The reaction of Italian scholars was particularly intense, because, when La Roncière pointed out that the map contained a depiction of the "Island of the Seven Cities" (which, in actual fact, is also found on many previous maps), he seemed to be embracing — at least at first, or reinforcing in any case — Vignaud's earlier theory that this island (instead of the East) had been Columbus's secret objective, as Don Ferdinand, presumably, would lead one to believe.

De Lollis, who was the first Italian to write on this subject, adopted a particularly polemical tone, stressing the fact that the map's cartouches were in excellent Latin, such "that Columbus never even dreamed of," and pointing out the differences between the "legend" concerning Iceland and the text reported by Don Ferdinand and Las Casas (where this island is said to be as large as England, whereas on the map it is shown with smaller dimensions, approximating the true ones). The use of the term *Frislandia* is also given some emphasis on the part of this author. The text of the "legend" concerning the Red Sea also differs from that of Columbus's *Annotations*; the latter, which is found in the *Epilogus Mappe Mundi*, in the chapter *De Mari*, is rather shorter than the passage accompanying the "legend" on the map. De Lollis does not point out, however, the grammatical mistake of *de ibi* and concludes that the map, which has "features too obviously archaic" in its representation of Africa, must be from before 1492 (which opinion, in fact, seems acceptable, but debatable).

Caraci's writing seems more thoughtful. After arguing against the existence of a "type [of map] like those drawn by Bartolomeo" (or that we know anything about it, in any case) and having reiterated the absurdity of Vignaud's theory, he maintained that the concept of the world as a whole reflected in the map does not at all match the corresponding concept held by the future Admiral. The map preserved in Paris must not have been "a document practical in nature," like the one Columbus used on his voyage, but rather a "study edition," perhaps the work of a scholar who borrowed many features from nautical charts and added information about the interior of the continents. Its date can be moved back to some time after the discovery of America. This can be justified by the affinities he observed between it and Caverio's famous map of 1502 (I believe, on the contrary, that we cannot hypothesize so late a date, since it would have been impossible not to take the New World into account, ten years after reaching it). In any case, the misshapen outline of the southeastern coast of Africa, as Caraci pointed out, together with the lack of place names along this stretch, confirms that the date was before 1498 (that is, before Vasco da Gama's expedition).

Rather than being produced for a transoceanic expedition, the small world map seems intended to show the ease of communications between Western Europe and India via the route around the Cape of Good Hope (so think Caraci and also Isnard). Even if we were to admit that the map was produced "in the environment in which Columbus lived, and perhaps by his inspiration," this scholar emphasizes that it does not "mesh, extrinsically or intrinsically, with what we can legitimately confirm about the ideas, goals, and circumstances that led to Columbus's great enterprise."

Almagià had the advantage of writing some time later, after the map and its attribution had already been discussed in several places. He is very cautious with regard to attributing the nautical chart to a Genoese or a Venetian (as Caraci suggested), and limits himself to affirming the Italian forms of many of its place names. He considers it "inadmissible" that the document was made in the sixteenth century, even in its very early years, believing it to date undoubtedly from before 1498. He stresses, however, the (relative) agreement between the small world map (of a somewhat archaic type and brought up to date only with regard to the findings of Portuguese voyages) and the main nautical chart, an object of the most minute attention.

As for the Atlantic islands, the ones in the middle of the ocean do not present anything substantially new compared to other maps of the fifteenth century. The location of the ones in northern waters, including *islante uel Thile, frilant*, and the *insula de septem civitatum* or "island of seven cities" (all of them depicted not far from the latitude of Ireland) suggests an echo of voyages long ago (rather than discoveries) by the Icelanders or other northern sailors. The cartouche placed next to Iceland on the main nautical chart does not at all seem to show, according to Almagià, a correlation between this document and Columbus's statement, cited earlier, that he had gone in person to *Thile* and had sailed beyond — which was perhaps an unjustified boast based on confusing *Thile* with *Frislandia* (that is, the Faeroe Islands). Rather, everything written in the cartouche is plainly said to be second-hand information (*ut referunt Anglici*, "as the English report"). Therefore, I would like to add, if the map in Paris were by Columbus, it would be proof that he went no further than Bristol to obtain knowledge of the northern islands.

In addition to recalling the cartouche beside the Cape Verde archipelago, Almagià also considers other cartouches that bear a resemblance to, or prove to be derived from, the text of d'Ailly's *Treatises*, including the one about the Red Sea with the familiar grammatical mistake (*de ibi* instead of *inde*). This is a detail that makes us stop and think, and the only one that truly carries weight, "in a surprising manner" (as Almagià says), in favor of La Roncière's theory. It is quite true — as my colleague Silvana Fasce, a Latinist at the University of Genoa, has graciously brought to my attention — that errors of this sort were anything but rare in late medieval Latin but it is the location of that *de ibi*, which does not appear in d'Ailly's text (whereas it is found in Columbus's *Annotations* and on the map), and which perhaps recalls Ligurian dialectical forms, that makes us think most carefully.

But instead of accepting the idea that this map was made by Columbus, who introduced into the cartouche we are discussing the mistake of *de ibi* that was already present in the *Annotations*, Almagià formulates the opposite theory — that the error already existed on the map, whose maker is unknown to us (but was Ligurian nonetheless?) which was owned by Columbus; he would have annotated d'Ailly with the map before his eyes, copying from it a part of the "legend," including the mistake, without noticing it.

Finally, a portion of Almagià's essay aims to show that the map under discussion is not at all, as La Roncière wrote, "the most genuine expression of the geographical concepts that Columbus had formed for himself in those years." Besides, the idea of a habitable earth entirely surrounded by the sea, and other general geographical concepts reflected in the map, were, in essence, part of a good education at the time, as it was formulated in d'Ailly's *Treatises*, with which many other people, including Columbus, were familiar.

The conclusions I think we can reach are the following: the map is certainly from the period of 1488-1498; it could have been made later — but not much later — than 1492 and is undoubtedly not the one displayed by Columbus to convince the King and Queen to carry out his project. It may have been produced in his environment, and he almost certainly had it in his possession, either because he had constructed and inspired it himself (or simply because he suggested the "legends," using the passages from d'Ailly that he had annotated or was in the process of annotating), or because he had used it in order to understand better that author's *Treatises*, drawing not only on those texts, but also on the map's "legends," as starting points for his *Annotations*. Equally well founded, I think, is the hypothesis that it could be the work of his brother Bartolomeo instead, though reflecting their ideas in common, since Christopher must have been busy with a thousand other matters in the years when the map was being made. In this case the work would have been executed outside the Iberian Peninsula and therefore without Christopher's direct participation, since Bartolomeo was not there during those years — unless the map was made later, that is, after Bartolomeo's return to Spain.

As we see, various theories can be formulated, all more or less equally acceptable. What is certain is that the map does not at all demonstrate that Columbus's goal on the first voyage was different from that of reaching the East; in any case the polemics over Vignaud's theses (which nobody any longer thinks valid) should be kept separate from the discussion of this cartographic document. And while examining it, we need to distinguish the part concerning the small world map from the part involving the main nautical chart.

* * *

Bartolomeo has also been credited with the sketches in Codex XIII of the Magliabechi Collection in the National Library in Florence. More than fifty years ago, however, Almagià showed that, although they were probably derived from a planisphere of his, they were produced not by him, but by the learned Venetian, Alessandro Zorzi. Before looking at the meaning of this depiction of the land masses — which dates back to the first decade of the sixteenth century, especially as regards the links between the West Indies and Asia — it seems appropriate to mention the characteristics and nature of these sketches (Plates XVIII a-d).

They are found in a miscellany of travelers' reports and letters, in four small volumes (a fifth seems to have been lost), partly in manuscript and partly printed, and known also by the name (truly inappropriate) of

"Alberico." The name of the collector of this miscellany, Alessandro Zorzi, can be made out with certainty (as Almagià says) in the *Informatione di Bartolomeo Colombo della Navigazione di Ponente et Garbin di Beragna nel Mondo Nuovo*, or *Bartolomeo Columbus's Information about the Voyage West and Southwest to Veragua in the New World*. After this text in the miscellany comes the one of Christopher Columbus's famous letter to the King and Queen from Jamaica on July 7, 1503. The three cartographic sketches of which we are speaking are drawn in the margins of some of these pages. Other rudimentary drawings (of the globe, for instance) and sketches concerning the recently discovered lands also appear in this miscellany.

Those, like Wieser, who claimed that the three depictions under discussion were Bartolomeo Columbus's work, based their opinion on a passage in the just cited *Information...*, in which it is stated that Zorzi had acquired, through a Roman friar, *uno disegnio de litti di tal terre* (that is, a drawing of the shores along which they had sailed during the fourth voyage) made by Bartolomeo in his own hand. But the drawing is not reproduced in the *Information...* itself, and one must leaf through the pages to reach the letter from Jamaica in order to find the sketches.

The problem is how to establish whether or not the sketches in the margins of this letter correspond to the *disegnio* drawn by Bartolomeo (or, rather, are a copy of it). The latter, in turn, should be identified with the map that Oviedo says Christopher Columbus's brother delivered to Diego Nicuesa, who took it with him on his 1509 expedition. The *disegnio* and the map, however, must have been a "special" depiction, so to say, of the lands and seas involved in the fourth voyage (hence we can imagine that they were very detailed), whereas the sketches in the margins of the letter from Jamaica are a different matter.

Taken together, in fact, they represent the entire equatorial band of the globe, within, very approximately, those boundaries. They are not just "extremely crude" (as Almagià says), but quite summary and schematic, and they undoubtedly sum up information about the world that was acquired who knows how, and bungled. They are not even distantly comparable to what an original survey of barely known lands by Bartolomeo Columbus, or any other navigator or cartographer, would be. The first sketch shows the southern part of Africa (with a gradation in latitude from 24° north to 24° south). Opposite, that is, to the west, but also toward the south, are the *ANTHIPODI*, on a land mass with roughly drawn contours. The second sketch is devoted to Asia, from the Middle East (beneath which stretches the eastern tip of the Horn of Africa) to the *SINARUM SITUS*, or REGION OF THE CHINESE, and a little beyond. The longitude extends from a little under 90° east to more than 180°. Between the equator and the Tropic of Capricorn are the *INDICUM MARE* and the *OCEANUS INDICUS*. The third sketch stretches from the eastern tip of Asia to the Iberian Peninsula and part of Africa; Asian territory is linked by a line of land to the *MONDO NOVO*, that is, to the continent of South America.

This is the sketch that should be linked directly to Columbus's discoveries on the fourth voyage, and hence to Bartolomeo's *disegnio*, but we must point out that all scholars deny that the sketches were made on the basis of data in the text of either the *Information*… or the letter from Jamaica. Indeed, the third sketch has very few (and general) features that could have come from a map made by Bartolomeo Columbus to illustrate the results of the fourth voyage. Even the place names (and the nomenclature in general) varies somewhat from those in the Columbian sources concerned with this sailing trip. The other two sketches must, therefore, be even less relevant to Columbus's undertakings. This is so even though Nordenskiöld, and a number of other scholars after him, considered these drawings to be Bartolomeo's works, with the result that they were inserted among the Columbian sources, in the belief, among other things, that the term "New World" derived from an intuition that germinated in the mind of the Columbus brothers during the fourth voyage.

In actuality, as Almagià correctly concludes, Alessandro Zorzi was a learned Venetian, certainly in contact with Angelo Trevisan, and a man who passionately kept up with advances in geographical knowledge and collected accounts of the discoveries made. He did this with the help of the so-called Ferrara Manuscript, which he marked with handwritten notes and drawings, including cartographic ones, from before the time the miscellany was gathered together. He continued to do this at least until 1538, while he was in Venice, and this work, now kept in Florence, grew out of this interest of his. But the sketches under discussion, which are certainly his work, do not expressly refer to the results of Columbus's fourth voyage (and perhaps not to the earlier ones either) and they "do not at all reflect Columbus's geographical concepts, but rather the ideas of Zorzi himself." Only "one of them… was perhaps drawn with a map by Bartolomeo Columbus before his eyes, a map in Zorzi's possession that has been lost" (to be more exact, I would say not "one of them," but "a rather small part of one of them").

In essence, this confirms (though it seems to me unnecessary) that Bartolomeo made surveys and constructed charts in order to give an account of the results of the voyages in which he participated. Zorzi kept at hand one of these charts concerning the fourth voyage, along with other maps by various makers, so that he might follow and interpret the travelers' reports that he was reading. Perhaps the chart was also used, in part, when drawing the third sketch, and so we cannot deny the possibility that some features derived from the chart were transferred to the drawing, but the ideas and geographical concepts are another matter. The name *Mondo Novo*, for instance, which is found already in the Ferrara Manuscript, should not be traced back to the Columbus brothers, but to ideas that Zorzi had formed for himself from very different sources.

Finally, we know that Bartolomeo, the *adelantado*, or governor, in Santo Domingo, had made *una carta y pintura de las Islas*, which he sent to King Ferdinand at the end of 1512 or in the first months of 1513. Peter Martyr of Anghiera reports that at the Council of the Indies in 1513 he saw, among other cartographic material, a map begun by Christopher Columbus on his fourth voyage *cui et frater eius Bartholomeus Colonus, Hispaniolae adelantadus, iudicium suum addidit; peragravit namque et ipse ea litora* ("to which his brother Bartolomeo Columbus, governor of Hispaniola, added his opinion; for he, too, traveled around these shores"). In addition to a printed map of which we shall speak shortly, two other maps are attributed to Bartolomeo, maps that can be defined as part of the evangelization of Hispaniola because of the depictions of churches that they contain. These are provided in some editions of the work of the same Peter Martyr, though not in all copies, but only a few.

One of the duties of the *adelantado*, in fact, was that of overseeing the building and maintenance of the island's churches. It is likely that he himself gave an account of this on a parchment manuscript map inserted at the end of the copy of the volume of *Oceani Decades* in the Seville edition of 1511 that is now kept in the Columbian Capitular Library in Seville. At that time the churches built, and therefore depicted, were few in number. Many more (about 15) appear on the map, also in manuscript and on parchment, that appears in the copy of *De Orbe Novo Decades* published in Alcalà de los Henares in 1516 and preserved in the University Library in Bologna.

It is probable, moreover, that it was from one of these documents — more likely the former, which was sent to the King — that the printed map was taken (the engraving was in wood); it is of the Greater Antilles and part of the Caribbean Sea, and was appended to some of the copies of the 1511 Seville edition of a part of Peter Martyr's work. This printed map has provoked debate because it shows, in the form of an island, a section of the coasts north of Cuba — that is to say, Florida — which is generally considered to have been discovered in 1513 instead. Now it is not unlikely that even before this discovery some information about the shores opposite Cuba had already reached the Spanish colonists on the island. But it makes more sense to suppose that after 1513 Peter Martyr himself, having easy access to the court and to public offices, had had published — in haste, with few additions and some errors — a printed map based on that of Bartolomeo Columbus. It would have been brought up to date in that period and inserted at an unspecified time after its publication into only some of the copies of his work (perhaps those as yet unsold). In any case the events surrounding this first edition include many episodes and shadowy areas that do not concern us here. What does concern us is to point out that this document proves that Bartolomeo Columbus continued to make maps until the last years of his life (in fact, he died, as we know, in 1514), and that this is the first "special" map (today we would call it "corographic") of a part of Central America for which undeniable evidence, indeed a copy, has come down to us.

3) *Columbus's cartographical concepts, as seen in cartography*

What has been said in the previous pages and paragraphs therefore confirms what we already knew, that both Columbus brothers were experts in the art of cartography, with an output that was anything but insignificant. But the uncertainty that prevails as to so many aspects of the lives and activities of these figures, and especially the fact that very little of their hard work has been preserved, has allowed various suppositions and countless stories to arise and persist, as is true also in other areas concerning Columbus (apart from the sketch of Haiti, for instance, nine or ten other maps have been attributed to Christopher, in all cases using arguments that, if they cannot be totally rejected, are anything but convincing and decisive; among these attributions is that of the hypothetical document from which the famous Turkish map of Piri Re'is is said to be derived). In any case, we are concerned here with examining how Columbus's cartographic preparation fits into his cultural formation, even though we will be able to pick out only a few definitive factors (from now on we will be speaking only of Christopher, except in cases where we need to proceed in another fashion).

This last topic has also been debated at length by several authors and from different points of view. The recent (or relatively recent) contributions of Luzzana Caraci, however, require that we refer back to them and see how they fit together. Thus we must identify a first, foundational, nucleus of Columbus's education dating back to the period of his first 25 years (approximately), which were passed in Genoa and

Savona and in the Mediterranean at any rate. Here Columbus learned the basics of reading and writing (especially Latin, which was useful to merchants and sailors for understanding and drawing up contracts, and to churchgoers for participating in religious services; in the common speech of Genoa at that time, as Taviani, in the wake of Pandiani and other local scholars, has pointed out, Italian was used very little or not at all). He also studied arithmetic, and, at a higher level, nautical arts, including cartography.

Columbus learned to sail, therefore, in Genoese and Ligurian circles and probably (indeed almost certainly) to construct nautical charts as well. Maritime skills, like commercial and financial ones (as we said before) must have been far advanced in Genoa in those decades. The future admiral must have been familiar with the use of instruments like the quadrant and the astrolabe (the nautical one, of course) even before he left the Mediterranean. Similarly, he must have been acquainted with the use of nautical charts and the methods of their construction. A very suitable environment for learning these things had existed in Genoa for centuries. Albino de Canepa is probably only one example among many of cartographers who were contemporaries and compatriots of Columbus. At Savona, too, where he settled for some time, cartography was not unknown, as the case mentioned earlier of Francesco Beccario shows (on the other hand, the notion that higher studies undertaken by Columbus in Pavia could have contributed to his preparation is pure fantasy; this was reported in that part of Don Ferdinand's *Histories* that Luzzana Caraci has demonstrated to be the result of a late manipulation of the text by an anonymous author).

There has been much more discussion and controversy about the second period of Columbus's formation, which he spent in a Portuguese environment, in Lisbon, from which he made periodic journeys and visits to Madeira, Porto Santo, Guinea, and perhaps the Azores. It is perfectly correct to say, with Luzzana Caraci, that "Columbus underwent life-changing experiences in this environment, which strained outward toward the Ocean and toward the Indies," but it says too little. Not only must he have had, during those years, the inspiration (as Taviani believes) for his great voyage to reach the east by traveling west, but he also went on from there to develop a practical and concrete plan — to the point that he presented it to King John II, as Taviani and Luzzana Caraci, among others, emphasize.

It is very hard to say which cultural tools, including cartographic ones, he could have used to develop this plan, but it is possible to clear the field of certain legendary theories that have been more or less hallowed by tradition. Even if Columbus had received as a gift from his mother-in-law nautical charts and notes previously belonging to her husband (who was never the great navigator that some have made him out to be), they could not have been very useful to him, since they would have been from a time 40 years earlier, a period when new discoveries along the west coasts of Africa were being made almost from year to year. Nor could he have profited from any possible meetings or contacts with Martin Behaim, who arrived in Lisbon just as Columbus was leaving, as we saw earlier, and who proves not to have had any particularly original geographical or cosmographical ideas.

There remains the burning issue of his correspondence with Toscanelli, whom Columbus saw, and perhaps received at his home in Lisbon, along with a map of the world, which Columbus is said to have stolen (and to have fled Portugal for this reason). His departure from Lisbon, of course, must be dated to 1485 or very shortly thereafter, whereas his brother Bartolomeo may have remained on the banks of the river Tagus. One of the two was certainly present in 1488 at the homecoming of the expedition of Bartolomeo Diaz and heard the report that they had rounded the southern tip of Africa (we are not entirely sure which of the two brothers it was, nor can we rule out the possibility that both were there). The Portuguese sailing trip to reach *Cabo Tormentoso* or "Cape of Storms" was 3100 leagues long, of course; according to Columbus the voyage to reach the East via the Atlantic would have been little more than half that. For this reason, also, he was led to continue improving and defending his plan.

Toscanelli's map has never been found (we have only a very approximate idea of it based on the indications contained in the letter that supposedly accompanied it), and so I do not think it very useful to debate it further. It is more helpful to recall that Columbus's calculation of the earth's circumference was a good deal smaller than that imagined by classical antiquity and accepted by his contemporaries (as well as smaller than in reality). His estimate was derived from measurements that he made in Guinea and then figured on the basis of a Roman mile, which is a lot shorter than the Arabic one that had been used to establish his model. Very interesting to me, however, is an observation by Luzzana Caraci, who has noted that, with regard to distances on the earth's surface, Columbus's geographical ideas, as they emerge from the usual sources, do not at all coincide with those of Toscanelli. After arriving at the coast of Cuba, for example, after a journey of 1142 leagues by his own calculations, he claimed that the continent of Asia lay before him. According to the Florentine physicist, on the contrary, they would have had to sail another 40°.

It is possible that Toscanelli was also influenced by the concepts of those classical authors who placed the world of the *Antoikoi* and the *Antipodes* in the West, but in my opinion it is going too far to claim, as has been done, that it was through him that these concepts were passed on to Columbus. If anything, we should ask whether he could have seen in Lisbon (or elsewhere in Portugal) any codices, or one of the first printed editions, of Ptolemy's works that were furnished with maps, including the usual world map, that is, with representations that would become Henricus Germanus Martellus's prototypes (as we know, the latter date to after 1478-1480, so that it is highly unlikely, but not impossible, that they were known in Lisbon during the years when the future admiral resided there). It is not impossible in itself, but there is nothing to prove it (Table XIX).

Rather than continue debating these subjects, I think we should emphasize the very useful experiences Christopher had in Portuguese circles (we cannot even exclude the possibility that the correspondence with Toscanelli, including the references to the map, had been "invented" after the first or second voyage, when Columbus needed to ennoble his work, so to say, and demonstrate its scientific basis). In Portugal he had contacts with a fleet that was used to ocean sailing as far as the equator and beyond, one accustomed to recognizing the system of the winds and currents. He also gathered facts and information about the existence of lands to the west from sailors from the European mainland and the islands, and he acquired a rich inheritance of knowledge by reading their *roteiros*, their nautical guides, and other similar writings.

If I must draw a conclusion, obviously on a purely hypothetical level, it is that Columbus's formation, as it matured during the Portuguese period of his life, was rather more practical and experimental than theoretical in nature. He also faced the great themes of the size of the earth's circumference and the shape and arrangement of the *oikumene* (the Portuguese discoveries along the African coastline must have made him — and not only him — stop and think), but I find it hard to believe that he could have deepened his understanding of them on the basis of classical, medieval, and contemporary texts. He would do that in Andalusia and Castille, instead, both because the discussion of his project lasted longer there than in Portugal, and because he found a more suitable environment for the development of a scientific system to support his ideas (at court, in the circle of the Geraldinis, and especially in the Franciscan monasteries).

* * *

The documentation of the Spanish phase of Columbus's cultural formation is more extensive (as we know and have mentioned earlier, a variety of books read, studied, and annotated by him are kept in the Columbian Capitular Library). The problems, however, become more complex, confirming, among other things, what Luzzana Caraci has been claiming for some time, namely, that Columbus's cosmographical and geographical ideas matured over time, and were also modified in part (with biblical elements and messianic motifs entering into his understanding). The writings in which he treats these ideas, or rather refers to them, are all from after 1496 and "are probably more a consequence of the discovery of America than a premise for it" as the same Luzzana Caraci writes, since they aim to defend the view that the lands discovered were part of Asia. Since we do not know the date of most of the *Annotations* found in the books belonging to Columbus and kept in the library mentioned earlier (a complete and thorough study of them has never been done), it makes perfect sense to assume that they go back to various times. Nor do we know anything of the study Columbus must have undertaken of maps and planispheres, comparing them to the theories and information that he came across in the books he was reading.

Until now it has been maintained, on the basis of indications in the letter said to have accompanied Toscanelli's map, that the latter had a kind of geographical graticule with vertical and horizontal lines (*recte* and *tranverse*) corresponding to parallels and meridians (assuming that the map ever existed, though one can imagine any world map used by Columbus). But did Columbus see and use it before his voyage — as is generally believed — or after it (and which one)?

We can obtain some very general and not decisive indications from the date of publication of the books annotated by Columbus. In general these dates are from the period after he left Portugal (or shortly before), even if the works were written earlier. Thus Cardinal d'Ailly's work was published in Louvain, probably in 1483. It contains 476 *Annotations* to *Ymago mundi*, while a smaller number (between 20 and 80 approximately) are made to various others of the 20 minor *Treatises*. Columbus, of course, must have read this work, and also the *Historia rerum ubique gestarum* by Pius II (Piccolomini), before his first voyage (the famous *Annotation* of "*Coenta*," however, which was studied earlier as a possible indication of the date of this labor of reading and annotating, does not have any chronological significance, because it reports a date contained in a passage by Abraham Zacuto, as Luzzana Caraci has shown). But this does not mean that he had acquired all his cosmographical and geographical ideas from these authors. In any case, the annotations to these works bring us back to 1485-1488, whereas those in other books, as we shall see, date to decidedly later.

Two of the *Annotations* to d'Ailly's *Treatises* refer specifically to cartography. One, on the location of an African city, reports the famous phrase, *vide in Ptholomeo et in quattuor cartis nostris*. Here, as we have seen before, *nostris* can be interpreted as "belonging to us." Another states, *et vide in nostris cartis a papiri, ubi est Spera*. This means — and it is a rather interesting detail — that Columbus, perhaps together with his brother, owned several maps that included a depiction of the globe and that these were not on parchment, but rather on paper.

We cannot fail to speak of Columbus's reading and study of Ptolemy's geographical work. Bernáldez attests that he had a copy of his *Geography* in the printed edition of 1478, one of the first to be furnished with plates of maps, among which there was always a world map. Logic would have it that the future admiral acquired it and consulted it before 1492; if the opposite were true, he would have obtained a later edition, perhaps with a more up to date cartographical apparatus. One can imagine that he owned and perhaps studied more than one copy, in different editions (they must have been in circulation in the Iberian Peninsula in the last two decades of the fifteenth century). I find it more difficult to believe, though the possibility cannot be totally excluded, that Columbus also saw one of the codices from which these printed editions were derived, including the well known manuscript world map of Henricus Germanus Martellus.

In the previous chapters I have not spoken of this work, which circulated widely even in the early years of the sixteenth century, especially in engraved editions; nor shall we speak of it (except for an occasional reference) in the following pages, since it belongs to what we might call "learned" cartography, which has very little (indeed nothing or almost nothing) to do with the Ligurian tradition. Of the manuscript planispheres just mentioned, six have come down to us (of which two, in fact, were inserted into codices of Ptolemy's work in the last decades of the fifteenth century). Being much alike, they have been studied and compared for some time so as to bring to light even small differences that could have some significance for the history of the depiction of the earth. They attest to the intellectual journey made and the difficulty with which Ptolemaic ideas were overcome, especially with regard to the depiction of Asia, including the notion that the Indian Ocean was landlocked and that the Indies could therefore not be reached by circumnavigating Africa.

We know nothing about the life of Martellus (Hammer in German) except that he worked in Italy, probably in Florence, in the latter part of

Plate XVIII a

dalbra Cibani · P · QVARTO · 70 ·

in.xxxvi.zorni forono racolte:meglior che mai manzaffi-
no. In questo lo Admirante per noticia haueua da qlli infu
lani che haueua feco mando.xxx.hoi a una prouincia di q
fta ifola dicta Cipangi:laqual in mezo de lifola era fituata:
muntuofa cum gran copia de oro. Quefti homini retornati
referireno mirabilita de richeze de qael loco:& che dal mon
te defcendeuan.iiii.fiumi che diuidon lifola in.iiii.pte.lun ua
uerfo leuante chiamato Suma.laltro in ponéte attibiunco.
et terzo attramontana dicto Jachem.el quarto a mezodi
Naiba chiamato.

forneto

Cipangi
p winita del oro

Suma y leuate
Attibumoy ponte
Iache p tramotan
Naiba p mezodi

¶ Como lo Admiráte ando ala Minera de loro. c.xcvii.

A per tronare al ppofito lo admirante facta q
fta Cita incincta de muro a di.xii. de Marzo fe
parti cu circha.a.cccc.a piedi & a cauallo fe mi
fe in camino per andare ala puincia de loro d
la parte de mezodi:& dapoi paffati monti:ualle:& fiumi de
uene in una pianura e principio de cimpagq:p laqual pianu
ra correno alcuni riuoli cu rena da oro.Intrato aduche lo ad
mirante per.lxxii.miglia dentro de lifola:& diftante dala fua
cita.zonfe in una riua dun gran fiume:& li in un colle emi
nente delibero far una forteza per poter piu figuraméte cer
care li fecreti pel paefe:& chiamo la forteza.S.Thoma ftá
do in qfta edificatió molti paefani ueneno alo admirante p
hauer fonagli:& altra fuftare che haueua:& lui alfi contro li
dimando che li portaffino de foro. Vnde in pocho tempo
andarono:& portorono affai quantita de oro: intra: liquali
un porto un grano de una onza:li noftri fe marauegliarono
de tal grandeza:tamen cum céni demonftrauano trouarfe

Cita edificata
12 marzo 1504
400 homini

Cimpagi

ibani

72 miglia

S. de Toma

oro d.j.p uno
Sonaio

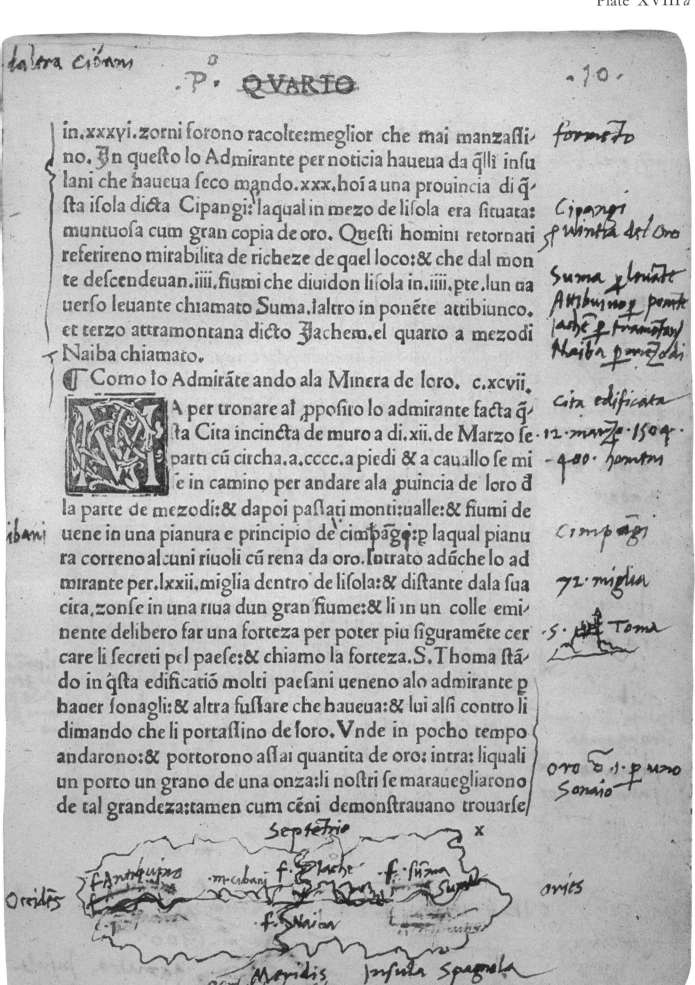

The sketches by Alessandro Zorzi, previously attributed to Bartholomew Columbus: Hispaniola; the Americas and the Western end of the Old World; Africa and Asia Minor; Asia.

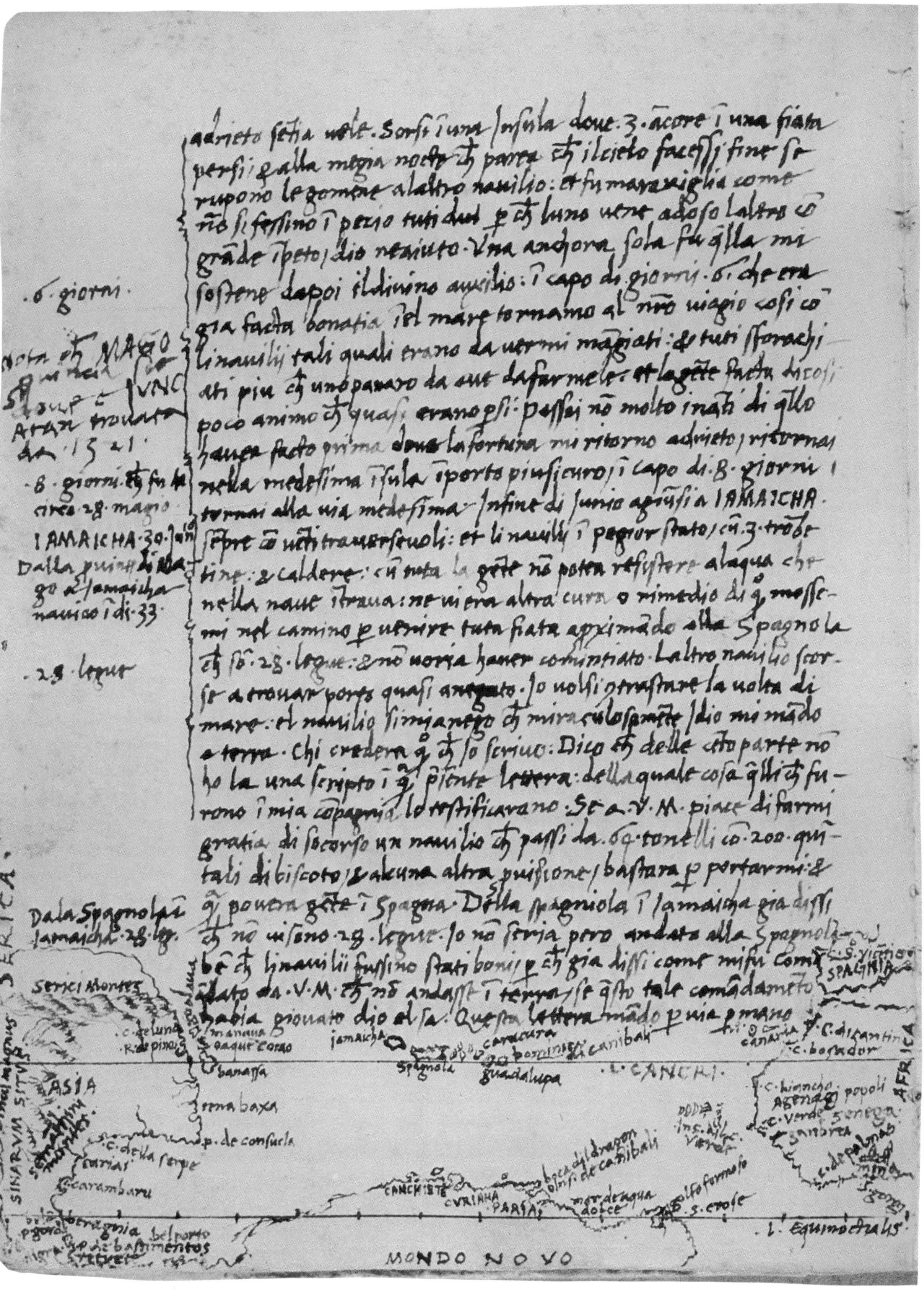

Plate XVIII *b*

adrieto setia uolt. Sorsi i una Insula doue .3. acore i una fiata
persi; e alla megia nocte ch parea ch ilcielo facessi fine si
ruppono le gomene alaltro nauilio: et fu marauiglia come
no si fessino i pezio tuti dui p ch luno uene adoso laltro co
grade ipeto; dio neaiuto. Una anchora sola fu qlla mi
sostene dapoi ildiuino auxilio: i capo di .6. giorni ch era
gia facta bonatia idel mare tornamo al nro uiagio cosi co
li nauilii tali quali erano da uermi magiati: & tuti sforachi
ati piu ch uno panaro da aue dasar mele: et lagte facta dicosi
poco animo ch quasi erano epsi: passei no molto inati di qllo
haue facto prima doue lafortuna mi ritorno adrieto; ritornai
nella medesima isula iporto piu sicuro; i capo di .8. giorni
tornai alla uia medesima: Infine di iunio agiusi a IAMAICHA
sepre co uenti trauersi euoli: et li nauilii i pegior stato; cu .3. trobe
tine. e caldere: cu nota la gte no potea resistere alaqua ch
nella naue itraua; ne ui era altra cura o rimedio di q; messe
mi nel camino p uenire tuta fiata aprimado alla Spagnola
ch so .28. legue: e no uorria hauer cominciato. Laltro nauilio scor
se a trouar porto quasi anegato. Io uolsi penstare la uolta di
mare: et nauilio simiante ch miraculosamte ;dio mi mado
a terra. Chi credera q ch io scriuo: Dico ch delle cto parte no
ho la una scripto i q; psente lettera: dellaquale cosa qlli ch fu
rono i mia copagnia lo testificarano. Se a .V. M. piace di farmi
gratia di socorso un nauilio ch passi da .64. tonelli co .200. qui
tali di biscoto; e alcuna altra puisione; bastara p portarmi &
q; pouera gte i Spagna. Della spagniola i iamaicha gia dissi
ch no uisono .28. legue. Io no scriua pero andato alla Spagnola
be ch li nauilii fussino stati boni; p ch gia dissi come misu coma
dato da .V. M. ch no andassi i terra; se qsto tale comadameto
habia giouato dio el sa. Questa lettera mado p uia p mano

Left margin notes:

.6. giorni.

nota ch MAGIO
su era i JUNO
A fan trouata
da .15 a .1

.8. giorni ch fu
circa .28. magio

IAMAICHA .30.
Dalla punta di cu
ba a Jamaicha
nauico i di .33

.28. legue

Dala Spagnola i
Jamaicha .28. lg.

Map labels:

BERICA

SINARVM SITVS

SERICA MONTES

ASIA

terra baxa

c. de luna
R. de pinos

mangi
p. de consuela

c. della serpe
curiay
c. carambaru

jamaicha

spagnola

caracura
guadalupa

bomini; canibali

L. CANCHI.

canaria

c. di cantina
c. boyador

c. biancho
c. verde
gambra

populi AGENA
senega

DODA
ins. dll
verde

CANCHISTE
CVRIANA
PARIA

boca dl dragon
i ilisi de canibali
agr deaqua
dolce

olfo formoso
S. croce

AFRICA

L. Equinoctialis

belporto
de bastimentos

MONDO NOVO

SPAGNIA
S. uicenu

Plate XVIII c

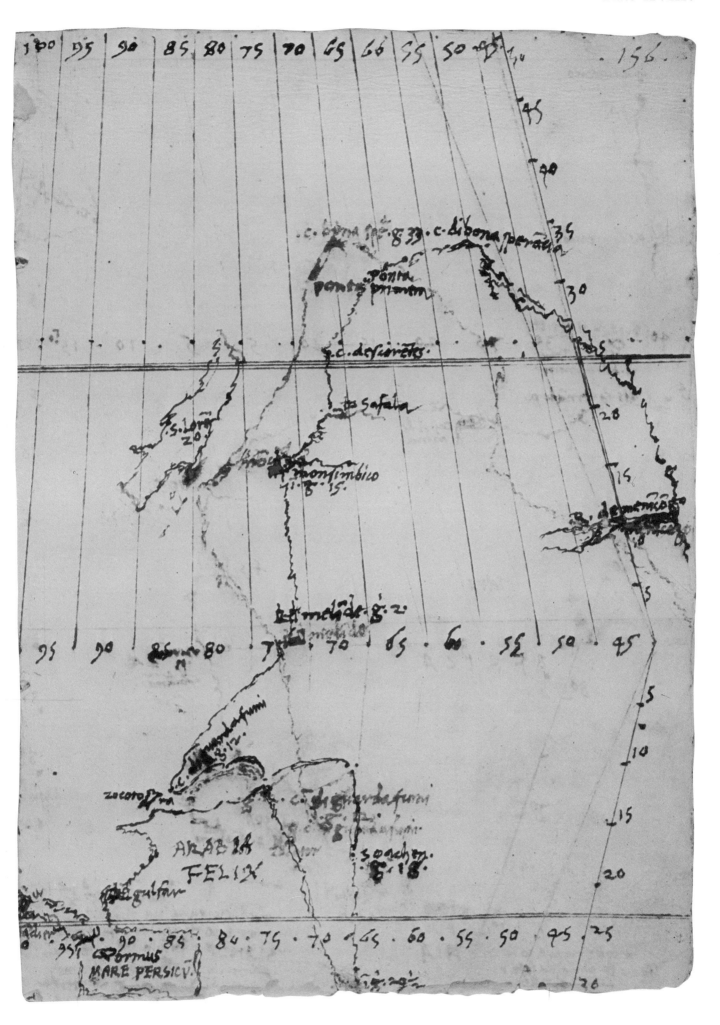

Plate XVIII *d*

·L°·III·°   ·57·

mare bollo nella dicta pu[n]tia di Cinquave. et che li | mar bollete
agiorni·x· uie il fiume GANGES appellato pare chesse | 10· quernatr
Tortox co̅ | tere stieno co̅ BERAGNA como sta Tortosa co̅ fonte Ra-| GANGES· flu
fonte Rubia | bia: Ouer pisa co̅ Venetia: Qua[n]do Jo mi parti da CARA-| BERAGNA
Pisa p Venet | BARY: et agonsi aquesti lochi ch ho dicto: trouai le gete| CARAMBARV
aquel medemo uso: saluo ch li spechi de oro ch hapeuano
li danano p tri sonagli de sparauiere p uno. Anchora ch
pesassino·x· ouer·xv· ducati luno: In tuti suoi usi sono como
quelli della Spagnola Insula. Lo oro ricogliono co̅ altra
arte b̅ ch luna et laltra no̅ habbia afare cu larte nostra.
Questo ch Joho dicto e qua[n]to ho inteso da qste gente. Ma hora
un roteino di qua[n]to ho uisto adso. Lo año·1494· nauicai I | 1494
24· gradi uerso ponente I termino di·6· hore· ch no̅ li fu | g· 24· m̅ 1360
fallo· p ch I quella hora fu Ecchipsi: el sole era I Libra | adi·14· septe̅ do-
et la luna I ariete. Tuto qsto ch Jo p parole intese da qste | menicha ho·19·m·45
gete Za lo haueuo Jo saputo logamente p scripto· p thole- | Ecclipsis: libra Ar-
meo credete hai hauere be satisfato a Marino: et adeso | ies. Ecclipsis lune
si troua sua scriptura be p̅piqua dal uero. p tholomeo | opi̅ñ di colombo
mete catigara a·12· hore logi dal suo Occide̅te | mal scripta
quale affirmo essere sopra capo Satu uice̅tio I porto gallo | hore·12·
gradi·2⅓ Marino I·15· hore costituite la tera: Questo mede- | hore·15·
mo Marino I Ethiopia scriue sopra la linea Equinoctiale
g·24 | piu de·24· gradi· Et adeso ch li portogalesi li nauicano:
g·15⅓ | lo trouano esser uero p tholomeo disse ch latera piu...
Eil primo   termino: ch no̅ abbassa piu de·15· gradi. ⅓

CARMA   indus   f. Gãges   INDIA EXTRA GANGEM·
NIA·   FLVVIV
                INDIA INTRA   M
                GANGEM·F·
                          Sinus Gãgeticus   Magnus
                                                   Sinus
L. Equinoctialis   Taprobana
90   100   110   120   130   140   150   160   170   180
              Samotra·Ins.   Aurea
INDICVM·MARE·   chersonesus

OCEANVS INDICVS·

·2·Capricor.

the fifteenth century. He was a prolific maker of maps, some Ptolemaic and some modern. Even though it was always obvious that he did not intend to move too far away from tradition (according to Almagià, he seems to have been a well informed mapmaker, a careful compiler able to bring in improvements, additions, and corrections, and an excellent cartographer), he introduced some major innovations. With regard to the northern part of Eurasia, he used the famous map by Clavus for Scandinavia and the adjoining countries. The shape and place names of southern Africa are based on the results of Portuguese voyages, including that of Bartolomeo Diaz (a cartouche in one of Martellus's planispheres refers to the *ultima navigatio Portugalensium anno Domini 1489*). The eastern part of Asia, especially the coastline, is also new.

While some of the planispheres included in Martellus's codices are purely Ptolemaic and still depict the Indian Ocean as landlocked to the south, the others show East Asia (which includes information going back to Marco Polo) as characterized by the existence of a fourth peninsula at the far end. While the northern coasts of the Indian Ocean as far as Cattigara retain the Ptolemaic configuration unchanged, the body of water, on the contrary, is open to the south, the earlier *Terra incognita secundum Ptolomeum* having disappeared. Almagià, whom we mentioned earlier, observes that the fourth Asian peninsula "comes into being... automatically." Indeed, to preserve the traditional outline of the remaining shores of southern Asia while opening the ocean to the south, it was necessary to extend the farthest part of East Asia to the east and south-east; it thereby become reachable by sea and much lengthened from north to south. In any case, even d'Ailly accepted the opinion of those who believed that India stretched far to the south (*usque Tropicum Capricorni...*), and the codex in the British Museum in London that contains Martellus's map is accompanied by the work entitled *Pii II Pontificis maximi descriptio*. The cartographer therefore had in mind the same authors whose works Columbus was poring over, as he sought to reconcile their theories (as well as those of Ptolemy) with the results of recent voyages.

This fourth Asian peninsula — which was thought to be narrow, at least in places (so that it could even be traversed easily with a short march) — appears also on Martin Behaim's globe and in a whole group of important documents (from the so-called King-Hamy map — or world map — to the Waldseemüller planisphere and to those by Rosselli, Bernardo Silvano, and Pietro Apiano). It is this peninsula that has been linked to Columbus's geographical ideas and concepts, adding fuel to many discussions and polemics. Some have gone so far as to think that it prefigured (so to say) the entire continent of South America as far as

Tierra del Fuego and the Strait of Magellan, with the result that De Gandia and others end up speaking of an awareness of the eastern side of that continent going back all the way to the Roman era. Luzzana Caraci has contested these theories in a very timely and convincing manner, showing that the shape Martellus gives to this fourth peninsula indicates only the "dearth of knowledge they had at that time about the far eastern fringe of the Asian continent," so that it makes sense that a very uncertain and strange depiction of it was given.

Once this issue is resolved, we face another one, rather more interesting for the purposes of this research. Almagià had already asked how far the *oikumene* stretched in degrees longitude, as depicted by Henricus Martellus, and he had affirmed that on the Ptolemaic world map in the Vatican Codex, which has longitude markings, it was 180° from the Fortunate Isles to Cattigara. In the Laurentian Codex, however, the antimeridian passes through Cattigara and part of the fourth peninsula, and in the one in the British Museum, which has no longitude markings, there is a piece of East Asia, beyond the territory that ought to correspond to the antimeridian, that can be estimated as stretching about 40° in longitude. The Eurasian mainland, therefore, would be 220° in extent, which corresponds exactly to Ptolemaic ideas.

As we know, however, the Eurasian mainland as far as Cattigara extended 225°, according to the measurements of Marinus of Tyre, which were the ones accepted by Columbus. Adding on the 40° of the farthest part of Asia we get 265°. That left 95°, equal to the width of the Atlantic, to complete the circuit of the globe. Almagià concludes, therefore, that a world map of the type Martellus made, but "modified... according to Marinus's measurements... represents the map that answers most faithfully to Columbus's concepts; or rather, more specifically, Columbus found a foundation or a support for his concepts about the dimensions and configuration of the earth and its habitable part in a world map of this kind, which he must have had before his eyes." This is all the more likely because such a depiction was in agreement with the theories expounded by Pius II and Pierre d'Ailly, nor did it contradict Toscanelli's letter and map. It agreed, in fact, with all of Columbus's previous geographical learning.

If all this is true (or likely) we have confirmation of something to which we referred earlier, namely, that Columbus found scientific support in Andalusia and Castille for the inspiration he had had while he lived on the banks of the Tagus. To this can be added the perfectly logical fact that of the two measurements of the earth's circumference indicated by Marinus of Tyre and by Ptolemy, he chose the first because it was more in keeping with his ideas and his goals. But the question remains: When did he see and obtain this world map of the Martellus type? Before 1492 — as most believe, and as Almagià also seems to maintain, though he leans toward a date after 1488 (that is, "later than what is generally believed") — or after?

I believe that no one can answer this question unless new documents turn up. Another consideration of Luzzana Caraci's seems interesting to me, however. She takes Martin Behaim's globe as her point of departure (on this subject I repeat that Columbus could possibly have heard of it only after 1492), in order to say that the attention paid by cartographers to the Atlantic islands (as we mentioned before) and the depictions of Asia much enlarged in the eastern and southeastern portion and with numerous offshore islands, attest to the spread of geographical concepts concerning the *oikumene*'s greater size (compared to medieval ideas) in the years immediately preceding the discovery of America, with the result that the age-old resistance to "the empty spaces" of the oceans was overcome. In other words, people expected to discover the New World, or rather, "new worlds."

* * *

Of course, planispheres like that of Henricus Germanus Martellus, as we said earlier, must have circulated around the Iberian Peninsula and been used both in the dispute over the line of the *raya*, and perhaps for Cabral's expedition (and maybe for others as well). The corresponding geographical concepts — which Columbus, convinced that he had reached Asia, continued to defend — were attracting opponents however. As Bernáldez attests, Columbus himself would pay the price in the discussions he would have to face on returning from his second voyage (that is, when there began to be more data about the newly discovered territories).

Thus Juan Gil, in a recent work, maintains that it was in 1497 that Columbus acquired new bibliographic materials in order to find arguments with which to meet those of his adversaries. As a result, many of the *Annotations* must go back to a rather late date, after the discussions about the feasibility of his plan for a transatlantic voyage and after the discovery of America. The annotations to Marco Polo's work are necessarily after 1496 or 1497 (the years when Columbus acquired it), while Marina Conti had shown earlier that his reading and annotation of Pliny's *Natural History* must have preceded his departure on the third voyage. Even an annotation to Pius II Piccolomini's *History* must be after 1492.

All this has only an indirect bearing, however, on Columbus's cartography. On the other hand, it is more pertinent, for the events of Columbus's fourth voyage, to call to mind the world maps of the Martellus type. While the Admiral was sailing along the eastern coasts of the isthmus of Central America, and while he was writing the letter mentioned above to the King and Queen from Jamaica in 1503, he must have had before his eyes one of those maps or planispheres that depicted the fourth Asian peninsula as narrow enough to imagine crossing it by land in a march of nine days, as he claims to have been told, or better yet, to seek out a strait or an arm of the sea by which to pass into the Indian Ocean. Columbus already knew of the results reached by Vespucci, Cabral, Bastidas, and others concerning the exploration of a continent to the south; he himself had theorized about it during his third voyage. For him, all that was lacking now was to find a sea route north of this territory in order to reach Cattigara and the mouth of the Ganges.

Luzzana Caraci has written about another subject connected to Henricus Martellus's planisphere, using as her point of departure an article by Davies. In it Davies defends a rather complicated and fanciful theory, according to which the world map acquired not long ago by Yale University would not be traced back to Martellus, as is commonly believed, but would be the work of Bartolomeo Colombus. He would have executed it in England and later (in 1489) stolen it and taken it to Spain (where a copy would have been made) and then to Italy, where Martellus would have copied it. It is obvious that such a theory needs documentation, which is entirely non-existent for now. The only useful element that can be extracted from this theory for the purposes of this study is the affirmation that not even in this manner are we able to identify a cartographic type that can be said to be that of Bartolomeo Columbus (nor that of Christopher either, therefore, who, according to Gallo's account, discussed with him the prospects for success of a voyage westward).

If what Luzzana Caraci writes is perfectly true — that a single map is not enough to allow us to speak of a "type" of document and to discern in it the reflection of geographical concepts — then we are left totally helpless, since we have at our disposal not even one map, but only a sketch (concerning a partial coastal survey) that issued positively from the hands of such prolific cartographers. Even the allusions Columbus made in 1494 to the *pintura* of the islands — in the letter already mentioned to the Catholic Kings — contribute nothing to our cartographic reconstruction of his geographical concepts, though they contain precious references, in the recent edition of the *Libro Copiador*, to gradations in latitude and longitude (which was new for the time).

There is no doubt, as we said before, and keeping Luzzana Caraci in mind, that Columbus's cosmographical and geographical ideas (and all his learning) must have been enriched, modified, and developed over time "as a consequence of the accumulated experiences of the four voyages." I do not think, however, that we can speak of an improvement in his concepts during the last ten years of his life. In fact one could imagine that as soon as there was a sufficient number of scientific proofs (or data held to be such) to defend his ideas and his rights (these are in addition to the theoretical arguments that he invoked even before the discovery) — perhaps on the eve of the third voyage — the Admiral closed himself off in a tenacious and obstinate insistence on claiming and trying to prove that the lands he had reached were part of Asia.

The reality is that even though Columbus accepted Marinus of Tyre's measurement of the earth's circumference, he must never have entirely freed himself from the influence of Ptolemaic ideas (and their related cartographic representations). For him, the continent discovered during his third voyage could perhaps be the same as the land with which Ptolemy bounded the Indian Ocean on the southeast, while "Cathay" could be discerned to the north in Cuba and "Cipango" in Hispaniola; from the sea offshore, via a strait, one "ought" to be able to arrive in the waters into which the Ganges flowed and on whose banks "Cattigara" arose. In essence, this was a return to Ptolemy. In this respect, perhaps, the Columbus of the fourth voyage had geographical ideas that were less advanced than those of Bartolomeo Diaz sixteen or seventeen years earlier.

CHAPTER IV

CONSEQUENCES
OF THE GREAT GEOGRAPHICAL DISCOVERIES
IN LIGURIAN CARTOGRAPHY

1) *A period of great cartographical production*

It stood to reason that the great geographical discoveries, along with the acquisition of so much information about the large and varied new territories, would stimulate a renewal of cartography and give rise to the production of many noteworthy works in the sixteenth century, with respect both to nautical documents (which we will deal with here) and to depictions of the interior of the continents (and hence to land maps). This occurred not only in Italy, but also in Portugal, in Spain, and elsewhere (Spain would go so far as to establish a *Padrón real* — that is, an official nautical chart of the new seas and the associated lands — which was constantly brought up to date with the findings of voyages; all cartographic documents were to be constructed using longitudes determined by the *Casa de Contratación* in Seville). Confronted with such a quantity of documents, we will have to follow rigorously selective and restrictive standards in the coming pages (so as not to distort the features of this essay), in the sense that we will discuss only Ligurian cartographers, even if they worked elsewhere, barely mentioning the less important and later ones.

Indeed, more than fifty nautical charts by Ligurian map makers have come down to us from that century, not including the anonymous ones that bear a definite Genoese imprint. In this field Liguria probably had an advantage at that time because of its location in the Western Mediterranean, that is, its relative proximity to the Atlantic. This century in fact witnessed a relative decline in cartography in the Adriatic (judging by the physical evidence that has been preserved), although there were still centers in Ancona, which boasted about fifteen signed works, and in Venice. Still on the topic of the Western Mediterranean, we should note that the Olives family moved from Majorca to Messina, where they founded a flourishing workshop; it would be active even into the seventeenth century, and from there (as well as from Naples) other maps by makers of Majorcan origin, such as those of Martinez, would reach Genoa.

The output of nautical charts in this century can essentially be divided into two types: planispheres, which were brought up to date and filled in from time to time, taking into account the discoveries and news about them; and individual charts depicting the Mediterranean (this was the most widespread type of Italian work, in the wake of the ancient medieval tradition), and also other bodies of water and coastal stretches. At the same time and immediately thereafter, however, there was a proliferation of atlases containing, in addition to planispheres, a series of maps of the Mediterranean and of seas and lands far and near. In actuality, the nautical cartography of this century attests to the fact that the isolation of the Mediterranean world (or Western Europe) from other areas of maritime activity had now broken down. Since navigation was still by sail power, however, certain environmental factors typical of coastal navigation remained in full force, even for ocean-going seamen. These included local climatic conditions, particular circumstances of winds, currents, and tides, and the coastal morphology, together with the opportunities it afforded for finding places of safe shelter that were also good for restoring water supplies — all of which explains the minute care with which these last features were represented.

The sizeable cartographic output of the sixteenth century — which was accompanied by an equally abundant production of globes, joined with the attainment of a much broader geographical outlook (compared to the past) — exhibited all the defects of the previous systems of projection in the difficulty it had in depicting the position and configuration of the newly discovered lands (it would be better to speak of the previous empirical systems, which were not true projections, but were used alongside those that do deserve the name). There were many attempts, taking various tacks, before the concept of loxodromics was accepted and applied and before Mercator made his maps, which were especially suited to navigation.

Thus cordiform projections appeared, such as the one Waldseemüller used when representing the Americas. Then came the equidistant oval ones utilized by Agnese. In Gastaldi's very famous world maps, however, the parallels were not equidistant, but were laid out with reference to the oval's smaller diameter. All the orientation lines in turn were shifted. The one through the Mediterranean was replaced by the equatorial line;

later, not one remained fixed. Finally, as Baldacci points out, the spread of Ptolemaic cartography at the hands of Humanism had shown the serious errors to which the application of the principle of using coordinates could lead, because it was so imperfect and there were no instruments for determining longitude. In this respect it would take decades to accumulate enough observations.

Thus, in the anonymous Italian world map known as the King-Hamy map, a straight line running from south to north with latitude markings on it appears for the first time (does this perhaps reflect remote Ptolemaic influences, or possibly bear witness to the maker's awareness that the earth is round?). In 1536 Battista Agnese would speak of the *linea meridiana tholomei*, and in 1562 Bartolomeo Olives would mention an *escala dos grados*. Even before this a double scale for distances had been used, since it was recognized that the representation suffered distortions with variations in latitude. Degrees of longitude, in turn, would be indicated more and more often, obviously along the line of the equator.

Now that there was a geographical graticule on the map, or gradations serving as points of reference for parallels and meridians, the wind roses and their associated "rhumb lines" were obviously becoming less important, especially at a time when navigation was increasingly based on an astronomical determination of the ship's position. Both would survive, however, the "rhumb lines" perhaps because they had some usefulness for indicating wind directions, while the wind roses ended up as an accessory, or merely decorative, feature. In the workshops of Lisbon and Seville, on the other hand, the network of winds would be laid down on the basis of degrees latitude, and perhaps with an estimation of degrees longitude.

Consequently, the sixteenth century witnessed the overcoming of the separation between nautical cartography, which we have been treating up to now, and learned cartography of the Ptolemaic type; by the same token it also saw the correction of many mistakes characterizing the one (the misorientation of the axis of the Mediterranean, for example) and the other (the exaggerated length of that body of water longitudinally). Strategems to compensate for mistakes due to magnetic declination — the scope of which was now well recognized — were probably introduced, if it is true that all Spanish nautical charts were deliberately distorted to account for the needle's deviation, as Alonso de Santa Cruz, writing in 1555, says. Nonetheless, mistakes would persist in nautical charts until Bartolomeo Crescenzio introduced a new model of nautical chart with "rhumb lines" of the winds — a "modern" one, so to speak, inasmuch as it was corrected in accordance with recent observations and had a graticule that was correctly oriented (in Baldacci's wellchosen phrase).

* * *

Other observations concern the decorative aspect, which became ever more conspicuous in the sixteenth century — almost as a prelude to the Baroque taste for "fullness" — as these features replaced the fantastic motifs derived from the whimsical imagination of the medieval cartographer. The roses, which had as many as 34 winds, were ever more colorful and ornate. The shape of the lily, which pointed north, became geometrical and lanceolate (in the seventeenth century it would assume strange shapes, such as that of a bunch of flowers). Graphic scales and scrolls for the inscriptions, often in the form of streamers, were also decorated. The perspectival views of cities were taken over from earlier prototypes and therefore turned out distorted at times. Maritime symbols, such as Greek crosses to indicate dangerous places, rocks, and shoals, became more frequent. On land, the pictures of animals proliferated; the Prunes family would become famous for their figures of a live ostrich with its neck in a knot. Drawings of ships and monsters, the latter repeating classical and medieval images, appeared on the sea, especially in the oceans. In addition to the usual religious depictions in the Holy Land, nautical charts began to show images of Madonnas and saints as well, generally on the neck of the parchment. The first one that we know of, that of Saint Christopher on the very well-known map by Juan de la Cosa (from 1500), brings us back again to the story of Columbus.

The fact is that in the sixteenth century nautical charts had become art objects as well, since collecting and owning such documents — nautical charts or land maps, planispheres and atlases — had come into fashion. In 1570 John Die wrote (in a passage quoted by Wallis and cited, in turn, by Astengo): "Some in order to adorn with them their halls, residences, rooms, galleries, studies, or libraries; some on account of things in the past, such as battles, earthquakes, heavenly lights and other such occurrences mentioned in history books, and thus to see, as if with their own eyes, the place, the neighboring regions, the distance from us, and other similar circumstances; some at present in order to see the great domain of the Turk, the vast empire of the Muscovite, and the small plot of land where Christianity (by profession of faith) is certainly known, which is little, I say, compared to the rest; some on account of their own journeys to distant lands or in order to understand the journeys of other people: all these delight in, love, acquire, and use nautical charts and geographical globes."

* _* *

The spread of the art of printing also contributed to the large market for works of cartography. Engravings from woodcuts had already made an early appearance, but with this method it was not possible to obtain the precise outlines that people were used to seeing in manuscript nautical charts; this is evident in the works, valuable nonetheless, of Pietro Coppo, the great Istrian cartographer and geographer. In this sense copper engravings gave better results and at a fairly reasonable price. In 1569 a nautical chart by Diogo Homem, published in a printed edition by Forlani in Venice, was a great success. But maps printed by typographical methods then had to be painted by hand, using water-colors. For this reason, as Astengo points out, maps drawn by hand on parchment and illuminated continued to be prized and therefore to be produced. At the end of the sixteenth century maps printed on paper took the upper hand, Dutch cartographers having now become the leaders in this market (and also in that of atlases). The Dutch were also responsible, however, for the surviving production of nautical charts and atlases on parchment — though they were still printed — such as the nautical chart of Europe by Cornelius Cleausz.

To all this were added concerns of a political nature, especially regarding the routes and seas of the territories recently reached and still little known. In the Iberian Peninsula nautical cartography had become a "matter of state." An official *Padrâo* existed also in Lisbon and was always kept up to date with information that navigators were obliged to report to state authorities. Compared to these measures the "privilege" that the Republic of Genoa granted to cartographers (usually to one at a time, as we will see in the case of Maggiolo), requiring them to remain in the city, meant very little. In any case, the system of "exclusivity" would collapse in the seventeenth century.

On the whole, therefore, the sixteenth century saw a considerable increase in the number of cartographers, along with a more substantial output than in the preceding centuries, including numerous copies and anonymous works. The predominance of the maritime interests of the Iberian states is reflected in the extensive development of cartography in Spain (where, however, Seville and other southern cities gradually prevailed over the Balearics and Catalonia) and in Portugal, as a result of decided advances in knowledge of the Atlantic. Cartographers' mobility was also greater than in the past. In spite of all precautionary measures on the part of governments intent on protecting the "state secrets" of nautical cartography, there were episodes of espionage and theft of maps (as must have been the case of Cantino and Caverio). In addition to obtaining works to copy, nations often tried to induce cartographers to move from one country to another by enticing them with the prospect of better pay. Some would move spontaneously, because of economic incentives or a particular period of depression in the maritime center where they were working. Thus the Olives family, as we saw earlier, would move from Majorca, whose port activities were on the decrease, to Messina. When even Messina saw its commerce ebb, Martinez, who was working there, would inundate Genoa with his works, a city that, on the contrary, must have continued to be a rich market in this respect.

2) *The first representations of America and Nicolò de Caverio*

The earliest maps to show the new lands beyond the Atlantic were constructed and circulated in Europe while Columbus was still alive, and indeed was still sailing. The very first one we know of today is the famous map by the Basque Juan de la Cosa, a traveling companion of the Admiral's, which is kept in the Naval Museum in Madrid. On it America is shown as two rather squat continental masses with quite imprecise outlines but solidly joined at the point where the ocean protrudes deeply, and there are many offshore islands. Such a representation must have corresponded (but with obvious distortions for the continental portions) to ideas the participants had about the new regions on their return trip from Columbus's second voyage or shortly thereafter. It makes sense that they had relatively accurate information only about the islands of Central America, but the intuition they had about the continent is significant (if it was a question of intuition and not a collection of legends).

The story of the so-called "map of Cantino," which can be dated with certainty to the period between December 1501 and October 1502, is well-known. In fact Alberto Cantino, the Duke of Ferrara's ambassador to Lisbon, had it made at just that time so as to keep Ercole I d'Este informed about the new discoveries. The map (in actuality, a very fine planisphere) arrived in Genoa at the home of the patrician Francesco Cattaneo, who had it sent on to Ferrara. Today it is held by the Estense Library in Modena.

It was clearly inspired by Portuguese models (as is shown by some of the place names), perhaps by the official *Padrâo* itself. It is characterized by the usual network of "rhumb lines" radiating from wind roses and includes a representation of parts of the New World: a stretch of coastline of the North American continent, the Caribbean Sea with the Greater and Lesser Antilles, and a stretch of the shores of South America from Venezuela to Brazil. To the north, in the Atlantic, Newfoundland is shown as the *Terra del Rey de portuguall*. A portion of Greenland is indicated, with the name *Apontad* (that is, the farthest point of Asia). The decorations are very conspicuous, including pictures of very tall, green trees, parrots, and other animals, along with city views, coats-of-arms, flags, and other embellishments.

We have mentioned this famous map, which has nothing to do with the Ligurian tradition, because the maker of another map very like it (and which must date to shortly after it) was, however, Genoese, namely Nicolò de Caverio, whose surname was often in the past misread as "de Canerio" or "Canerio" (here, as earlier, in the case of de Pareto and de Canepa, I prefer to retain the "de" before the surname out of greater fidelity to the sources, even if the preposition only serves to indicate their belonging to a family). Revelli has traced a handful of archival documents that indicate that he belonged to a family that lived in Genoa from 1488 to 1529 (at least as far as we can ascertain) and that in Quinto he even owned real estate adjacent to the holdings of the Columbuses and Antonio Gallo, the chancellor and chronicler of the Admiral's first two voyages, whom we mentioned earlier. The map, held in the National Library in Paris is signed (*Opus Nicolay de Cauerio Januensis*), but not dated (Plate XX).

The map must certainly go back, however, to 1502 or a period immediately thereafter, since, again according to Revelli, the representation of Central America corresponds to the geographical concepts that Columbus had at the beginning of the fourth voyage. There are also correlations with the so-called Contarini-Rosselli planisphere of 1506. The map was certainly made while taking into account the results of the first three voyages of Columbus and those of Hojeda, Juan de la Cosa, and Vespucci. As in Cantino's map, Cuba is represented twice: as an island (*insulla issabella*) and as a peninsular promontory of the continent, approximately corresponding to Florida. This duplication, which is also found in later documents such as those of Waldseemüller, can be explained by the different opinions of Columbus; when he arrived there on his first voyage he thought he had reached "Cipango," whereas by the end of the second he was convinced he had gotten to Asia, of which

Cuba must have been an outcropping, or rather a peninsula. As for the rest of the New World, the only difference, compared to Cantino's map, is a somewhat greater number of place names along the Brazilian coasts represented.

De Caverio's map, which is the first from a Ligurian workship to show the American territories, is also the first we know of, even in other countries, to include a scale of latitudes, from 55° to 70° north, on the left side of the parchment. This is an innovation clearly linked to the spread of celestial navigation, which brings us back to Portuguese models. We know, in fact, that Portuguese ships' commanders and pilots, such as Vasco da Gama, for instance, calculated, even from land, the latitude of the places reached. Another peculiarity of this chart-planisphere is the presence of a small world map surrounded by the heavenly spheres in a wind rose situated in Africa at the center of a network of "rhumb lines." This document undoubtedly had a great influence on the cartography of the Renaissance, since we find its coastal outlines and its place names in a number of other important planispheres.

All this leads one to reflect on at least two points: What prototypes did De Caverio use when constructing his chart-planisphere? Who, in fact, was he, that he was able to command such widespread circulation of his work? We cannot answer the first question, except through suppositions. Revelli's hypothesis is only that — that the cartographer may have had at his disposal some Columbian data, possibly furnished by the Admiral himself, who could have sent news about his discoveries to Gallo and his cousins in Quinto (perhaps via Nicolò Oderico or Francesco Rivarolo, who took it upon themselves to see that the "Codex [Book] of Privileges" got to Genoa). Even if this could have happened, however, it is obvious that one cannot construct so complex a planisphere on the basis of information in a letter or even by using a sketch of some kind. My supposition (which remains only that, however) seems more reasonable to me, namely that while the so-called "map of Cantino" was in Genoa awaiting the courier that would take it to Ferrara, the nobleman Francesco Cattaneo allowed De Caverio to see and copy it. The latter would have added only a few new elements, derived perhaps from the information and letters just mentioned. This could explain the minor differences between this chart-planisphere and the one now kept in Modena.

It certainly does not follow that De Caverio ever left Genoa, and still less that he went to Lisbon or any place else in Portugal (though we know nothing of his life). In 1505 a person bearing his name was in Quinto, for business with Antonio Gallo. All this conflicts with the image of a cartographer well known in the world, where his works circulated and became famous — an image such as to justify the influence of his planisphere on later ones. One could also suppose that this influence was exerted by a previous Portuguese prototype, now lost, to which we could relate both the "map of Cantino" and this document (though it has not yet been sufficiently studied) (Plate XXI).

To complete these remarks about cartography in the Columbian era, we must refer to another famous world map or planisphere, the so-called King-Hamy map, already mentioned and held by the Huntington Library in San Marino, California. It is anonymous and undated, but certainly by an Italian hand, though no one has ever been able to prove that it came from a Genoese workshop. For the purposes of this research it should be mentioned, because the representation of the continent's isthmus in Central America, and, even more, the depiction of Asia, with its fourth eastern peninsula carefully outlined and expanded a long distance toward the south, can be linked to the geographical concepts held by Columbus in the last period of his life. Indeed, the planisphere is believed to date from after 1502, that is, to the years of the fourth voyage and the epilog of the Admiral's existence.

3) *The Da Maiolo dynasty and the prolific output of Battista Agnese*

The history of Genoese and Ligurian cartography in the sixteenth century is dominated by the presence and industry of a family of "masters," who obviously passed down the principles and secrets of the profession from father to son. Fortunately we are aided in our study of them by archival documents, including those published by Ferretto. We are referring to the Da Maiolo (or De Maiolo) family, usually known as Maggiolo, originally from Rapallo or its surroundings. The place name of "Maiolo," meaning the shoots of the vine, is, in fact, rather widespread in coastal Liguria, but the family — or rather one of the families of this name — to which the cartographers belonged, seem to have come from a place between Rapallo and Zoagli.

The first of them was Vesconte, who, after probably growing up in Genoa, had already left by 1511, since he signed an atlas in Naples calling himself *civis Janue* (this would be followed by a map and an atlas in 1512). A few years later, however, apparently in 1518, he returned to the Ligurian capital by invitation of the doge, Ottaviano Fregoso, since he made another similar work there in 1519, including a planisphere that extends in longitude from the island of Cuba to well beyond the Ganges, and in latitude from Labrador to the Cape of Saint Augustine (or rather as far as the mouth of the Rio de la Plata, but placed several degrees north of its true location).

In 1520 the Republic of Genoa granted to Vesconte Maggiolo a regular annual stipend because he was "experienced in the manufacture of sailing charts and other necessities for navigation," so that he had a right to the title of *Magister cartarum pro navigando*. The payment — specified to begin in the following year — would be for life, that is, even when he would no longer be able to practice his profession. But the payments did not come regularly, since, as a document published by Staglieno shows, he made a complaint about them in 1523. In it he pointed out that he was responsible not only for his own numerous progeny, but also for that of his deceased brother Antonio, and he threatened to leave town. All this he did in order to request not only his stipend, but also tax exemptions, which were not granted.

In 1525 the name of his son, Giovanni Antonio, appeared next to his own as maker of a map constructed in Genoa (the signature reads *Vesconte et Joannes de Maiollo*). In 1527 Vesconte alone made a famous map on which the words *Terra nova descoberta per Christoforo Colombo Ianuensum* are written over Central America; a cartouche refers to *Magalanes Portogese* and his passage through the strait of that name. The 1530's were also years of intense production for Vesconte, some of his maps from this period having been preserved. A contract signed by him in 1534 with a well known Genoese editor seems not to have led anywhere, however; it was for the execution of a world map that the editor must have had engraved and printed (in this same time period Vesconte also became the owner of real estate in the outskirts of Genoa). The last maps and the last atlas of his that have come down to us are from 1547, 1548, and 1549. In March of 1551 he was dead. But the stipend awarded to him was collected by his son Giacomo, who, in 1544, pledged to the doge that he would reside in Genoa and practice the *artem fabricandi cartas* there (the stipend would be collected until 1605).

This very abundant output has been only partially studied. Here it will be sufficient to point out those aspects of it that may reflect the spread of geographical concepts going back to Columbus or Vespucci, or that concern the cartographic interpretation of information arising from the explorations made in the years when Vesconte was active. In the atlas made in Naples in 1511, for instance, and now held in the John Carter Brown Library in Providence, the sixth map is a planisphere, on which the maker, as Caraci writes, "clearly intended to depict, opposite the old world, the newly discovered lands beyond the Atlantic, showing at the same time the entire sailing route around Africa." The type of projection, in fact, has a certain originality compared to other more or less contemporary world map, and it is not easy to say from what model the maker could have taken his inspiration. Perhaps this work was derived from an Italian prototype, now lost, that other cartographers also must have had in mind (Pl. XXII).

Other features — concerning the parts of the new lands that are represented, with their infrequent place names — also show the originality of this document. The northern part of America appears in it as the eastern tip of Asia (it is labeled *India Occidentale*), while the southern sector, from the isthmus of Darién to the *terra de brazille*, is depicted as separate, including a portion of the Greater and Lesser Antilles. Caraci thought that Vesconte had, among other sources, a Roman edition of Ptolemy (which obviously had no bearing on the representation of the New World). He also maintained that Vesconte believed the discoveries of Cabot and Corte Real to pertain to Asia; it must have been an open question whether these discoveries, as opposed to those of the Spanish and Portuguese in Central and South America, had led to the identification of a free-standing continental mass or of another part of that same Asia.

Very soon, however, Vesconte had to change his mind about how to depict America. Indeed, without taking other earlier documents into account, it seems significant that in his 1527 map all of America except for Labrador (and obviously the Caribbean islands) is shown as a nearly continuous continental mass, which becomes narrow in the middle and very curved. The *Terra Florida* appears as a promontory of it, opposite Cuba and southeast of an isthmus, to the northwest of which is *Francesca* (with the flag with three fleur-de-lis). We called this a nearly continuous land mass, because in it, to the south of an island labeled *Juchatan*, is an opening marked *Stretto dubitoso*, or "dubious strait," through which the Atlantic Ocean supposedly joined with the Indian Ocean (or rather with the Pacific, as we would correctly say today).

Another interesting work by Vesconte is the small atlas, also made in Genoa and now held by the National Library in Florence. Caraci drew attention to it in his time, pointing out that it was unfinished (this fact could provide further evidence that, at least in this instance, the "rhumb lines" were laid out before the actual geographical outline of the map was made, though in the case of copies this argument can be turned upside down). Two of the final maps are devoted to the American continent. In the first the coastlines are delineated from Florida to the Strait of Magellan, where the outline of the shore is interrupted, resuming in Peru and ending in Mexico (Cuba, *Hispaniola*, and the course of the Amazon River are shown with few or no place names, but what there is is "purely Sevillan in character"). In the second map the Atlantic coast of America extends from Labrador to Florida. Since these maps are among the ones not finished by the map maker, this atlas, which has innovations compared to Vesconte's earlier works, shows only that he kept up to date about the most recent geographical discoveries and took them into account in the documents he produced even in those years when he must have been quite old.

Giacomo Maggiolo made his debut, as far as we know, with a 1551 map that shows he had already achieved maturity. His brother Giovanni Antonio, of whom only three maps, dating from the period 1565 to 1575, have come down to us, perhaps moved, at least for a time, to Naples, where the family continued to own the house his father had lived in earlier (in Genoa, however, they resided in the Molo quarter). Giovanni Antonio's son would be Baldassare, also a cartographer; we know of documents he made in Genoa in the last decades of the century. Baldassare's brother, in turn (Giacomo evidently had had no sons), was Cornelio, who laid a claim before the Senate in 1607 for the "privilege" of exercising the profession of cartographer that had earlier been granted to Vesconte, Giacomo, and Giovanni Antonio; these having died, the Senate had decided to assign it to one Gerolamo Costo from Sestri Ponente. Cornelio reminded them that it was he who had done everything during the last years of Giacomo's life, and that "he was already in peaceful possession of all the writs and instruments necessary for the said profession, with which he served with every perfection, as his works bear witness, which not only all Genoese sailors use, but also the Florentines, the Romans, the French, the Savoyards, and other nations." Therefore, since by now even Costo was dead, he requested the aforementioned "privilege" for himself and his three male children.

Only after a second appeal, in 1611, was this granted, but Cornelio died in 1614. One of his sons, Giovanni Antonio the Younger, then asked to succeed him; the Senate conceded this to him, though it cut the stipend in half. When he was murdered a year later, it was his brother Nicolò who asked for the same privilege (it was in the latter's petition to the Senate, in 1644, that we find the complaint that there had come into the city "outsiders, who without being approved for this profession have the impudence to sell and manufacture nautical charts, compasses, hour-glasses, etc.," thereby causing him harm). The long family line of these cartographers came to an end with Cornelio the Younger, who, at the death of Nicolò in 1650, declared himself "very well qualified" for the exercise of that profession to which "there remains no one else at present to attend." We do not know the outcome, however, of his request for the "privilege" and stipend.

Of the considerable output left behind by these descendants of Vesconte Maggiolo certain works by Giacomo deserve attention, especially his maps of 1561, 1563, and 1564, although they are richer in decorative elements than they are in elements involved in this research; Capacci was right to underline his fine qualities as an illuminator. In any case the works of those years that have come down to us are obviously "study editions" derived from the same prototype, except for minor or totally insignificant variations. All three of the documents from the dates cited show the Mediterranean and a considerable portion of the Atlantic, where, however, the pictures of ships with sails unfurled are more conspicuous than the islands.

The 1563 map owned by the Société de Géographie in Paris is noted for its partial scale of the northern latitudes. Here it is very obvious that the representation of Northern Europe (Denmark and Scandinavia) is derived mainly from an edition of Ptolemy from almost a century earlier, with some adjustments, suggested perhaps by consulting later maps (but this does not concern the purposes of this essay). Worth mentioning here, however, is the (rather small) world map placed in the center of the Saharan area of the 1561 map held at the Civic Naval Museum in the Pegli district of Genoa (there is not a trace of one, however, in the 1564 map at the Berio Civic Library in Genoa). The depiction is clear and well done, and its derivation is uncertain (as Capacci writes), with an obviously incomplete coastal outline of the Americas. But the shape of the two continental masses is shown in modern fashion, so to speak. Thus, seventy years after Columbus's discovery, we have come a long way, as we might expect, from the uncertainties and the travails that afflicted the Admiral in the last years of his life.

* * *

Battista Agnese, who was active, as far as we know, from 1514 to 1564, should also be placed among the Genoese cartographers of this century (though the apprentices in his workshop and the people who carried on his work may have continued producing maps even after the death of the master, using his models). He was the maker of a large number of maps and atlases, the latter containing as many as 32 and 36 plates. We know for a fact that he was born in Genoa, because some of his documents are signed *Baptista Agnese Januensis*, but we do not know whether he received his training as a cartographer in the Ligurian capital (this is only a probability). It is also certain that at a young age he must have moved to Venice; there he started and managed an important shop, where he made all the important products known to us (although several that prove to be undoubtedly from his hand carry no indication as to their maker, date, and place of execution).

Caraci has called his output "the richest collection of manuscript nautical charts and atlases, of all the products of the sixteenth century, that can be attributed with certainty to a single draftsman or his school," while noting that "the commercial element... doubtless must have carried great weight" for a part of such activity. He adds that "there are very good reasons to believe that, even though not everything that bears the name of Agnese can have been put together by him, physically or not, it is still in reality his work or that of his shop, and much of what has come down to us without his signature is, by the internal features of the design and content, undoubtedly his."

This is not the place to speak of that part of Agnese's work that consists of nautical charts, depicting usually the Mediterranean and a portion of the Atlantic (that is, still — after so much time — the territory of the so-called "standard portolan"). The maps in his various atlases referring to the Americas, however, deserve mention. I am thinking in particular of the atlases made after 1550, indeed probably much later, such as the one I studied previously in the Civic Library in Bergamo; this work is unfinished, so that its construction is thought to have been interrupted by the death of its maker.

In this type of atlas four maps are usually set aside for America, beginning with the central section, then passing on to the northern one, and finally to the southern portion (naturally depicting the Atlantic islands, as well, and the parts of the Old World that are on the ocean). If the method of drawing up the coastal contours on these maps is the same as that used for the Mediterranean and the territory of the so-called "standard portolan," including a wealth of details, the basic arrangement is, on the contrary, entirely different, because there is no network of "rhumb lines" corresponding to the wind directions, although polychrome wind roses do appear on them, in addition to the scale, of course, on the lines indicating the equator and the Tropics of Cancer and Capricorn. The "dividing line between the Castilians and the Portuguese" is also shown on it (Pl. XXIII).

Geographical features abound concerning the eastern seaboard of the two Americas, along with some offshore islands or groups of islands, but inscriptions such as *Mare Incognita* and *Terra Incognita* also appear in various places. On the other hand, in some of Agnese's works the representation of geographical features on the American side of the Atlantic is behind the times; this happened in the case of the Yucatan, which is still shown as an island in a 1554 atlas, whereas documents from other map makers depicted it correctly, as a peninsula, as early as 1529 (it is shown in the Bergamo atlas as a penisula, though quite distorted in appearance compared to reality — which confirms the quite late date of this atlas, as well).

On the whole, however, we cannot deny Agnese credit for having kept up to date with the majority of the most recent geographical discoveries of his time. Through his manuscript maps, which differed from those derived from medieval nautical charts, he publicized the results of the most recent geographical accomplishments, such as those that followed Magellan's circumnavigation. The itinerary of this expedition, passing through the Moluccas, is traced in a quite detailed manner on the atlas maps that depict the planisphere. It is repeated with such frequency that it led Magnaghi to claim that it was a kind of trademark for the works of Agnese and his co-workers.

It should also be said that, as in so many other cases we have seen, this cartographer's works — judging by the examples that have come down to us — must have been intended more for cultural and decorative purposes than for the practical goals of navigation, since they were destined for amateurs, influential people, the well educated, and libraries (for one thing, the scale of his maps is too small for nautical use). In any case, during the century when the art of printing was spreading, Agnese remained tied to the manuscript tradition, and through it he was able to make a not insignificant contribution to the dissemination of the new geographical learning.

For the Mediterranean and the Old World he often attained modest or poor results from his attempt to reconcile models of nautical cartography with Ptolemaic ones (or perhaps, more correctly, with one or more of the fifteenth century prototypes of the "new" or "modern" maps in the first editions of Ptolemy); for example, Agnese's depiction of Italy proves to be a step backward with respect to that of medieval nautical charts. Nonetheless, in the case of the Americas he assembles and provides a rich collection of information, which he aptly inserts into a representation drawn by a sure hand, though it still essentially repeats models of the same type. In any case, the work of this Genoese, transplanted to Venice for unknown reasons, also assisted the advance of cartography and cannot be ignored here.

4) *Toward the decline*

Beginning in the last decades of the sixteenth century the environment in Genoa and Liguria no longer provided cartographers of significance producing notable works. It is impossible to say whether this was in some way connected to the various crises undergone by the city and the region, and also by their maritime enterprises, or whether it is attributable to competition, felt in the Ligurian region as well, from cartographers from other lands, including those of Iberian origin living in Messina, like the Olives family (soon Italianized into Oliva) and Martinez, to name only the makers of maps that have been preserved in Liguria.

Alongside these maps Italian collections also hold works by Ligurian makers of little importance and (we may safely say) no originality. Examples include Francesco Scotti (or Scotto?), the maker of a nautical atlas in 1573, and Giacomo Scotto from Levanto (perhaps a relative of the former), who was making a nautical chart in Civitavecchia in 1589 (an earlier one of his dates to 1578) and who compiled an atlas, also nautical, of seven maps in Naples in 1593. We know nothing about them, incidentally, nor about Carlo da Corte, a Genoese, who made another nautical chart in Genoa, also in 1593. A figure of greater, but still relative, importance was perhaps Girolamo Costo, a Genoese and the maker of an undated map (though it is certainly from the last years of the sixteenth century) whose sobriety of decorative elements (poverty, we might even perhaps say) we cannot fail to note, along with the presence of two scales of distances, one, almost diagonal, in the Iberian Peninsula, and the other, horizontal, just north of the Danube.

A map like the one by Costo, held by the Società Ligure di Storia Patria in Genoa, could perhaps have been intended for nautical purposes precisely because of its emphasis on the essentials (though the scrolls for the scales and the margins of the document bear a floral decoration that already foreshadows those that would become fashionable in the seventeenth century). As in almost all the maps mentioned above, only the Mediterranean area is represented, along with the adjacent lands and seas. Hence even if they were used for navigation, it was of the kind confined to the Old World, and indeed to only a part of Europe, or rather to the countries habitually visited by sailors and local merchants, with some routes undoubtedly on the open sea, while other stretches, even long ones perhaps, were by coastal navigation. On these routes representations of the American coasts of the Atlantic served no purpose, nor did those of the Pacific and its associated territories. Indeed, for crossing the oceans increasingly widespread use would be made of Mercator's maps, whose projections, especially suitable (as we know) for nautical purposes, radically renewed cartography. On the other hand, printed engravings took the upper hand over the decades, greatly contributing to the dissemination and use of cartographic documents of whatever type.

At almost the same time and for a period thereafter Ortelius's atlases (the first edition of the *Theatrum Orbis Terrarum* dates from 1570) and those of his successors contributed greatly, through land cartography, to advances in modern geographical understanding; the great centers for the development and production of these works were in the Low Countries. In the Mediterranean, and indeed in Italy at this time, the most significant work for the purposes of this essay was that of Bartolomeo Crescenzio, who combined the results of previous experiments in his *Nautica Mediterranea* in 1607. With regard to cartography his first concern was to "locate correctly" the various coasts and islands and the different ports, which can only be done by establishing the latitude and longitude. This led to the "straightening up" or correct orientation of the network of "rhumb lines" of which Baldacci spoke, as we said before. But this method, Crescenzio wrote, was "totally unknown to the Pilots of the Mediterranean sea," which was "perhaps the reason that their map up until now has slumbered so shamefully under such great errors."

* * *

Even in the seventeenth century, therefore, there were in Italian territories a number of pilots accustomed to navigating by sight and with a compass, "by means of lookouts and estimations (an opinion is not a judgment, since opinions are often faulty)." Among them we should certainly place Guglielmo Saetone of Albissola Marina. Toward the end of the century he authored a *Stella guidante de' Pilotti e marinai*, that is, a manuscript nautical atlas (though it would perhaps be better to call it a portolan atlas, since in addition to maps, of which there are more than eighty, it also included an array of information typical of portolans). It has been preserved in two copies, one from 1681-1683 in the Braidense Library in Milan (probably this is the definitive presentation copy dedicated to Ippolito Centurione), the other, from 1682-1683, in the Archivio Comunale of his home town (this is perhaps the copy the author made and kept for himself; it turns out, in fact, to be less complex and especially less meticulous than the first one).

In addition to several maps giving an overview of large portions of the Mediterranean on a scale of between 1:3 and 1:4 million approximately, this work also depicts, using a scale with a much smaller reduction factor and with many minute details, the coasts of the Western Mediterranean, starting from the Gulf of Cadiz beyond the Strait of Gibraltar to the eastern part of the Italian peninsula in the Adriatic basin as far as Ancona,. The *Stella*... thus summed up the concrete experiences of the entire life of a sailor from a very small maritime town (it turns out, for example, that by age 18 he had already sailed along the French coasts; when he compiled these atlases he was past 60). He comes across as a simple, shrewd man who uses the sparing and undoubtedly practical language of coastal navigation such as he had conducted it throughout the trials and toils of everyday life. But these experiences of his are limited to the Western Mediterranean and, at most, the Adriatic, with no opening even toward the Eastern Mediterranean and the Aegean, let alone the Atlantic. In an outlying environment away from the innovations and echoes of modern culture there persisted, therefore, nautical techniques and a cartography (with a correspondingly limited geographical outlook) destined for an irreversible decline.

* * *

The works of Ghisolfo and Monno, which are from a distinctly earlier date by the way, should be placed on a different level, as being of interest for the history of Ligurian cartography (Ligurian at least in the broad sense, since Monno was a "surgeon" from Monaco [Montecarlo], which then belonged to the Republic of Genoa). Francesco Ghisolfo (or Ghisolfi or Gisolfi), whom some have claimed to be a disciple of Battista Agnese, was the maker of two unsigned and undated nautical atlases. The attribution of one of them, however, is very easy, since a poetic composition by Francesco Martinelli on the back of the last map praises Ghisolfo as the "maker of the present book." By comparison and analogy one then arrives at the attribution of the second one, which is held in the University Library in Genoa. As regards the date, however, we can only say that they are believed to be from the end of the sixteenth century, or perhaps (but less probably) from the very early seventeenth century.

These products were certainly not intended for use by sailors. The poem mentioned above speaks of a "book," that is, of a work obviously intended for libraries and the learned. The copy in Genoa was perhaps made for the Doria family, to whom we know it belonged for a long time. The fine decorations forming a continuous border on the margins of the maps testify to the same thing (whereas there are no conspicuous decorative features in the center of the maps except for the wind roses, which are delicately illuminated).

The usual plates at the beginning — devoted to astronomical features, including solar declinations — are followed by a nautical *map-pamundi* of the lands known at the end of the sixteenth century and by various maps with the traditional characteristics of nautical charts referring to the Old World, from Scandinavia to the Sahara and from the Atlantic to the Middle East (with the Mediterranean basin still in the center, therefore). The work ends with non-nautical planispheres, using an oval projection with whole and half zones. In the representation, nautical in nature, of the known world, the abundance of toponyms, even for recently reached lands in the Americas, stands out against a background of the usual network of "rhumb lines." The only coastal stretch that lacks them is the Pacific seaboard of Central America. South of the Strait of Magellan is drawn a large continental mass that continues both to the west and to the east, extending its coastal outline to the two corners of the map, to emerge again at the Tropic of Capricorn, almost as though it was intended to form the boundary of a landlocked sea (or rather a sea that, according to Ptolemaic conceptions, was understood as landlocked). To the north, after a deep indentation on the eastern seaboard, North America is joined on the west to a continental mass that is certainly that of Asia.

Another learned work is that of Giovanni Francesco Monno, dated 1633 and entitled *Arte della vera navegatione... Con un portolano con le coste figurate... Et Carta Mediterranea con il giusto luogo de gradi et vera via de venti* (preserved in the University Library in Genoa). We know nothing about the maker, since no biographical item concerning him has ever been traced in any archival document. One can only imagine that he was an enthusiast for navigational studies and a person well educated in matters of geographical knowledge. We know of another similar work by him from an earlier date (1620), held by Oxford University, which may be the first draft of the one in Genoa.

In addition to a treatise on astronomy and navigation and a portolan furnished with inset maps similar to those in island map collections, the latter work contains seven maps, all having the usual characteristics of nautical charts and still involving the area of the "standard portolan," hence the Old World. The last three of these pay particular attention to the Eastern Mediterranean (two being oriented with the south at the top). With this refined and (at least technically speaking) erudite work we are quite far removed from those aspects of the cartographic tradition that paved the way for Columbus's enterprise, and also from those that reflect the first results of the broadening of geographic knowledge that it brought about.

It is only for completeness' sake — or rather to avoid criticisms due to what might look like forgetfulness but isn't — that we mention here the Cavallini family (Francesco and Pietro, the latter being perhaps the son of the former), who lived in the seventeenth century and worked in Livorno producing nautical charts. It has been asserted that the father was of Genoese origin but later moved to that Tuscan city. That surname was and is very common, however, in the district of Massa and the adjacent area. In any case, their activity, though worthy of note, was largely and predominantly inspired by the marine culture of the Medici port, which was then being greatly expanded.

CHAPTER V

FINAL CONSIDERATIONS

If we are to draw any conclusions from what has been said up to now, we must make a clear distinction between what has been examined and studied over the past 150 years and more concerning the nautical cartography of the past — reaching results quite peacefully and generally accepted (except for a few details of secondary importance on the whole) by all those who were or are involved in it — and the problems associated with Columbus's cartography. The latter are still open at this time, since they are linked with the geographical concepts held by the Admiral and with his learning (I would add that the opportunity afforded by this quincentennary of the discovery of America has made only partial contributions to their solution, or even to a deepening of our understanding).

In the first place, then, we can say that nautical cartography introduced decisive innovations with respect to geographical understanding at that time. It arose in the thirteenth century as a result of the spread of the use of the compass in navigation, and it provided the first works known to us that were already assembled and joined together into overview maps between (perhaps) the end of the thirteenth and (for certain) the beginning of the fourteenth century. In the first decades of the latter century, there were already in circulation map collections like Vesconte's atlases, which aimed to depict the whole world then known. The planispheres in particular, of which we have examples from that period or shortly thereafter, were directed to the latter goal.

If the whole history of cartography can be considered to be the history of the image of the earth, as a fruit of human experience, then nautical charts — drawn up by sight and with the help of a compass without worrying about projection and magnetic declination — represent the final result of a legacy of data accumulated by trial and error through day-to-day events in the lives of sailors in the Mediterranean. The possibility of empirically representing the world on a plane surface did not contradict the cosmographical theories of the time, as we have seen, nor did the idea of a round earth, which was then commonly accepted in learned circles; it was believed that the size of the *oikumene* was insignificant and that for small areas a part of the rounded surface of the earth could be laid out in rudimentary fashion on a plane without posing any problems.

We have seen, of course, that what would be called the territory of the "standard portolan," in the Old World, was already well defined in the fourteenth century as far as data and mode of representation were concerned. Memories, very much alive, of Marco Polo, together with the multiple involvements to which they gave rise, led to particular consideration being paid to oriental matters. In contrast to the abundance of details about the Mediterranean shorelines already present in nautical charts, slight attention was paid to the northern regions and the Atlantic, except for the coastal stretches visited by Italian sailors (including those of northwest Africa, a traditional goal of Ligurian merchants). Greater notice was taken of the western ocean, with its real and imaginary islands, in cartographic documents of the fifteenth century (this, too, seems to me to be a sign of the times).

In the latter century map collections, which go by the modern name of atlases, also assumed a definite shape. They were shown earlier to be derived from several nautical charts (with fewer place names than the latter, probably because a selection was made in order to encourage an overall depiction). In time they would be designed from the start as self-contained works, independent of nautical charts. With the passing decades they would also begin to acquire features arising from the dissemination of the rediscovered codices of Ptolemy.

Some time ago Giovanni Marinelli, having pointed out that the geographical map can "represent a point of focus and synthesis in the history of thought and human activity... suitable for establishing the phases of progress and regress in the manifestation of such thought and activity," warned against accepting "a cartographic depiction of a historical area distant from us in time... as reliable documentation of the data it presents." This is because the sources used by the cartographer are different, as is the critical scrutiny to which he may have subjected them. Thus the cartographic document should undergo not only an examination of its external characteristics, but also an internal investigation. What was stated a long time ago by one of the masters of Italian geography remains valid today, when, in the area of medieval nautical cartography, we set out to explore the originality of the Ligurian tradition.

Genoa, of course, was a center of cartographic production, being a hub of lively and important marine and mercantile activity in the Middle

Ages, open to everything new, as is attested by the development of trade and the tools used in that field. On the other hand, Genoa was never a great cultural center. After an early development of certain poetical genres, the experimental "arts," which today would belong with the natural and medical sciences, emerged in the thirteenth century from among all the secular professions and established themselves. Here, as in other fields, the applied aspect very quickly prevailed.

In this environment nautical sciences, including cartography, must have found favorable conditions for their development and establishment. Evidence for this is given, among other things, by the fact that the cartographers about whom we have information turn out to be from families of a fairly high social level, or they were clergymen (a class then held in great esteem). This was well before the time when, through petitions and complaints to the Senate, they acquired tax exemptions and "privileges" to the point of obtaining a true monopoly, in some cases a perquisite handed down from father to son.

By long-standing tradition, therefore, Genoa was a center for nautical cartography, but it is useless to argue about which works or models were earliest, since a "first nautical chart" must never have existed. Such documents were in reality the manifestation of a common nautical culture in the Mediterranean, just as a number of words and expressions in the kind of lingua franca spoken in the ports were held in common. Naturally there were exchanges of information and a trade in ideas in these centuries, as well as a movement of cartographers between Genoa, Venice, and the ports of the Catalan and Majorcan area. Other cities and areas were very soon added to these.

It is equally well recognized that we know little about Arab influence, which must have been anything but insignificant, on the development of nautical cartography in "Christian" countries. In Genoa the opportunity to communicate in writing or orally with Muslim circles was always assured by the governing bodies. We are less well informed, probably because of the reticence of official sources, about the contribution the Jewish element must have made to the city's economic and cultural life (in this case, too, it must not have been negligible).

Then there is an aspect of political geography that we must assess. Genoa never had a large area of "its own sea" in front of the city and the Rivieras (at its greatest extent, at the time of the medieval "conventions" with coastal cities, it stretched from *Barchinonia usque ad Caput Corvi*, "from Barcelona to Cape Corvo;" thus it was a coastal sea). This was precisely because the city did not have behind it, in the Republic, an extensive political and territorial organization of which it was clearly in control. Thus we cannot apply to Genoa that Venetian concept, reflected in Ramusio, of the sea as a territorial and economic basis for the state. On the other hand Genoa did have various "seas of its own," but these were far removed from the territory of the metropolis: the Black Sea, part of the Greek archipelago, the Eastern Mediterranean, and for a certain stretch and in a certain period, the sea off the northwest coasts of Africa. This, too, had an influence, obviously a negative one, on the history of its tradition of nautical cartography, just as the city's recurring political crises and their economic effects must have been among the causes of the dispersion of its cartographers throughout the Mediterranean world. Similarly, the lack of a stable political power, of a "court," and of a university program, induced many learned people to emigrate from Genoa.

Other events in the city's life felt the effects of economic policy. More than once crises in progress required monetary monometalism, which led to the search for gold as a raw material in various parts of Africa, including initiatives (like that of Antonio Malfante) that had consequences for the history of exploration. Of course, new geographical information was converted into advances in cartography, which were in turn useful for the study and planning of new expeditions. These, in broad strokes, are the characteristics of the fifteenth century. During this period we do not find a great number either of Ligurian cartographers or of their works (although some are significant and interesting), and yet this is the century in which the dogmatic presuppositions on which medieval learning was based were overcome, including the limitation of geographical knowledge to large parts of the Old World.

But the fifteenth century is also the period of Humanism and of the rediscovery of Ptolemy, at first through manuscripts and then through printed editions, later furnished with maps that were very quickly redone. These "novelties" came relatively late to Genoa, since even though a certain stir of interest in the classics could be detected in the city, it would be the late sixteenth century before we encounter the only significant figure in Genoese Humanism, Agostino Giustiniani.

In the fifteenth century the concept that the earth was round was even more generally accepted than previously; it was combined with fragments of medieval theoretical principles (such as the inaccessibility of the "Antipodes," the uninhabitability of the intertropical band because of "excess of heat" — which, however, favored the formation of minerals — and the idea of the Earthly Paradise, situated on a mountain with abundant water in the far east). This concept had aroused the first concerns about problems relating to projections (through the application of which one could depict ever larger pieces of the earth's surface). This in turn had stimulated the construction of globes (following a tradition that slowed down but was never interrupted in the Middle Ages, especially in the Arab world). After this the century closed with the first great geographical discoveries, which then continued into the sixteenth century, bringing with them a radical broadening and renewal of geographical understanding.

There is not much point in discussing here the later history of the Ligurian cartographic tradition — with Genoese circles being dominated in the sixteenth century by the Maggiolo dynasty with its monopoly, with the prevalence of Iberian (including Portuguese) cartography, which must have made itself felt in the Western Mediterranean, and with the ascendancy of Venice and Ancona in the rest of that body of water, resulting in Battista Agnese's decision, for one reason or the other perhaps, to move to Venice. Nor is it worth discussing what happened later, when the spread of printed engravings created a crisis for manuscript production, when the traditional nautical charts were gradually replaced by those of Mercator with their so much greater practical navigational utility, when modern atlases with their detailed and more or less faithful rendering of the interior of the continents arose and proliferated. These are just so many causes of and moments in the decline of Ligurian nautical cartography.

In Genoa as elsewhere information about the new territories arrived more or less promptly. But by far the greatest portion of nautical charts produced in the city continued to be those concerning the Old World, that is, the Mediterranean and the neighboring seas. Obviously these were the favorite basins of Genoese sailors, who, when undertaking ocean voyages, preferred to come to the Iberian shipping industry (later the port cities and commercial centers of the Low Countries and England would take the upper hand instead).

In the seventeenth century Ligurian nautical cartography would provide only scholarly works or products intended for ornamentation and decoration, that is, not destined for navigational purposes, with the exception of a few examples, like that of Guglielmo Saetone, which show the survival of outdated techniques in outlying areas.

* * *

If we think of Columbus, however, the first question to ask concerns what contribution the Ligurian tradition of nautical cartography may have made to his cultural formation. One contribution was certainly that of manual ability, through drawing and calligraphy, an ability tested in the workshops of the Genoese masters, where he handled charts corresponding to the so-called "standard portolans," and where he may have learned to make them and perhaps had the occasion to admire a planisphere.

Hence when we speak of Columbus's cultural formation, correctly claiming it for Genoa (at least in part), we should specify that it consisted of having learned to read and write there (in Latin, the language used for contracts in commerce and shipping) and to do arithmetic. He also perhaps acquired a few rudiments of the sciences, including cosmography; he more probably learned nautical cartography, and he certainly obtained a wide nautical experience. When Columbus left the Mediterranean, as Taviani states, he was a man able to command a ship on all the routes of that body of water.

It was in Portugal, as we have said, that Columbus's great educational and cultural progress was made (using "culture" in the wide sense). His nautical experience was broadened and brought to completion thanks to all the ideas he acquired regarding Atlantic navigation. His geographical and astronomical horizons were enlarged as a result of voyages to the north, to Guinea, and to the Portuguese islands in the Atlantic. Observations that he made along the west coast of Africa, including naturalistic ones about phenomena and people, would recur often in his writings, even in much later ones having to do with his four trips to America. But did Columbus, on the shores of the Atlantic, only intuit the possibility of getting to the east by sailing west, or did he develop it further on the basis of studies and geographical theories? What progress he may have made in theoretical understanding, in fact, with cosmographical and geographical studies, remains an entirely open question. Did he see and read the work of Marco Polo in Lisbon? Did he consult and reflect on the local cartographic documents? Did he have the means to read any treatises by classical authors? Did he confront the learned men of the area, disputing their traditional ideas about ocean voyages? Perhaps so, at least in part, but any assumption is and remains possible while we lack precise indications from sources. We have considered the possible correspondence with Toscanelli, and it is undisputed that Christopher's great efforts at study and theoretical preparation were made in Andalusia and Castille after 1485-1486.

There is even greater uncertainty with regard to his brother Bartolomeo. Indeed we do not know when he moved from Savona to Portugal. It is fairly certain that he remained there until 1488, exercising the profession of cartographer. Then he must have gone to England and thence to France, where the news of the discovery of America reached him in 1493; as a result he decided to go to Spain, whence he rejoined Christopher the following year in *Hispaniola*. During his long stay in the West Indies in the office of *adelantado* he seems to have shown talent as an industrious administrator, but not as a subtle or clever politician. During the fourth voyage he proved to be a tough and shrewd sailor, but in a subordinate role to Christopher.

Of the extant cartographic documents attributed to the Columbus brothers, one that is almost certainly the work of Christopher (the "Haiti sketch") tells us essentially nothing, because it only confirms what is said in many other sources, namely that he knew how to construct nautical charts, making surveys by sight and with the compass. Disputes revolve around two other documents, the so-called "*Mappamundi* of Columbus" in Paris and Alessandro Zorzi's sketches in a manuscript now held in Florence.

The data concerning the document in Paris are well known: it was made between 1488 (or more probably 1489) and 1498 (or 1499 at the latest); one of its cartouches contains a typically Ligurian grammatical error that occurs again in an *Annotation* by Columbus (or one of the Columbus brothers). So, whether the map borrowed the text from the *Annotation* or whether the latter was instead copied from the "legend," this work can with certainty be traced back, if not to one of the Columbus brothers, at least to someone in their "entourage" who had access to their books and documents. But when, more precisely, can it have been made? If it was after the first or second voyage, it would also have included the American territories. Since they are absent, it must be from before 1493. It could have been done by Bartolomeo, perhaps outside the Iberian Peninsula, and then brought in by him. Christopher could then have borrowed the "legend," converting it into an *Annotation* after 1496. This hypothesis seems reasonable to me, but it remains only a hypothesis.

Alessandro Zorzi's sketches have obvious references to the fourth voyage and are believed by Luzzana Caraci, even in a very recent work, to be derived from a drawing by Bartolomeo Columbus. In my opinion, this is not at all certain, even though they undoubtedly reflect the ideas the Columbus brothers had about the relationship between the new lands and the eastern tip of Asia, as they took shape over the course of the third and fourth voyages. Thus the sketches must have been made after 1504, and they bring us back to Ptolemaic concepts that Christopher must have acquired through the work of Henricus Germanus Martellus (this is the very sensible view of Almagià). In the last part of his life, therefore, the Admiral, thanks to the most recent discoveries, departed from the traditional ideas reflected in planispheres derived from nautical cartography in order to go back to classical authors, indeed to that one (Ptolemy) of whom so many editions were circulating throughout Western Europe, furnished with "new maps" that attempted to reconcile the *auctoritates* of the past with recent experiences.

There still remains the famous, and hypothetical, map of Paolo dal Pozzo Toscanelli, of which no one knows anything exact, with the result that anyone can say what he thinks (or what fits best with his theories). It is certain, however, that it was not on the basis of this map that Columbus planned his enterprise, nor did he use it on the first voyage. This is indicated in the *Journal*, because he utilized more than one map for such purposes. So say the sources, and in this I agree with Luzzana Caraci.

These are questions that, in the present state of study, no one can answer. However, these themes go well beyond the Ligurian tradition of nautical cartography that had provided the young Christopher Columbus with the first elements of his profession as a sailor.

BIBLIOGRAPHIC REFERENCES

(compiled by MARIA GRAZIA BORRELLI)

Bibliography on the history of cartography is vast, especially if it is extended to cover the development of geographical thought. Even though we wished to consider only those writings that refer to Ligurian documents, or to those that are comparable (or influenced by them), I have had to examine hundreds of works. How boundless the bibliography on Columbus is, finally, is shown by the recent listings made by Simonetta Conti, which include thousands of entries.

This survey is bounded, therefore, by some very precise limits, even though it also has to make up for the lack of citations and bibliographic references in the text (they are lacking so as not to weigh down the reading of the text, as well as to conform to the general criteria set for the *Nuova Raccolta Colombiana*).

Among these writings on the history of cartography and geography, therefore, I have omitted those (though they are not numerous) that are concerned only marginally with the period under discussion. I have taken into consideration, however, those that deal with issues, relating to preceding periods that are useful (and indeed necessary) to explain events and features in cartography and geographical thought at the time of Columbus.

References to works and treatises on general cartography have been restricted to those that contain chapters or introductions that are historical and theoretical in nature, especially if they discuss the writings of Italian authors and give more coverage to the output that flourished in this country. Similarly, works about the history of geography are considered only insofar as they show how the evolution of thought may have been reflected in cartographic representations.

Moreover, with regard to classical antiquity and the medieval period before the explosion of nautical cartography, I have not cited works about individual cartographic documents that are valuable only as generic forerunners to those examined in this book. Rather, a citation is provided only for those writings that contain specific references to the works discussed here.

A great deal more space had to be devoted to works about the birth and development of late-medieval nautical cartography, and also to the period — particularly the sixteenth century — when, in Liguria and elsewhere, cartographic works brought together and reproduced the results of the great geographical discoveries. This continues up to the time of the seventeenth-century decline in hand-compiled production. For these topics, I have often listed writings about individual maps or specific issues.

Finally, it should be said that, as far as possible, the present bibliography has been organized according to the standards set by similar bibliographies in the volumes published thus far in the *Nuova Raccolta Colombiana* (for example, not in chronological, but in alphabetical order, a chronological sequence being used only when two or more works by the same author are cited in series).

The principal Italian bibliographies on Columbus:

BOSCOLO, G. *Saggio di bibliografia colombiana.* Saggi e documenti 2, vol. 1. Genoa: Civico Istituto Colombiano, 1981.

CONTI, S. *Bibliografia Colombiana 1793-1990.* Genoa: Cassa di Risparmio di Genova e Imperia, 1990. Contains 8409 titles.

DE PAOLI, G., LUCIA, M.G. and G. GALLIANO, *Contributi alla bibliografia colombiana.* Pubblicazioni dell'Istituto di Scienze Geografiche dell'Università di Genova, vol. 34. Genoa, 1980.

SALONE, A.M. "Opere colombiane della Biblioteca Universitaria di Genova." In *A Compagna.* Genoa, 1987.

Of the volumes of the *Nuova Raccolta Colombiana* published as of the date of compilation of this bibliography we list the following, in chronological order, because they contain features concerning the biographies of the Columbus brothers, as well as their cartographic activity and Christopher's cultural education:

COLUMBUS, C. *Log.* Edited by P.E. TAVIANI and C. VARELA. 2 vols. Nuova Raccolta Colombiana, 1. Rome: Istituto Poligrafico e Zecca dello Stato, 1988.

LUNARDI, E.; MAGIONCALDA, E. and MAZZACANE, R., eds. *La scoperta del Nuovo Mondo negli scritti di Pietro Martire d'Anghiera.* Nuova Raccolta Colombiana, 4. Ibid., 1988.

UNALI, A., ed. *Le scoperte di Cristoforo Colombo nelle testimonianze di Diego Chanca e di Alvarez Andrés Bernáldez.* Nuova Raccolta Colombiana, 7. Ibid., 1990.

TAVIANI, P.E. and LUZZANA CARACI, I., eds. *Le Historie della vita e dei fatti dell'Ammiraglio Don Cristoforo Colombo di Fernando Colombo.* 2 vols. Nuova Raccolta Colombiana, 8. Ibid., 1990.

GIUNTA, F. *Le scoperte di Cristoforo Colombo nei testi di Fernández de Oviedo.* Nuova Raccolta Colombiana, 10. Ibid., 1990.

FERRO, G., ed. *La Liguria e Genova al tempo di Colombo.* 2 vols. Nuova Raccolta Colombiana, 11. Ibid., 1990.

MANZANO MANZANO, J. *Cristoforo Colombo: sette anni decisivi della sua vita (1585-1492)* (translation from the Spanish). Nuova Raccolta Colombiana, no. 15. Ibid., 1990.

FERRO, G.; FALDINI, L. and MILANESI, M., eds. *Iconografia Colombiana.* Nuova Raccolta Colombiana. In collaboration with the Istituto dell'Enciclopedia Italiana. Ibid., 1991. The sections relating to cartography will be indicat/ed under their various authors in the following pages.

HISTORY OF CARTOGRAPHY, WITH GENERAL REFERENCES TO THE HISTORY OF GEOGRAPHICAL THOUGHT

As was said earlier, I have chosen, from among these general works, those that are the most complete, those that establish the closest connections between the history of cartography and the evolution of geographical thought, and those that devote the most space to the themes of this research. I have also alluded to some writings on questions of general cartography.

Lexikon zur Geschichte der Kartographie von den Anfängen bis zum ersten Weltkrieg. 2 vols. Die Kartographie und ihre Randgebiete. Enzyklopädie, C/182. Vienna: Franz Deuticke, 1986.

ALMAGIÀ, R. "Storia della geografia." In *Storia delle scienze*, edited by N. ABBAGNANO, 1: 185-303. Turin: UTET, 1962.

ARENTZEN, J. *Imago Mundi Cartographica: Studien zur Bildlichkeit mittelalterlicher Welt- und Ökumenekarten unter besonderer Berücksichtigung des Zusammenwirkens von Text und Bild.* Münstersche Mittelalter-Schriften, 53. Munich: Wilhelm Fink, 1984.

BAGROW, L. *Istoriya geograficheskoy karty. Ocherk i ukazatel' literatury* [The history of the geographical map: Review and survey of the literature]. Petrograd: Arkheologicheskim Institution, 1918. From this work were derived a *History of Cartography* published in London in the years after World War II and a German edition published in Berlin (by Safari-Verlag) in 1951. Moreover, the two following works were also drawn from it.

BAGROW, L. *Meister der Kartographie.* Berlin: Safari-Verlag, 1963.

BAGROW, L. *History of Cartography.* Edited by R. A. SKELTON and C. A. WATTS. London, 1964. Revised edition. Chicago: Precedent Publishing, 1985.

BLAKEMORE, M. J. "Cartography." In *The Dictionary of Human Geography*, edited by R. J. JOHNSTON, 29-33. Oxford: Blackwell, 1981.

BRICKER, C. *A History of Cartography: 2500 Years of Maps and Mapmakers.* London: Thames and Hudson, 1969. [Originally published by Elsevier, 1958].

BROWN, L. A. *The Story of Maps.* Boston: Little Brown, 1949. Reprint. New York: Dover, 1979.

CAMPBELL, T. *Mappe Antiche.* Milan: Sugarco, s.d. [Earlier edition. New York: Cross River Press, 1981].

CARACI, G. "Cartografia." In *Enciclopedia Italiana* 9: 230-237. Rome: Giovanni Treccani, 1929-1939.

CASSIDY, V. "Geography and Cartography, Western European." In *Dictionary of the Middle Ages*, 395-399. Edited by J. R. STRAYER. New York: Charles Scribner's Sons, 1982.

CLIVIO MARZOLI, C., ed. "Imago et Mensura mundi." *Atti del IX Congresso Internazionale di Storia della Cartografia.* 2 vols. Rome: Enciclopedia Italiana, 1985. Various contributions relevant to the aims of this research are indicated under the authors' names.

CRONE, G. R. *Maps and Their Makers: An Introduction to the History of Cartography.* 1st ed. London: Hutchinson, 1953. 5th ed. Hamden, CT: Archon Books, 1978.

CUENIN, R. *Cartographie générale.* 2 vols. Paris: Editions Eyrolles, 1972-1973.

DAINVILLE, F. de. *La cartographie reflet de l'histoire.* Gex: Slatkine, 1986.

DALY, C. P. "On the Early History of Cartography, or What We Know of Maps and Map-making before the Time of Mercator." *Bulletin de la Société de Géographie* 9 (1879): 1-40.

DUHEM, P. *Le système du monde. Histoire des doctrines cosmologiques de Platon à Copernic.* 10 vols. Paris: Hermann, 1913-1959.

ECKERT, M. "Die Kartographie als Wissenschaft." *Zeitschrift der Gesellschaft für Erdkunde zu Berlin* (1907): 539-555.

ECKERT. M. *Die Kartenwissenschaft. Forschungen und Grundlagen zu einer Kartographie als Wissenschaft.* 2 vols. Berlin and Leipzig: Walter de Gruyter, 1921-1925.

FERRO, G. and LUZZANA CARACI, I. *Ai confini dell'orizzonte. Storia delle esplorazioni e della geografia.* Milan: Mursia, 1979. 2nd ed. 1991.

HARLEY, J.B. "L'histoire de la cartographie comme discours." *Préfaces* 5 (1987-1988): 70-75.

HARLEY, J.B. "The Map and the Development of the History of Cartography." In HARLEY, J.B. and WOODWARD, D., eds. *The History of Cartography.* Chicago: University of Chicago Press, 1987. A work in several volumes, of which at the present only the first two have been published. It contains contributions by various authors, of which the more significant are cited under the respective authors' names.

KISH, G. *La carte image de civilisation.* Paris: Denil, 1980.

LEITHAUSER, J.G. *Mappae mundi: Die Geistige Eroberung der Welt.* Berlin: Safari-Verlag, 1958.

LEWIS, G.M. "The Origins of Cartography." In HARLEY, J.B. and WOODWARD, D., eds. *The History of Cartography.* Op. cit., 50-53.

LIBAULT, A. *Histoire de la cartographie.* Paris: Chaix, 1959.

NEBENZAHL, K. *Atlas of Columbus and the Great Discovery.* Chicago, New York, and San Francisco: Rand McNally, 1990. (Despite the title this is a historical survey of cartography from Ptolemy to Mercator, and it is rich in reproductions of *mappaemundi* and maps). Italian edition: *Atlante di Colombo e le Grandi Scoperte.* Milan: Sugarco, 1990.

PINCHEMEL, P. "Géographie et cartographie, réflexions historiques et épistémologiques." *Bulletin de l'Association de Géographes Français* 463 (1979): 239-247.

QUAINI, M. *Appunti di Storia della Cartografia.* Genoa: Libr. Ed. M. Bozzi, 1967.

RAISZ, E. Principles of Cartography. New York: McGraw Hill, 1962.

RANDLES, W.G.L. *De la terre plate au globe terrestre. Une mutation épistémologique rapide (1480-1520).* Cahiers des Annales, 38. Paris: Colin, 1980. Italian edition: *Dalla terra piatta al globo terrestre. Una mutazione epistemologica rapida, 1480-1520.* Florence: Sansoni, 1986.

ROBINSON, A., SALE, R. and J. MORRISON, *Elements of Cartography.* 4th ed. New York and Chichester: John Wiley, 1978.

SANTAREM, M.F. *Estudios de cartografía antiga.* 2 vols. Lisbon: Lamas, 1919-1920.

SESTINI, A. *Cartografia generale.* Bologna: Patron, 1981.

SKELTON, R.A. *Explorers' Maps: Chapters in the Cartographic Record of Geographical Discovery.* London: Routledge and Kegan Paul, 1958.

SKELTON, R.A. *Maps: A Historical Survey of Their Study and Collecting.* Chicago: University of Chicago Press, 1972.

TOOLEY, R.V. *Maps and Map-makers.* London: B.T. Batsford, 1970.

THROWER, M.J.W. *Maps and Man: An Examination of Cartography in Relation to Culture and Civilization.* Englewood Cliffs, NJ: Prentice Hall, 1972.

UNGER, E. "From the Cosmos Picture to the World Map." *Imago Mundi* 2 (1937): 1-7.

WILFORD, J.N. *The Mapmakers.* London: Junction Books, 1981.

WOODWARD, D. "The Study of Cartography: A Suggested Framework." *American Cartographer* 1 (1974): 101-115.

WOODWARD, D. "La cartographie et la méthode artistique." *Préfaces* 5 (1987-1988): 84-88.

To this section can be added certain works devoted to the history of cartography in specific areas or to cartographers from individual countries or regions, such as the following:

ALMAGIÀ, R. "Alcuni nuovi contributi alla storia della cartografia." *Rivista Geografica Italiana* 65 (1958): 368-372.

CORTESÃO, A. *Cartografía e Cartografos Portugueses dos Seculos XV e XVI.* 2 vols. Lisbon: Seara Nova, 1935.

CORTESÃO, A. *A History of Portuguese Cartography.* 2 vols. Coimbra: Junta de Investigações do Ultramar-Lisboa, 1969-71. Original title: *Historia da Cartografía Portuguesa.* 2 vols. Lisbon: AECA, 1969-1970.

DENUCÉ, J.A. *Les origines de la cartographie portugaise et les cartes des Reinel.* Ghent, 1908. Reprint, Amsterdam: Meridian, 1963.

PINHEIRO MARQUES, A. *Origem e Desenvolvimento da Cartografía Portuguesa na epoca dos descobrimentos.* Lisbon: Casa da Moeda, 1987.

QUAINI, M. "L'Italia dei cartografi." *Storia d'Italia* 6: 5-52. Turin: Einaudi, 1976.

QUAINI, M. *Carte e cartografi in Liguria.* Genoa: SAGEP, 1986.

REY PASTOR, J. and E.G. CAMARERO, *La Cartografía Mallorquina.* Madrid: Departamento de Historia y Filosofía de la Ciencia, 1960.

SKELTON, R.A. *The European Image and Mapping of America 1000-1600.* Minneapolis: University of Minnesota, 1964.

WORKS MAINLY TECHNICAL OR SEMIOLOGICAL IN NATURE

Reference should also be made to certain general works that are more specialized and technical in nature, and were mentioned during the course of this research, such as those that deal with spheres, projections, semiology, and iconography, albeit generally.

AVEZAC, A. D'. "Coup d'oeil historique sur la projection des cartes géographiques." *Bulletin de la Société de Géographie,* Series 5, vol. 5 (1863): 257-361, 437-485.

DAINVILLE, F. DE. *Le langage des géographes*. Paris: A. et J. Picard, 1964.

ELIADE, MIRCEA. *Images and Symbols: Studies in Religious Symbolism*. Translated by P. Mairet. S.l.: Harvill Press, 1961.

FIORINI, M. *Le proiezioni delle carte geografiche*. Bologna: Zanichelli, 1881.

FIORINI, M. "Le sfere cosmografiche e specialmente le sfere terrestri." *Bollettino della Società Geografica Italiana* 30 (1893): 862-888; 31 (1894): 121-132, 271-281, 331-349, 415-435.

HARLEY, J.B. "The Iconology of Early Maps." *Imago et Mensura Mundi...* Op. cit. Vol 1: 29-38.

LOWENTHAL. D. ed. "Geography, Experience, and Imagination: Towards a Geographical Epistemology." *Annals of the Association of American Geography* 51 (1961): 241-260.

ULLA, E. "Color in Cartography: An Historical Survey." In *Art and Cartography: Six Historical Essays*, edited by D. Woodward. Chicago: University of Chicago Press, 1987.

WRIGHT, J.K. "Notes on the Knowledge of Latitudes and Longitudes in the Middle Ages." *Isis* 5 (1923): 75-98.

COLLECTIONS, INVENTORIES, AND CATALOGS OF MAPS, ATLASES, SPHERES, GLOBES, AND OVERALL CARTOGRAPHIC WORKS RELATING TO SEVERAL CENTURIES

Of the numerous collections, inventories, and editions containing more than one map (including non-nautical ones) published over time, and often decorated with reproductions and illustrations of high value and effectiveness, only the principal ones and those having the greatest scientific value are reported here, especially if they are introduced by texts providing a systematic treatment.

ALMAGIÀ, R. *Monumenta Italiae Cartographica*. Florence: Istituto Geografico Militare, 1929.

ALMAGIÀ, R. *Monumenta Cartographica Vaticana*. 4 vols. Rome: Biblioteca Apostolica Vaticana, 1944-1945.

ALMAGIÀ, R. *Documenti Cartografici dello Stato Pontificio*. Rome: Biblioteca Apostolica Vaticana, 1960.

BERCHET, G. "Portolani esistenti nelle principali biblioteche di Venezia." *Giornale Militare per la Marina* 11 (1865): 1-11.

CAPACCI, A. *Museo navale di Pegli*. Documenti geocartografici nelle Biblioteche e negli Archivi privati e pubblici della Liguria, no. 1: *Catalogazione di cimeli cartografici*, 3. Florence: Leo S. Olschki, 1990.

CARACI, G. *Tabulae Geographicae vetustiores in Italia adservatae*. 3 vols. Florence: Otto Lange, 1926.

CASANOVA, L. "Inventario dei portolani e delle carte nautiche del Museo Correr." *Bollettino dei Musei Civici Veneziani* 3-4 (1957): 17-36.

CORTESÂO, A. *Cartografía Portuguesa Antiga*. Lisbon: Coleçâo Henriquina, 1960.

CORTESÃO, A. and A. MOTA, (TEXEIRA DA). *Portugaliae monumenta cartographica.* 6 vols. Lisbon, 1960.

DE SIMONI, C. "Elenco di carte e atlanti nautici di autore genovese oppure in Genova fatti e conservati." *Giornale Ligustico* 2 (1875): 1-67.

DESTOMBES, M. *Catalogue des cartes gravées aux XVe siècle. Rapport de la Commission pour la Bibliographie des Cartes Anciennes.* Paris: UGI, 1952.

FERNÁNDEZ DE NAVARRETE, M. *Biblioteca Maritima Española.* 2 vols. Madrid, 1851. Facsimile reproduction. New York: Burt Franklin, 1968.

FERNÁNDEZ DURO, C. *Noticia breve de las cartas y planos existentes en la biblioteca particular de S.M. el Rey.* Madrid, 1889.

FONCIN, M.R.; DESTOMBES, M. and RONCIÉRE, M. DE LA. *Catalogue des cartes nautiques sur vélin conservées au Département des Cartes et Plans.* Paris: Bibliothèque Nationale, 1963.

FRABETTI, P. *Carte nautiche italiane dal XIV al XVII secolo conservate in Emilia Romagna.* Archivi e Biblioteche Pubbliche. Florence: Olschki, 1978.

HARRISSE, H. *Biblioteca Americana Vetustissima. A description of works relating to America, published between the years 1492 and 1551...* Vol 1. New York: G. P. Philes, 1866. Vol. 2: *Additions.* Paris: Livr. Tross, 1872. Also contains references to cartography.

JOMARD, E.F. *Les Monuments de la géographie ou recueil d'anciennes cartes publiées en fac-simile de la grandeur des originaux.* Paris: Duprat, 1846-1862.

KAMAL, Y. *Monumenta Cartographica Africae et Aegypti.* 5 vols. Cairo, 1926-1951.

MARCEL, G. *Reproductions de cartes et de globes relatifs à la découverte de l'Amérique du XVIe au XVIIIe siècle, avec texte explicatif.* Recueil de voyages et de documents pour servir à l'histoire de la cartographie. Paris: Ernest Leroux, 1893.

MOLLAT, M. and M. DE LA RONCIÉRE, *Les Portulans, Cartes maritimes du XIIIe au XVIIe siècle.* Fribourg: Office du Livre, 1984. English edition. *Sea Charts of the Early Explorers: 13th to 17th Century.* Translated by L. DETHAN. New York: Thames and Hudson, 1984.

NORDENSKIÖLD, A.E. *Facsimile Atlas to the Early History of Cartography with Reproduction of the Most Important Maps Printed in the XV and XVI Centuries.* Translated from the original Swedish by J.A. EKELOF and C.R. MARKHAM. Stockholm, 1889. New editon with introduction by J.B. Post. New York: Dover Publications, 1973.

ONGANIA, F. *Raccolta di mappamondi e carte nautiche dal XIII al XVI secolo.* Venice, 1875-1881.

SANTAREM, M.F. *Atlas composé des cartes des XIV, XV, XVI, XVII siècles pour la plupart inédites, et devant servir de preuves à l'ouvrage sur la priorité de la découverte de la côte occidentale d'Afrique au delà du Cap Bojador par les Portugais.* Paris, 1841. Facsimile reprint edited by L. DE ALBUQUERQUE. Lisbon: Administração do Porto de Lisboa, 1989.

SANTAREM, M.F. *Atlas composé de mappamondes, de portulans et de cartes hydrographiques et historiques depuis le VIe jusqu'au XVIIe siècle.* Paris, 1849. Reprinted edited by of H. WALLIS, A.H. SIJMONS, and R. MULLER. Amsterdam, 1985.

SANZ, C. ed. *Biblioteca Americana Vetustissima. Mapas Antiguas del Mundo (Siglos XV-XVI).* S.e., s.d.

SHIRLEY, R.W. *The Mapping of the World: Early Printed World Maps 1472-1700*. London: Holland Press, 1983.

UZIELLI, G. and P. AMAT DI SAN FILIPPO, *Studi biografici e bibliografici sulla storia della geografia in Italia. Part II: Mappamondi, carte nautiche, portolani ed altri monumenti cartografici specialmente italiani dei secoli XIII-XVIII*. Rome: Società Geografica Italiana, 1882-1884. Reprint. Amsterdam: Meridian, 1967.

VILLIERS, J.A.J. DE. "Famous Maps in the British Museum." *The Geographical Journal* 44 (1914): 160-188.

WIEDER, F.C. *Monumenta Cartographica*. The Hague, 1925-1933.

The following writings, on the other hand, deal with spheres or globes, terrestrial and celestial, in general:

BONELLI, M.L. *Catalogo dei globi antichi conservati in Italia*. Facs. 1: Blaeu; Facs. 2: Coronelli. Florence: Istituto e Museo di Storia della Scienza, 1957-1960.

FIORINI, M. *Sfere terrestri e celesti di autore italiano oppure fatte e conservate in Italia*. Rome: Società Geografica Italiana, 1889. See also the later contributions by the same author, published in the *Bollettino della Società Geografica Italiana*.

LUZIO, L. "I globi antichi conservati in Italia con particolare riguardo a quelli di G. Blaew." *Atti XVI Congresso Geografico Italiano, Padova-Venezia 1954*, 753-758.

STEVENSON, E.L. *Terrestrial and Celestial Globes: Their History and Construc/tion, Including a Consideration of Their Value as Aids in the Study of Geography and Astronomy*. 2 vols. Publications of the Hispanic Society of America 86. New Haven: Yale University Press, 1921. Reprint. New York and London: Johnson Reprint Corporation, 1971.

From among the cartographical exhibition catalogues, only the following, of greater geographical interest for the theme of this research, are cited, in chronological order:

STAGLIENO, M. and L.T. BELGRANO, *Catalogo dell'esposizione artistico-archeologico-industriale aperta nelle sale dell'Accademia Ligustica la primavera del 1868*. Genoa: Tip. Sordo-muti, 1868.

Catalogo Generale della Prima Mostra Geografica Italiana, 7-30 settembre 1892 on the occasion of the First Congresso Geografico Italiano in Genoa, September 18-25, 1892. Genova: Fratelli Pagano, 1892.

CARACI, G. *Catalogo della Mostra di Carte, di Manoscritti e di Stampe di interesse geografico*. *Atti VIII Congresso Geografico Italiano* (Florence, 1921), 3: 94-95.

LABÓ, M. "Catalogo della Mostra della scuola cartografica genovese." *Atti del IX Congresso Geografico Italiano* (Genoa, 1924), 3: 134-135.

FAVA, D. and C. MONTAGNANI, eds. *Mostra Colombiana e Americana della R. Biblioteca Estense*. Modena: Biblioteca Estense, 1925.

GNOLI, T. "Catalogo ragionato della Mostra Geografica retrospettiva della Biblioteca Braidense." *Atti X Congresso Geografico Italiano, Milan 1927*, Appendix 2: 145-185.

MAGRINI, G.; PICOTTI, M. and REVELLI, P. *La partecipazione italiana alla mostra oceanografica internazionale di Siviglia, 1929*. Genoa: SIAG, 1937. Especially relevant is the section written by P. REVELLI, "Nota illustrativa," 173-184.

REVELLI, P., ed. *Mostra Colombiana Internazionale (Genova, Palazzo San Giorgio, 12 ottobre 1950-12 ottobre 1951): Elenco illustrativo*. Genoa: Società d'Arte Poligrafica, 1950.

GASPARRINI LEPORACE, T., ed. *Catalogo della Mostra "L'Asia nella cartografia degli occidentali."* Venezia: Tip. G. Garzia, 1954.

Raccolta di carte e documenti esposti alla mostra tenuta nel V Centenario della nascita di A. Vespucci, pts. 3 and 4. Florence: Tip. Giuntina, 1954.

MARTINI, G.D., ed. *Mostra Vespucciana*. Florence: Tip. Giuntina, 1954.

BIBLIOTECA NAZIONALE MARCIANA, ARCHIVIO DI STATO. *Mostra dei viaggiatori veneti del Quattrocento e del Cinquecento. Catalogo della Mostra*. Venice: Biblioteca Nazionale Marciana, 1957.

CODAZZI, A. "Catalogo delle edizioni esposte della *Geografia* di Tolomeo." *Atti del XX Congresso Geografico Italiano (Rome, 1967)*, 1: 207-218.

Manoscritti cartografici e strumenti scientifici nella Biblioteca Vaticana, secoli XIV-XVII: Catalogo della Mostra. Rome: Biblioteca Apostolica Vaticana, 1981.

PIERSANTELLI, G. *Presentazione al catalogo della 'Mostra di manoscritti e libri rari della Biblioteca Berio di Genova," 9 maggio-8 giugno 1969*. Genoa: SAGEP, 1969.

SECCHI, L., ed. *Navigazione e carte nautiche nei secoli XIII-XVI: Catalogo della Mostra*. Genoa: Comune di Genova, Servizio Beni Culturali, 1983.

BIBLIOTECA CIVICA BERTOLIANA. *Teatro del cielo e della terra: Mappamondi, carte nautiche e atlanti della Biblioteca Civica Bertoliana dal XV al XVIII secolo. Catalogo della Mostra*. Vicenza: Biblioteca Civica Bertoliana, 1984.

THE CONCEPT OF THE EARTH AND ITS REPRESENTATIONS
IN THE CLASSICAL ERA

Of the vast existing literature the following writings are those containing the most references to themes discussed in this book and to authors who influenced medieval cartography:

ALMAGIÀ, R. "La geografia nell'età classica." *La Geografia* 2 (1914): 330-348. Republished in ALMAGIÀ, R. *Scritti geografici 1905-1957*, 325-41. Rome: Ed. Cremonese, 1961.

AUJAC, G. *La Géographie dans le monde antique*. Paris: PUF, 1975.

AUJAC, G. "Les représentations de l'espace, géographique ou cosmologique, dans l'Antiquité." *Pallas 28, Annales publiées trimest. par l'Université de Toulouse-Le Mirail* 17 (1981): 3-14.

BAGROW, L. "The Origin of Ptolemy's Geographia." *Geographiska Annaler* 27 (1945): 318-387.

BEAZLEY, C.R. *The Dawn of Modern Geography: A History of Exploration and Geographical Science from the Conversion of the Roman Empire to A.D. 900*. 3 vols. London: J. Murray, 1897-1906.

BERGER, H. "Entwicklung der Geographie der Erdkugel bei den Hellenen." *Die Grenzboten. Zeitschrift für Politik, Literatur und Kunst* 39 (1880): 403-417.

BERGER, H. *Geschichte der wissenschaftliche Erdkunde der Griechen.* 2nd ed. Leipzig: Verlag von Veiten & Comp., 1903. Reprint. Berlin: W. de Gruyter, 1966.

BUNBURY, E.H. *A History of Ancient Geography among the Greeks and Romans from the Earliest Ages till the Fall of the Roman Empire.* 2 vols. 2nd ed. S.l.: 1883. Reprint. New York: Dover, 1959.

CAMPBELL, T. *Early Maps.* New York: Abbeville Press, 1981.

CEBRIAN K. *Geschichte der Kartographie. Ein Betrag zur Entwicklung des Kartenbildes und Kartenwesens.* Gotha: Perthes, 1922.

DELATTE, A., ed. *Les portulans grecs.* Bibliothèque de la Faculté de Philosophie et Lettres de l'Université de Liège 107 (1947).

DELGEUR, L. "La cartographie chez les Anciens." *Bulletin de la Société Royale de Géographie d'Anvers* 5 (1880): 117-146. Republished in *Acta Cartographica* 3 (1969): 1-48.

DILKE, O.A.W. "The Culmination of Greek Cartography in Ptolemy." In *The History of Cartography*, edited by J.B. HARLEY and D. WOODWARD, op. cit., 177-200.

GIROD, R. "Vision et représentation géographique chex les Anciens." *Littérature greco-romaine et géographie historique. Mélanges offerts à Roger Dion.* In Caesarodunum 9 bis. Paris: Picard, 1974.

GUARNIERI, G. *Le correnti del pensiero geografico nell'antichità classica e il loro contributo alla cartografia nautica medioevale.* 2 vols. Pisa: Ed. Giardini, 1968-1969.

GUNDLACH, R. "Landkarte." In *Lexikon der Ägyptologie*, edited by W. HELCK and E. OTTO, 922-923. 3 vols. Wiesbaden: O. Harrassowitz, 1975.

HARLEY, J.B. and D. WOODWARD, "The Foundation of Theoretical Cartography in Archaic and Classical Greece." In *The History of Cartography*, edited by J.B. HARLEY and D. WOODWARD, op. cit., 130-147.

HARLEY, J.B. and D. WOODWARD, "Greek Cartography in the Early Roman World." In *The History of Cartography*, edited by J.B. HARLEY and D. WOODWARD, op. cit., 161-176.

HARLEY, J.B. and WOODWARD, D. "The Growth of an Empirical Cartography in Hellenistic Greece." In *The History of Cartography*, edited by J.B. HARLEY and D. WOODWARD, op, cit., 148-160.

HEATHCOTE (DE VAUDRY), N.H. "Early Nautical Charts." *Annals of Science* 1 (1936): 1-28.

HEIDEL, W.A. *The Frame of Ancient Greek Maps.* New York: American Geographical Society, 1937.

HENNIG, R. *Terrae Incognitae.* 4 vols. Leiden: E.J. Brill, 1938-1950.

JANNI, P. *La mappa e il periplo. Cartografia antica e spazio odologico.* Pubblicazioni della Facoltà di Lettere e Filosofia, Università di Macerata, no. 19. Rome: Bretschneider, 1984.

LUKERMANN, F. "The Conception of Location in Classical Geography." *Annals of the Association of American Geographers* 51 (1961): 194-209.

MILLER, K. *Die Peutingersche Tafel.* Ravensburg: F.A. Brockhaus, 1887-1888. Facsimile reprint. Stuttgart, 1962.

MILLER, K. *Mappaemundi: Die ältesten Weltkarten.* 6 vols. Stuttgart: J. Roth, 1962.

MILLER, K. *Itineraria Romana.* Stuttgart: Strecker und Schröder, 1916.

MORI, Associazione. "Osservazioni sulla cartografia romana in relazione colla cartografia tolemaica e colle carte nautiche medievali." *Atti del III Congresso Nazionale di Studi Romani* 1: 565-575. 5 vols. Rome: Cappelli, 1934. Republished in Associazione MORI. *Scritti Geografici*, 167-180. Pisa: C. Cursi, 1960.

MUHLY, J.D. "Ancient Cartography: Man's Earliest Attempts to Represent His World." *Expedition* 10 (1977): 26-31.

PAGANI, L. "Introduction." In *Cosmographia. Tavola della Geografia di Tolomeo.* Torriana (FO): Stella Polare Editrice, 1990.

PERETTI, A. *Il Periplo di Scilace. Studio sul primo portolano del Mediterraneo.* Pisa: Ed. Giardini, 1979.

POLASCHEK, E. "Ptolemy's *Geography*, in a New Light." *Imago Mundi* 14 (1959): 17-37.

PRONTERA, F. ed. *Geografia e geografi nel mondo antico. Guida storica e critica.* Rome and Bari: Universale Laterza, 1983.

PRONTERA, F. "Géographie et mythes dans l'isolario des Grecs." In *Géographie du Moyen Age et de la Renaissance*, edited by M. PELLETIER, 169-179. Paris: Ed. du Comité des Travaux Historiques et Scientifiques, 1979.

RONCONI, A. "Per l'onomastica dei mari." *Studi italiani di filologia classica* 9 (1931): 193-242, 257-331.

SCHNABEL, P. *Text und Karten des Ptolomäus.* Leipzig: F.K. Koehlers Antiquarium, 1938.

SCHUTTE, G. *Ptolemy's Maps of Northern Europe: A Reconstruction of the Prototypes.* Copenhagen: Royal Danish Geographical Society, 1917.

STAHL, W.H. *Ptolemy's Geography: A Select Bibliography.* New York: New York Public Library, 1953.

THOMSON, J.O. *History of Ancient Geography.* Cambridge: Cambridge University Press, 1948. Reprint. New York: Biblo and Tannen, 1965.

TOZER, H.F. *A History of Ancient Geography.* 2nd ed. 1897. Reprint. New York: Biblo and Tannen, 1964.

TUDEER, L.O.T. "On the Origin of Maps Attached to Ptolemy's Geography." *Journal of Hellenic Studies* 37 (1917): 62-70.

VERNANT, J.P. "Géometrie et astronomie sphérique dans la première cosmologie grecque." *La Pensée* 109 (1913): 82-93.

GEOGRAPHY AND REPRESENTATIONS OF THE EARTH IN THE MIDDLE AGES

In this case also we will limit ourselves to citing works with a quite broad outlook, works that deal especially with the evolution of geographical thought and the resulting ways of depicting the earth.

ALAVI, S.M.Z. *Geography in the Middle Ages.* Delhi: Sterling, 1966.

ANDREWS, M.C. "The Study and Classification of Medieval Mappae Mundi." *Archeologia* 75 (1925-1926): 61-76.

BALDACCI, O. "Ecumene ed emisferi circolari." *Bollettino della Società Geografica Italiana* 102 (1965): 1-16.

BALDACCI, O. "L'ecumene a 'mandorla'." *Geografia* 6 (1983): 132-139.

BALDACCI, O. "Geoecumeni quadrangolari." *Geografia* 6 (1983): 80-86.

BEAZLEY, C.R. "New Light on Some Medieval Maps." *The Geographical Journal* 14 (1899): 620-629; 15 (1900): 130-141, 378-389; 16 (1901): 319-329.

BLASQUEZ Y DELGADO AGUILERA, A. "Estudio acerca de la cartografía española en la Edad Media acompañado de varias mapas." *Boletín de la Real Sociedad Geografica* 48 (1906): 190-237.

BOFFITO, G. *Intorno alla 'quaestio de aqua et terra' attribuita a Dante. La controversia dell'acqua e della terra prima e dopo Dante.* Memorie della R. Accademia delle Scienze di Torino, series 2, vol. 51 (1902).

BRINCKEN, A.D. VON DEN. "Mappa mundi und Chronographia." *Deutsches Archiv für die Erforschung des Mittelalters* 24 (1968): 118-186.

BULL, W.E. and H.F. WILLAIMS, *Semeianca del Mundo: A Medieval Description of the World.* Berkeley and Los Angeles: University of California Press, 1959.

CAPELLO, C.F. "Il mappamondo medioevale di Vercelli." *Atti XVII Congresso Geografico Italiano, Bari 1957,* 3: 577-585.

CAPELLO, C.F. *Il mappamondo medioevale di Vercelli (1191-1218?).* Memorie e Studi Geografici, vol. 10. Turin: Università degli Studi di Torino, 1976.

DESTOMBES, M. ed. *Mappemondes A. D. 1200-1500. Catalogue préparé par la Commission des Cartes Anciennes de l'Union Géographique Internationale.* Amsterdam: N. Israel, 1964.

DURAZZO, P. *Il Paradiso Terrestre nelle carte medioevali.* Mantua, 1886. Reprint. Bologna: Arnaldo Forni Editore, 1979.

GARFAGNINI, G. *Cosmologie medioevali.* Storia della Scienza, vol. 4. Turin: Loescher, 1978.

GOBBO, I. "Il pensiero geografico di S. Alberto Magno." In *Scritti vari, Facoltà di Magistero di Torino,* 1: 1-83. Turin: Ed. Gheroni, 1950.

GRIBAUDI, P. "La Geografia di S. Isidoro di Siviglia. Contributo alla storia della Geografia nel medioevo." *Memorie della R. Accademia delle Scienze di Torino,* series 2, vol. 56 (1906): 1-76.

GRIBAUDI, P. *Per la storia della geografia specialmente nel medioevo.* Turin: Clausen, 1906. Reprint. GRIBAUDI, P. *Scritti di varia geografia. Laboratorio di Geogr. Econ. "Piero Gribaudi," Fac. di Economio e Commercio, Università di Torino,* 21-72. Turin: Giappichelli Ed., 1955.

HASKINS, C.H. *Studies in the History of Mediaeval Science.* Cambridge: Harvard University Press, 1924. Republished in New York: Fr. Ungar Publ., 1960.

KIMBLE, G.H.T. *Geography in the Middle Ages.* London: Methuen, 1938.

LAGO, L. *Le conoscenze sul ciclo dell'acqua nell'antichità classica e nell'evo medio.* Pubblicazioni dell'Istituto di Geografia della Facoltà di Magistero dell'Università degli Studi di Trieste, extra series 1. Trieste: Ed. Lint, 1983.

LE GOFF, J. "L'Occident médiéval et l'Océan Indien, un horizon onirique." *Travaux du sixième Colloque Internationale d'Histoire Maritime, Méditerranée, et Océan Indien, Venezia, 20-24 settembre 1970*, 317-336. Paris: SEVPEN, 1970.

LEAR, F. S. "Saint Isidore and Mediaeval Science." *The Rice Institute Technical Learning Pamphlets* 23 (Houston 1936): 75-105.

LELEWEL, J. *Géographie du Moyen Age.* 4 vols. Brussels: J. Pilliet, 1852-1857. Reprint, Amsterdam: Meridian, 1966.

LOSACCO, U. "Pensiero scientifico e osservazioni naturali di Restoro d'Arezzo." *Rivista Geografica Italiana* 50 (1943): 31-61.

MARINELLI, G. "La Geografia e i Padri della Chiesa." *Bollettino della Società Geografica Italiana*, series 2, vol. 7 (1890): 472-498, 532-573. Reprint. *Scritti minori di G. Marinelli* 1: 281-393. Florence: Le Monnier, s.d.

MARINELLI, G. "Un nuovo lavoro sulla storia della geografia medievale." *Bollettino della Società Geografica Italiana*, series 3, vol. 3 (1890): 232-238. Reprint. *Scritti minori di G. Marinelli*, op. cit., vol. 1: 439-448.

MELON, A. "La etapa isidoriana en la geografía medieval." Arbor 28 (1954): 456-467.

MENÉNDEZ PIDAL, G. "Mozárabes y asturianos en la cultura de la Edad Media." *Boletín de la Real Academia de la Historia 134* (1954): 137-291.

MOORE, E. "La geografia di Dante." Edited by G. BOFFITO and E. SANESI. *Rivista Geografica Italiana* 12 (1905): 92-101, 204-215.

MORI, Associazione. "La geografia di Dante." *Archivio di Storia della Scienza* (Rome, 1921): 57-69. Republished in ASSOCIAZIONE MORI. *Scritti Geografici*, op. cit., 117-131.

PELLETIER, M., ed. *Géographie du monde au Moyen Age et à la Renaissance.* Paris: Ed. du Comité des Travaux Historiques et Scientifiques, 1989.

POOLE, R. L. *Illustrations of the History of Medieval Thought and Learning.* London: Williams and Norgate, 1884.

REVELLI, P. *L'Italia nella Divina Commedia.* Milan: Fratelli Treves, 1923.

RUBERG, U. "Mappae Mundi des Mittelalters im Zusammenwirken von Text und Bild." In *Text und Bild, Aspekte des Zusammenwirkens zweier Künste in Mittelalter und früher Neuzeit*, edited by C. MEIER and U. RUBERG, 550-592. Wiesbaden: Ludwig Reichert, 1980.

TILMANN, S. J. P. *An Appraisal of the Geographical Works of Albertus Magnus and His Contributions to Geographical Thought.* Ann Arbor: University of Michigan, 1971.

TIMBLE, G. H. T. *Geography in the Middle Ages.* London, 1938.

UHDEN, R. "Die Weltkarte des Isidorus von Sevilla." *Mnemosyne, Biblioteca classica batava*, series 3, vol. 3 (Leiden 1936): 1-28.

WOODWARD, D. "Medieval Mappaemundi." In *The History of Cartography*, edited by J. B. HARLEY and D. WOODWARD, op. cit., 286-370.

WRIGHT, J. K. *The Geographical Lore of the Time of the Crusades: A Study in the History of Medieval Science and Tradition in Western Europe.* American Geographical Society Research Series, vol. 15. New York, 1925. Rev. ed. New York: Dover Publications, 1965.

NAUTICAL CARTOGRAPHY:
WORKS AND ISSUES OF A GENERAL NATURE

For now we shall limit ourselves to citing the works that, even under differ/ent titles, deal with nautical cartography in the Middle Ages and the modern period. These writings address particular themes and issues having to do with the various aspects common to such cartographic production, without entering into a detailed examination of individual charts (or groups of charts). Naturally we have paid particular attention to works that are considered to be examples of Italian and Ligurian documents.

ALBUQUERQUE, L. DE. *Ciência e Experiencia nos Descobrimentos Portugueses.* Lisbon: Biblioteca Breve, 1983.

ALBUQUERQUE, L. DE. "Considerações sobre a Carta-Portulano." *Revista Univers. de Coimbra* 31 (1984). Reprinted under the title "Observations on the Portulan-Chart." *Mare Librum* 1 (Lisbon 1990): 117-129.

ALMAGIÀ, R. "Intorno alla più antica cartografia nautica catalana." *Bollettino della Società Geografica Italiana*, series 7, vol. 10 (1945): 20-27.

ALMAGIÀ, R. "Per un nuovo repertorio di carte nautiche italiane conservate in Italia (secoli XII-XVII)." *Atti XVII Congresso Geografico Italiano, Bari 1957*, 427-341. Bari: Cressati, 1957.

AMAT DI SAN FILIPPO, P. "Recenti ritrovamenti di carte nautiche in Parigi, in Londra ed in Firenze." *Bollettino della Società Geografica Italiana*, series 3, vol. 1 (1888): 268-278. Reprint. *Acta Cartographica* 9 (1970): 1-11.

BALDACCI, O. "La cartonautica medioevale precolombiana." *Atti del Convegno Internazionale di Studi Colombiani, Genova 13-14 ottobre 1973*, 123-126. Genoa: Civico Istituto Colombiano, 1974.

BALDACCI, O. "Il grande asse del Mediterraneo nelle carte nautiche di tipo medioevale." Bollettino A. I. C. 47 (1979): 49-56.

BALDACCI, O. *Introduzione allo studio delle geocarte nautiche di tipo medioevale e la raccolta della Biblioteca Comunale di Siena.* Documenti geocartografici nelle Biblioteche e negli Archivi privati e pubblici della Toscana, no. 3: *Catalogazione di cimeli cartografici*, 4, op, cit., 1990.

BRINKEN, A.D. VON DEN. "Portolane als Quellen der Vexillologie." *Archiv für Diplomatiek: Schriftgeschichte Siegel und Wappenkunde* 24 (1978): 408-426.

CAMPBELL, T. "Portolan Charts from the Late Thirteenth Century to 1500." In *The History of Cartography*, edited by J.B. HARLEY and D. WOODWARD, op. cit., 371-463.

CANALE, M.G. *Storia del commercio dei viaggi, delle scoperte e carte nautiche.* Genoa: Tip. Sociale, 1866.

CARACI, G. "The First Nautical Cartography and the Relationship between Italian and Majorcan Cartographers." *Eighth General Assembly and Seventeenth International Congress, Washington D.C., 1952: Abstracts of Papers*, 12-13. Washington, D.C.: International Geographical Union, 1952.

CARACI, G. "Italiani e Catalani nella primitiva cartografia nautica medievale." *Memorie Geografiche dell'Istituto di Scienze Geografiche e Cartografiche* 5 (Rome 1959): 131-140.

Ample references to particular questions, such as the Dalort-Dulcert relationship, are included in this volume of almost 400 pages.

CARACI, G. "A conferma del già detto. Ancora sulla paternità delle carte nautiche anonime." *Memorie Geografiche dell'Istituto di Scienze Geografiche e Cartografiche* 6 (Rome 1960): 131-140.

CARACI, G. *Viaggi fra Venezia e il Levante fino al XIV secolo e relativa produzione cartografica in Venezia e il Levante fino al secolo XV*, Vol 1. Florence: Olschki, 1973.

CLOS-ARCEDUC, A. "L'Enigme des portulans. Etude sur la projection et la mode de construction des cartes à rhumbs du XIVe et du XVe siècle." *Bulletin du Comité des Travaux Historiques et Scientifiques. Section de Géographie* 69 (1956): 215-231.

CONTI, S. "Portolano e carta nautica: confronto toponomastico." In *Imago et Mensura Mundi...*, op, cit., 55-60.

DAMIANI, G., ed. *Navigazione e carte nautiche nei secoli XIII-XVI*. Genoa: Museo Navale di Pegli, 1978.

DE SIMONI, C. "Intorno ai cartografici italiani e ai loro lavori specialmente nautici." *Atti dell'Accademia Pontificale dei Nuovi Lincei*. Rome, 1885.

DE SIMONI, C. "Le carte nautiche italiane del Medio Evo: a proposito di un libro del prof. Fischer." *Atti della Società Ligure di Storia Patria* 19 (1888): 225-266.

FISCHER, T. *Sammlung mittelalterlicher Welt- und Seekarten italienischen Ursprungs und aus italienischen Bibliotheken und Archiven*. Venice: F. Ongania, 1886. Reprint. Amsterdam: Meridian, 1961.

FISCHER, T. *Raccolta di mappamondi e carte nautiche dal XIII al XVI secolo*. Venice: F. Ongania, 1871-1881.

FRABETTI, P. "Carte nautiche manoscritte di autore italiano conservate nella città di Bologna." *Atti XVII Congresso Geografico Italiano, Bari 1957*, 2: 433-438.

FRABETTI, P. "Ulteriori ricerche sulle carte nautiche manoscritte di autore italiano conservate in Emilia Romagna." *Atti XVIII Congresso Geografico Italiano, Trieste 1961*, 2: 105-107.

FREISLEBEN, H.C. "The Still Undiscovered Origin of the Portolan Charts." *Navigation: Journal of the Institute of Navigation* 24 (1983): 124-129.

FREISLEBEN, H.C. "The Origin of Portolan Charts." *Navigation: Journal of the Institute of Navigation*, 37 (1984): 194-199.

GELCICH, E. "Kompass und Seekarten." In *Hamburgische Festschrift zur Erinnerung an die Entdeckung Amerikas*, 1 (1892), pt. 2: 23-43.

GODINHO, V.M., ed. *Documentos sobre a Expansão Portuguesa*, 3 vols. Lisbon: Editorial Gleba, 1943-1956.

GUARNIERI, G. *Il Mediterraneo nella storia della cartografia nautica medievale. Con un catalogo delle carte portolaniche*. Livorno: S.T.E.T., 1933.

GUARNIERI, G. *Geografia e cartografia nautica nella loro evoluzione storica e scientifica*. Genoa: s.e., 1956. See also a book by the same author, already cited in the section on classical antiquity: *Le correnti del pensiero geografico nell'antichità classica e il loro contributo alla cartografia nautica medioevale*.

HOWSE, D. and M. SANDERSON, *The Sea Chart: An Historical Survey Based on the Collections in the National Maritime Museum*. Newton Abbot: David and Charles, 1967.

KAHANE, H.; KAHANE, R. and BREMNER, L. *Glossario degli antichi portolani italiani*. Quaderni dell'Archivio Linguistico Veneto. Florence, 1967.

KOBERER, W., ed. *Das rechte Fundament der Seefahrt*. S.l.: Hoffman & Campe, 1982.

KOEMAN, C. *Land- und Seekarten in Mittlealter und in der Frühen Neuzeit*. Wolfenbütteler Forschungen, vol. 7. Munich, 1980.

KRETSCHMER, K.C.H. *Die italienischen Portolane des Mittelalters. Ein Beitrag zur Geschichte der Kartographie und Nautik*. Veröffentlichungen des Instituts für Meereskunde und des Geographischen Institut an der Universität Berlin, vol. 13. Berlin, 1909. Reprint. Hildesheim: Georg Holms, 1962.

LANMAN. J.T. "On the Origin of Portolan Charts." Paper presented at the Eleventh International Conference on the History of Cartography, Ottawa, 1985. Published in an expanded version in *The Hermon Dunlop Smith Center for the History of Cartography*, Occasional Publications, vol. 2. Chicago: The Newberry Library, 1987.

LUCA, G. DE. "Carte nautiche del medio evo disegnate in Italia." *Atti dell'Accademia Pontiana* (1866): 3-35. Reprint. *Acta Cartographica* 4 (1969): 314-348.

MAGNAGHI, A. "Sulle origini del portolano normale nel medio evo e della cartografia dell'Europa Occidentale." *Memorie Geografiche* 8 (Florence, 1909): 115-187.

MAGNAGHI, A. "Nautiche, Carte." In *Enciclopedia Italiana* 24, op. cit., 323-331.

MARINELLI, G. "Venezia nella storia della geografia cartografica ed esploratrice." *Atti del Reale Istituto Veneto di Scienze, Lettere ed Arti*, series 6, vol. 7 (1888-1889): 933-1000.

MARINELLI, G. "Recente ritrovamento di carte nautiche e planisferi." *Rivista Geografica Italiana* 4 (1897): 454-456.

MOLLAT DU JOURDIN, M. and P. ADAM, eds. "Les aspects internationaux de la découverte océanique aux XVe et XVIe siècle." *Actes du Vème Colloque Internationale d'Histoire Maritime*. Paris: SEVPEN, 1966.

MONTEIRO VELHO ARRUDA, M. *As Ilhas Ocidentais na cartografía medieval*. Coleçao de Documentos Relativos ao Descobrimento e Povoamento dos Açores. Ponte Delgado: 1st ed., 1932; 2nd ed., 1977.

MOTA, A. TEXEIRA DA. "Influence de la cartographie portugaise sur la cartographie européenne à l'époque des découvertes." *Actes du Vème Colloque Internationale d'Histoire Maritime: Les aspects internationaux de la découverte océanique aux XVe et XVIe siècle*, edited by M. MOLLAT DU JOURDIN and P. ADAM, 377-429. Paris: SEVPEN, 1966.

NORDENSKIÖLD, A.E. *Periplus: An Essay on the Early History of Charts and Sailing-Directions*. Translated by F.A. BATHER and P.A. NORSTEDT. Stockholm, 1897.

PAGANI, L. "Il territorio tra il Mar Nero e il Mar Caspio nella cartografia nautica italiana." *Atti I Congresso Cultura Transoceanica, Istituto Univ. Bergamo*, 19-39. Genoa, 1984.

PASTINE, O. "Se la più antica carta nautica medioevale sia di autore genovese." *Bollettino Ligustico* 1 (1949), fasc. 1-3, 79-82.

PESCHEL, O. "Uber eine italienische Weltkarte aus der Mitte des 16. Jahrhunderts." *Jahresbericht des Vereins von Freunden der Erdkunde zu Leipzig* 9 (1871): 59-64.

PORENA, F. "La collezione di carte nautiche di T. Fischer." *Bollettino della Società Geografica Italiana* 24 (1887): 381-388.

PUTMAN, R. *Early Sea Charts*. New York: Abbeville Press, 1983.

RANDLES, W.G.L. "De la carte-portulan méditerranéenne à la carte marine du monde des grandes découvertes: la crise de la cartographie au XVIe siècle." In PELLETIER, M., ed., op, cit., 125-131.

REPARAZ, G. DE. *Catalunya a les mars. Navegants, mercaders i cartògrafs catalans de l'Etad Mitjana i del Renaixement (Contribucio a l'estudi de la història del comerc i de la navegacio de la Mediterrània)*. Barcelona: Mentova, 1930.

REVELLI, P. *Cristoforo Colombo e la scuola cartografica genovese*. 2 vols. Genoa: SIAG, 1937. The first volume is a complete treatment of the subjects indicated in the title. The second volume, cited earlier, is devoted to *La partecipazione italiana alla Mostra Oceanografica di Siviglia* and contains only casual references to the themes of medieval nautical cartography.

RONCIÈRE, C. DE LA. "Les portulans italiens." In *Les portulans de la Bibliothèque de Lyon*, fasc. 8. Lyons: Bibliothèque de la Ville, 1929.

RONCIÈRE, M. DE LA. "Les cartes marines de l'époque des grandes découvertes.' Revue d'Histoire Économique et Sociale 45 (1967): 5-28.

RUGE, S. *Über Compas und Compaskarten*. Dresden: Separat Abdruck aus dem Programm der Handels-Lehranstalt, 1868.

STEGER, E. *Untersuchungen über italienische Seekarten des Mittelalters auf Grund der kartometrischen Methode*. Dissertation, Göttingen, 1896.

STEVENSON, E.L. *Portolan Charts: Their Origin and Characteristics, with a Descriptive List of Those Belonging to the Hispanic Society of America*. New York: s. e., 1911.

TAYLOR, E.G.R. "Early Charts and the Origin of the Compass Rose." Navigation: Journal of the Institute of Navigation 4 (1951): 351-356.

TRIAS, L.R. *La Aportación Científica de Mallorquines y Portugueses a la Cartografía Nautica en los Siglos XIV al XVI*. Madrid: Instituto Histórico de Marina, 1964.

UHDEN, R. "Die antiken Grundlagen der mittelalterlichen Seekarten." *Imago Mundi* 1 (1935): 1-19.

WAGNER, H. *Das Rätsel der Kompasskarten*. Bremen, 1895.

WAGNER, H. "The Origin of the Medieval Nautical Charts." *Report of the Sixth International Geographical Congress, London 1895*, 695-703. London: Royal Geographical Society, 1896. Reprint. *Acta Cartographica* 5 (1969): 476-483.

WAGNER, H. "Der Ursprung der Kleinen Seemeile auf den mittelalterlichen Seekarten der Italiener." *Nachrichten der Königlichen Gesellschaft der Wissenschaften, Göttingen, Philo-histor. Klasse 1900*, 271-285.

WIEDEMANN, R. *Zur Geschichte des Kompasses bei den Arabern*. Verhandlungen der Deutschen Physikalischen Gesellschaft, vol. 9. Braunschweig, 1908.

WINTER, H. "Das katalanische Problem in der älteren Kartographie." *Ibero-Amerikanisches Archiv* 14 (1940-1941): 89-126.

WINTER, H. "The True Position of Hermann Wagner in the Controversy of the Compass Chart." *Imago Mundi* 5 (1948): 21-26.

WINTER, H. "Catalan Portolan Maps and Their Place in the Total View of Cartographic Development." *Imago Mundi* 11 (1954): 1-12.

WINTER, H. "The Origin of the Sea Chart." *Imago Mundi* 13 (1956): 39-52.

ZURLA, P. *Sulle antiche mappe lavorate in Venezia.* Venice, 1818. Also contains large sections that are general in nature.

NAVIGATIONAL TECHNIQUES, INSTRUMENTS, AND NAUTICAL AIDS

Even though we sought to limit the number of works, often technical in nature, cited in this section, those that have been consulted or used and that are connected to the transformation of nautical cartography are numerous. In this respect we have had to be quite selective, dwelling especially on the perspective of the late Middle Ages and of the period of the great geographical discoveries. We will have to return to certain specific issues later on.

ALBUQUERQUE, L. DE. *Os Guias Nauticas de Munich a Evora.* Agrupamento de Est. de Cart. Antiga. Lisbon: Junta de Invest. do Ultramar, 1965.

ALBUQUERQUE, L. DE. *Sobre a observação de estrelas na nautica dos descobrimentos.* In Agrupamento de Est. de Cart. Antiga, Sec. de Coimbra, op. cit., no. 7. Coimbra, 1965.

ALBUQUERQUE, L. DE. *A determinação da declinação solar na nautica dos descobrimentos.* In Agrupamento de Est. de Cart. Antiga, Sec. de Coimbra, op. cit., no. 16. Coimbra, 1966.

ALBUQUERQUE, L. DE. *Tratado da Agulha de Marear de João de Lisboa, reconstituição do seu texto seguida de uma versão francesa com anotações.* In Centro de Est. de Cart. Antiga, op. cit., Serie Separatas 150. Coimbra, 1982.

ALMAGIÀ, R. *La dottrina della marea nell'antichità classica e nel medio evo.* In R. Accademia Lincei, no. 302 (Rome 1905).

AVEZAC, M.A.P. D'. "Aperçus historiques sur la rose des vents." *Bollettino della Società Geografica Italiana* 11 (1874): 377-416.

BALDACCI, O. "Tecnica nautica tra medio evo ed età moderna." *Atti III Convegno Internazionale di Studi Colombiani, Genova 7 e 8 ottobre 1977*, op. cit., 65-90.

BAROZZI, P. "Navigazione e navi in età colombiana." *La Casana* 31 (1989): 22-27.

BAUR, L.A. "The Earliest Values of the Magnetic Declination." In *Terrestrial Magnetism and Atmospheric Electricity.* Baltimore, 1908.

BENSAUDE, J. "L'astronomie nautique au Portugal à l'époque des grandes découvertes." In *Histoire de la science nautique portugaise*, vol. 1/7: 1-290. Berne, 1912. This second monumental work in 5 volumes had various editors (C. Kuhn, J. B. Orbenetter, M. Dreschel) in more than one city (Munich, Berne) in 1912-1915.

BERTELLI, T. "Sopra Pietro Peregrino di Maricourt e la sua Epistola de Magnete." *Bollettino di Bibliografia e di Storia delle Scienze matematiche e fisiche* 1 (1868): 70-89.

BERTELLI, T. *La declinazione magnetica e la sua variazione nello spazio scoperta da Cristoforo Colombo*. Raccolta di Documenti e Studi pubblicati dalla R. Commissione Colombiana, pt. 4, vol. 2. Rome: M.P.I., 1892.

BERTELLI, T. "Studi storici intorno alla bussola nautica." *Memorie della Pontificale Accademia Nuovi Lincei* 9 (1893).

BERTELLI, T. "Discussione sulla leggenda di Fl. Gioia inventore della bussola." *Rivista di Fisica, Matematica e Scienza Naturale* 1 (1901): 529-601.

BERTELLI, T. "Sulle recenti controversie intorno all'origine della bussola." *Rivista Geografica Italiana* 10 (1902): 281-298, 409-424.

BERTELLI, T. "La leggenda di Flavio Gioia inventore della bussola." *Rivista Geografica Italiana* 11 (1903): 105-122.

BERTELLI, T. "Sulle recenti controversie intorno all'origine della bussola nautica." *Memorie della Pontificale Accademia Nuovi Lincei* 20 (1903): 1-52.

BERTOLOTTO, G. "Il trattato sull'Astrolabio di Andaló de Negro." *Atti della Società Ligure di Storia Patria* 25 (1894): 49-144.

BREUSING, A. "Flavio Gioia und der Schiffkompass." *Zeitschrift der Gesellschaft für Erdkunde zu Berlin*, 1868.

CORTESÃO, A. *Contribution of the Portuguese to Scientific Navigation and Cartography*. Agrupamento de Est. de Cart. Antiga, Sec. de Coimbra, no. 92. Coimbra, 1974.

CORTESÃO, A. *Nautical Science and the Renaissance*. Agrupamento de Est. de Cart. Antiga, Sec. de Coimbra, no. 94. Coimbra, 1974.

CORTESÃO, J. *Historia dos Descobrimentos Portugueses*. 2 vols. Lisbon: Arcadia, 1960-1962. Another edition published under the title *Os Descobrimentos Portugueses*. Lisbon: n. d. (but from 1960). Both editions make many references to techniques of navigation and the use of nautical charts.

COSTA, A. FONTURA DA. "Ciéncia nautica portuguesa. Cartografia e cartógrafos." *Congreso do Mundo Portugues*, vol. 3/1, sect. 1: 537-577. Lisbon, 1940.

COSTA, A. FONTURA DA. *A Nautica dos Descobrimentos*. Lisbon: AGU, 1956.

COUTINHO, C.V.G. *A nautica dos descobrimentos*. 2 vols. Lisbon: Agencia Gen. Ultramar, 1951-1952.

CUSA, S. "Sulla denominazione dei venti e dei punti cardinali, e specialmente di nord, est, sud, ovest." *Atti III Congreso Geografico Internazionale, Venezia 1881*, 1: 375-415. Rome: Società Geografica Italiana, 1884.

DE ALBERTIS, E.A. *Le costruzioni navali e l'arte della navigazione al tempo di Cristoforo Colombo*. Raccolta di documenti e studi pubblicati dalla Regia Commissione Colombiana, pt. 4, vol. 1. Rome, 1892.

FERRAND, G., ed. *Instructions nautiques et routiers arabes et portugais des XVe et XVIe siècles*. 3 vols. See especially vol. 3: *Introduction à l'astronomie nautique arabe*. Paris: Librairie Orientaliste Paul Geuthner, 1928.

FORMALEONI, V. *Saggio sulla nautica antica dei Veneziani con illustrazione d'alcune carte idrografiche antiche della Biblioteca di San Marco, che dimostrano l'isole Antille prima della scoperta di Cristoforo Colombo.* Venice: 1783.

GALFRASCOLI, G.O. "Nautica y ciencias geográficas en la época de Colón." *Atti del III Convegno Internazionale di Studi Colombiani*, Genova 1977, op. cit., 235-255.

GOVI, G. *La ragione del martilogio, ossia il metodo adoperato dai navigatori del secolo XV per calcolare i loro viaggi sul mare.* Atti della R. Accademia dei Lincei, fasc. 9 (1889).

HUMBOLDT, A. VON. *Examen critique de l'histoire de la géographie du Nouveau Continent et des progrès de l'astronomie nautique au XVe et XVIe siècles.* 4 vols. Paris: Gide, 1836-1839.

LAGUARDA TRIAS, R. *Interpretacion de los vestigos del uso de un metodo de navegacion preastronomica en el Atlantico.* Agrupamento de Est. de Cart. Antiga, Sec. de Coimbra, op. cit., no. 48. Coimbra, 1970.

MADDISON, F. *Medieval Scientific Instruments and the Development of Navigational Instruments in the XVth and XVIth Centuries.* Agrupamento de Est. de Cart. Antiga, Sec. de Coimbra, op. cit., no. 3. Coimbra, 1969.

MOTA, A. TEIXEIRA DA. "A Arte de navegar no Mediterraneo nos séculos XIII-XVII e a criaçâo da navegaçâo astronomica no Atlantico e no Indico." *Anais do Clube Militar Naval*, 5-27. Lisbon, 1957. Republished in *Travaux du IIe Colloque Internationale d'Histoire Maritime, Le navire et l'économie maritime du Moyen Age au XVIIIe siècle*, edited by M. MOLLAT DU JOURDIN, 127-154. Paris: SEVPEN, 1958.

MOTA, A. TEIXEIRA DA. *A Evoluçâo da Ciéncia nautica durante os séculos XV-XVI na cartografía portuguesa da época.* In Agrupamento de Estud. de Cart. Antiga, Sec. de Lisboa, no. 3, op. cit. Lisbon, 1961.

POLO, C. DE. "*Arte del navigare.* Manuscrit inédit daté de 1464-1465." *Bulletin du Bibliophile* 4 (1981): 453-461.

PORENA, F. "Un'ultima parola su Flavio Gioia e la bussola." *Rivista Geografica Italiana* 11 (1903): 314-334.

POULLE, E. *Les conditions de la navigation astronomique au XVe siècle.* Agrupamento de Est. de Cart. Antiga, Sec. de Coimbra, op. cit., no. 27, Coimbra, 1969.

RAMOS PÉRES, D. *Los contactos transatlánticos decisivos como precedentes del viaje de Colón.* Valladolid: Casa Museo de Colón, 1972.

RONCIÈRE, C. DE LA. "Un inventaire de bord en 1294 et les origines de la navigation hautière." *Bulletin de l'Ecole des Cartes* 58 (1897): 394-409.

SINGER, C.; HOLMYARD, E.J.; HALL, A.R. and WILLIAMS, T.I., eds. *Storia della Tecnologia.* 7 vols. Turin: Ed. Boringhieri, 1964 [original ed. *A History of Technology.* Oxford: Clarendon Press, 1958].

TIBBETTS, G.R. *The Navigational Theory of the Arabs in the Fifteenth and Sixteenth Centuries.* Agrupamento de Est. de Cart. Antiga. Sec. de Coimbra, op. cit., no. 26. Coimbra, 1969.

WATERS, D. *The Sea or Mariner's Astrolabe*. Agrupamento de Est. de Cart. Antiga, Sec. de Coimbra, op. cit., no. 15. Coimbra, 1966.

It seems appropriate to point out here some Italian editions of medieval portolans, such as the following:

AZZURRI, G. *Carta di navigare. Introduzione, testo e note.* Edited by O. BAZZURRO. Studi e Testi. Serie Geografia, no. 3. Genoa: Civico Istituto Colombiano, 1985.

MOTZO, B.R. *Il compasso da navigare. Opera italiana della metà del secolo XIII.* Annali della Facoltà di Lettere e Filosofia dell'Università degli Studi di Cagliari, vol. 8. Cagliari, 1947.

TERROSU ASOLE, A. *Il Portolano di Grazia Pauli. Opera italiana del secolo XIV trascritta a cura di Bacchisio R. Motzo.* Cagliari: Istituto Geografia, Università degli Studi di Cagliari, 1987.

Finally we cite the general treatises — mainly works from the sixteenth and seventeenth centuries about the nautical arts — or even comprehensive encyclopedias, as it were, of science. They also contain sections, relevant as well to earlier centuries, devoted to nautical charts as navigational instruments.

CORONELLI, V. *Specchio del Mare.* Venice, 1963.

CORTES, M. *Breve compendio de la sphera y de la arte de navegar.* Seville, 1556. English translation by R. EDEN.

CRESCENZIO, B. *Nautica mediterranea.* Rome: Bartolomeo Bonfadino, 1693.

CUNINGHAM, W. *The Cosmological Glasse, containing the pleasant principles of Cosmographie, Geographie, Hidrographie or Navigation.* London: John Day, 1559.

DUDLEY, D.R. *Dell'Arcano del Mare di D. Ruberto Dudleo duca di Nortumbria e Conte di Varich, Libri sei.* 3 vols. Florence: F. Onofri, 1646-1647. The second book in particular discusses *Carte sue generali e de' Portolani...*

FALERIO, F. *Tratado de la sphera y del arte del marear, con el regimento de las alturas.* Seville, 1535.

FOURNIER, G. *Hidrographie contenant la théorie et la pratique de la navigation.* Paris, 1679.

LULLO, R. *Arbor Scientiae*, 1515. Reprint. *Obras escojidas de filósofos.* Bibl. de Autores Españoles, no. 65 (Madrid, 1905): 83-139.

MONNO, G.F. *Arte della vera navigatione...*, 1633.

NUNES, P. (PETRI NONII SALACIENSIS). *De arte atque ratione navigandi libri duo.* Conimbricae [Coimbra], 1573.

RICCIOLI, G.B. *Geographiae et Hidrographiae reformatae libri duodecim.* Bononiae [Bologna], 1661.

SNELLIUS. *Tiphis Batavus, sive Histiodromiae, de navium cursibus et re navali.* Lugduni Batavorum [Leiden], 1624.

Finally, we should cite a medieval chronicle on the use of the compass:

DE NANGIS, G. *Gesta Sancti Ludovici.* Recueil des Historiens des Gaules et de la France, vol. 20. Paris, 1840.

NAUTICAL CHARTS OF THE EARLY CENTURIES, ESPECIALLY ITALIAN AND GENOESE ONES

Cited here are writings concerning single charts or groups of them, especially those of Italian or Genoese manufacture, from the early centuries (that is, up to the eve of the age of Columbus). In some cases, however, we are dealing with writings about groups of charts from different times; these therefore, may go beyond the designated period. Certain authors and issues of particular importance will be mentioned separately later.

ALMAGIÀ, R. *Planisferi, carte nautiche e affini dal secolo XIV al XVII esistenti nella Biblioteca Apostolica Vaticana.* Monumenta cartografica Vaticana, op. cit., vol. 1-2.

ALMAGIÀ, R. "Quelques questions au sujet des cartes nautiques et des portulans d'après les recherches récentes." *Arch. Internat. d'Hist. des Sciences* 2 (1948): 237-246.

ALMAGIÀ, R. "Intorno ad alcune carte nautiche italiane conservate negli Stati Uniti." *Atti Accademia Lincei, Rendiconti Classe di Scienze Morali, Storiche e Filologiche* (Rome, 1952): 356-366.

ARMIGNACCO, V. "Una carta nautica della Biblioteca dell'Accademia Etrusca di Cortona." *Rivista Geografica Italiana* 64 (1957): 185-223.

BUCHON, J.A.C. and J. TASTU, "Notice d'un atlas en langue catalane, manuscrit de l'an 1375." *Notices et extraits des manuscrits de la Bibliothèque du Roi et d'autres bibliothèques* 14 (1841): 1-152.

CAPACCI, A. "Reperti cartonautici manoscritti conservati in Liguria." *Atti del IV Convegno Internazionale di Studi Colombiani, Genova 1985,* 2: 205-208. Genoa: Civico Istituto Colombiano, 1987.

CARACI, G. "Un gruppo di carte e atlanti nautici conservati a Genova." *La Bibliofilia* 38 (1936): 149-182.

CARACI, G. "Le carte nautiche anonime conservate nelle biblioteche e negli archivi di Roma." *Memorie Geogr. Fac. Magistero* 6 (Rome, 1960): 157-162.

CLOS-ARCEDUC, M.L. *L'enigme des portulans. Études sur la projection des cartes à rumbs du XVIe siècle.* Rouen and Caen: Congrès des Sociétés Savantes, 1956.

CODAZZI, A. *Storia delle carte geografiche da Anassimandro alla rinascita di Tolomeo nel secolo XV.* Milan: La Goliardica, 1959.

DUKEN, J. "Reconstruction of the Portulan Chart of G. Carignano." *Imago Mundi* 40 (1988): 77-85.

DURO, C.F. "Noticia de algunas cartas de marear, manuscritas, de pilotos españoles, que han ido a parar a bibliotecas estranjeras." *Boletín de la Sociedad Geográfica de Madrid* 7 (1879): 253-262; 9 (1881): 334-335; 12 (1882): 80-82, 153-161, 445-447; 15 (1883): 134-143.

DURO, C.F. "Noticia breve de las cartas y planos existentes en la Biblioteca Particular de S.M. el Rey." *Boletín de la Sociedad Geográfica de Madrid* 26 (1889): 361-396; 27 (s.d.): 102-165.

ERRERA, C. "Atlanti e carte nautiche dal secolo XIV al XVII conservate nelle biblioteche pubbliche e private di Milano." *Rivista Geografica Italiana* 3 (1896): 91-96. Reprint. *Acta Cartographica* 8 (1970): 225-252.

FRABETTI, P. "Carte nautiche manoscritte di autore italiano conservate nella città di Bologna." *Atti XVII Congresso Geografico Italiano, Bari 1957*, 2: 433-438.

FREISLEBEN, H. "Map of the World of Sea Charts? The Catalan Mappamundi of 1375." *Navigation: Journal of the Institute of Navigation* 36 (1983): 124-129.

GENTILLI, G. "Di alcune carte nautiche dei secoli XV-XVII conservate a Firenze nella biblioteca del Principe Piero Ginori-Conti." *Rivista Geografica Italiana* 43 (1936): 253-292.

GROSJEAN, G. *The Catalan Atlas of the Year 1375*. Dietikon and Zurich: Urs Graf, 1978.

LONGHENA, M. "Atlanti e carte nautiche dal secolo XIV al XVII conservati nella Biblioteca e nell'Archivio di Parma." *Arch. Stor. per le prov. parmensi* 7 (1907): 168-169.

MORI, Associazione. "Di una carta nautica italiana del secolo XIV recentemente scoperta ed illustrata." *Rivista Marittima* 33 (1900): 353-364.

PIERSANTELLI, G. "La cartografia genovese nel medio evo (note ed appunti per una più completa storia della pittura medioevale)." *Bollettino del Civico Istituto Colombiano* 3 (1955): 67-85.

QUAINI, M. "Catalogna e Liguria nella cartografia nautica e nei portolani medievali." *Atti del Primo Congresso Storico Liguria-Catalogna: Ventimiglia-Bordighera-Albenga-Finale-Genova, 14-19 ottobre 1969*, 549-571. Bordighera: Istituto Internazionale di Studi Liguri, 1974.

RISTOW, W. and R.A. SKELTON, *Nautical Charts on Vellum in the Library of Congress*. Washington, 1977.

ROMANO, V. "Sulla validità della Carta Pisana." *Atti dell'Accademia Pontaniana* 32 (1983): 89-99.

RONCIÈRE, C. DE LA. *L'Atlas de Charles V dérive-t-il d'un prototype catalan?* Bibl. de l'Ecole des Cartes, no. 64 (1903).

YOELI, P. "Abraham and Yehuda Cresques and the Catalan Atlas." *Cartographic Journal* 7 (1970): 17-27.

On certain issues the literature is particularly abundant. The following writings, for example, discuss Vesconte, his relations with Marin Sanudo, and the Tamar Luxoro Atlas, which Revelli, in the work cited above, *Cristoforo Colombo e la scuola cartografica genovese*, along with other authors, attributes to him:

DE SIMONI, C. "Nuovi studi sull'Atlante Luxoro." *Atti della Società Ligure di Storia Patria* 5 (1867): 177-184.

DE SIMONI, C. "Una carta della Terra Santa del secolo XIV, Marino Sanudo e Pietro Vesconte." *Archivio Storico Italiano* (1893): 241-258.

DE SIMONI, C. and L. BELGRANO, "Atlante idrografico del Medio Evo posseduto dal prof. Tamar Luxoro." *Atti della Società Ligure di Storia Patria* 5 (1867): 5-168.

DEGENHART, B. and A. SCHMITT, "Marino Sanudo und Paolino Veneto." *Römisches Jahrbuch für Kunstgeschichte* 14 (1973): 1-137.

GEROLA, G. "Le carte nautiche di Pietro Vesconte dal punto di vista araldico." *Atti del II Congresso di Studi Coloniali, Napoli 1934*, 2: 102-103.

KRETSCH, K. "Marino Sanudo der Áltere und die Karten des P. Vesconte." *Zeitschrift der Gesellschaft für Erdkunde* 26 (1891): 352-370.

MAGNOCAVALLO, A. "I codici del *Liber Secretorum Fidelium Crucis*." *Rendiconti R. Istituto Lombardo* 31 (1898): 113-127.

MAGNOCAVALLO, M. "La carta *de mari mediterraneo*, di Marin Sanudo il Vecchio." *Bollettino della Società Geografica Italiana* 9 (1902): 438-449.

MARINELLI, G. *Venezia nella storia della geografia cartografica ed esploratrice*. Florence: Ricci, 1907.

MATKOVICH, P.P. "Alte handschriftliche Schiffskarten in der kaiserlichen Hof-Bibliothek in Wien." *Programm des K.K. Gymnasium...*, 3-8. Agram, 1860.

PAGANI, L. *Pietro Vesconte. Carte nautiche, Studio introduttivo*. Introduction by O. MAZAL. Gorle (BG): Grafia Gutemberg, 1977. Pagani's essay is on pages 5-46.

PAMPALONI, C. "L'Atlante nautico cosidetto *Luxoro*." Note in *Carte nautiche da musei e biblioteche della Liguria*, edited by G. FERRO, op. cit., 32.

PIERSANTELLI, G. "L'Atlante Luxoro." In *Miscellanea di Geografia Storica e di Storia della Geografia nel primo centenario della nascita di Paolo Revelli*, 115-141. Genoa: Bozzi, 1971.

ROCHRICHT. "Marin Sanudo senior als Kartograph Palästinas." *Zeitschrift des deutschen Palästina Verein* 21 (1898): 83-126.

In addition to the volume, already cited, by G. CARACI, *Italiani e Catalani nella primitiva cartografia nautica medioevale*, the following works also discuss the long-standing question of the Dalorto-Dulcert link:

DURO, C.F. "Descubrimento de una carta de marear, española, del año 1339. Su autor Angelino Dulceri o Dulcert." *Boletín de la Real Academia de Historia* (1888): 287-319.

GALLOIS, L. "Sui mappamondi del Dalorto e del Dulcert." *Rivista Geografica Italiana* 12 (1905): 1-7.

HAMY, E.-T. "Le mappamonde d'Angelino Dulcert, de Majorque (1339)." *Bulletin de Géographie Historique et Descriptive* (1886): 354-366.

HAMY, E.-T. *Le mappamonde d'Angelino Dulceti de Maiorque (1339)*. Paris: Deux Ed., 1903.

HINKS, A.R. *The Portolan Chart of Angelino de Dalorto MCCCXXV, with a Note on the Surviving Charts and Atlas of the Fourteenth Century*. London: Royal Geographical Society, 1929. With a facsimile reproduction in color of the chart.

MAGNAGHI, A. "Angellinus de Dalorto, cartografo italiano della prima metà del secolo XIV." *Rivista Geografica Italiana* 4 (1897): 282-294, 361-369.

MAGNAGHI, A. "Il mappamondo del genovese Angellinus de Dalorto (1325), Contributo alla storia della cartografia medievale." *Atti del III Congr. Geogr. Ital., Firenze 1899*, 2: 506-543.

MAGNAGHI, A. "Alcuni osservazioni intorno ad uno studio recente sul mappamondo di Angelino Dalorto (1325)." *Rivista Geografica Italiana* 41 (1934): 1-27.

MARCEL, G. "Note sur une carte catalane de Dulceri antérieure à l'atlas catalan de 1375." *Comptes rendus de la Société de Géographie* (Paris, 1887): 28-35.

NAUTICAL CARTOGRAPHY, ESPECIALLY GENOESE, OF THE FIFTEENTH CENTURY

Given the considerable output of this century, it is to be expected that the writings listed in this section are also numerous. We have therefore favored works containing references to Columbus and the Ligurian tradition, once again relegating to a subsection the citations concerning topics of more specific interest. In general we have taken into account writings about cartographic documents up to and including the 1490's, but excluding those about Columbus's cartographic knowledge, as these will be cited later.

ALMAGIÀ, R. "Il mappamondo di Albertin de Virga." *Rivista Geografica Italiana* 21 (1914): 92-96.

AMAT DI SAN FILIPPO, P. *Del Planisfero di Bartolomeo Pareto del 1455 e di altre quattro carte nautiche*. Memorie della Società Geografica. Rome, 1878.

ASTENGO, C. "Un cartografo a Savona nel primo Quattrocento." *Sabazia*, 2 (1987): 6-8. The article is about Francesco Beccari.

BARATTA, M. "La carta nautica di Albino Canepa." *Bollettino della Reale Società Geografica Italiana*, series 5, vol. 2 (1915): 721-746.

BARBIERI, G. "Una carta nautica sconosciuta del 1449 di Gabriel de Vallsecha." *Rivista Geografica Italiana* 58 (1951): 97-104.

BERCHET, G. *Il planisfero di Giovanni Leardo dell'anno 1452, fac-simile*. Paper read at R. Istituto Veneto de Scienze, Lettere ed Arti, 25 April 1880. Venice: F. Ongania, 1880.

CARACI, G. "An Unknown Chart of Grazioso Benincasa, 1468." *Imago Mundi* 7 (1950): 18-31.

CARACI, G. "A proposito di una nuova carta di Gabriel de Vallsecha e dei rapporti fra la cartografia nautica italiana e quella maiorchina." *Bollettino della Società Geografica Italiana* 89 (1952): 388-412.

CLOUZOT, E. "Le Carte Marine d'Andrea Benincasa (1476)." *Le Globe* 82 (1943): 129-137.

CORTESÃO, A. *The Nautical Chart of 1424 and the Early Discovery and Cartographical Representation of America: A Study of the History of Early Navigation and Cartography*. Coimbra: University of Coimbra, 1954.

DURAZZO, P. *Il planisfero di Giovanni Leardo*. Mantua: Tip. Eredi Segua, 1885.

DÜRST, A. "Seekarte des Iehuda ben Zara (Borgiano VII) 1497." Notes on the corresponding edition in facsimile in *Codices e Vaticanis selecti quam simillime expressi iussu Joannis Pauli PP II consilio et opera curatorum Bibliothecae Vaticanae*, vol. 55. Zurich: Belser Verlag, 1983.

ERRERA, C. "Della carta di Andrea Bianco del 1448 e di una supposta scoperta del Brasile nel 1447." *Memorie della Società Geografica Italiana* 5 (1895): 202-225.

FERRO, G. "La tradizione cartografica genovese e Albino de Canepa." Notes on *La carta nautica di Albino Canepa 1480*. Milan: Jaca Book, 1990.

FERRO, G. "La carta nautica di Albino de Canepa del 1480." *Bollettino della Società Geografica Italiana*, series 9, vol. 8 (1991): 231-242. Translated into english by L.F. Farina and M. Beckwith.

GENTILLI, G. "Di alcune carte nautiche dei secoli XV-XVII conservate a Firenze nella biblioteca del Principe Piero Ginori-Conti." *Rivista Geografica Italiana* 43 (1936): 253-292.

HAMY, E.-T. "Note sur des fragments d'une carte marine catalane du XVe siècle, ayant servi de signets dans les notules d'un notaire de Perpignan (1531-1556)." *Bulletin de Géographie Historique et Descriptive* (1897): 23-31.

KISG, G. "Two Fifteenth-century Maps of *Zipangu*: Notes on the Early Cartography of Japan." *Erdkunde* 41 (1966): 206-214.

LOPES PEGNA, M. "Nota alla carta nautica di Gabriel de Vallsecha." *Rivista Geografica Italiana* 59 (1952): 47.

LUZZANA CARACI, I. *Le Americhe annunciate*. Reggio Emilia: Coopsette, 1991.

PESCHEL, O. *Der Atlas des Andrea Bianco vom Jahre 1436 in zehn Tafeln*. Münster: Venedig, 1869.

PESCHEL, O. *Prefazione all'Atlante di Andrea Bianco*. Venice, 1871.

PETTI BALBI, G. "Nel mondo dei cartografi: Battista Beccari maestro a Genova nel 1427." In *Columbeis I*. Istituto di Filologia Classica e Medievale, Facoltà di Lettere, Università di Genova, 1986.

"Pro Bartolomeo Pareto." *Atti della Società Ligure di Storia Patria* 4 (1866): 494-496.

REVELLI, P. "Una nuova carta di Batista Beccari (Batista Becharius)?" *Bollettino della Società Geografica Italiana* 88 (1951): 156-166.

ROSSI, E. "Una carta nautica araba inedita di Ibrahim al-Murs — datata 865 Egira — 1461 Dopo Christo." *Comptes rendus du Congrès International de Géographie* [11th International Congress, Cairo 1925] 5 (1926): 90-95.

SALINARI, M. "Le carte nautiche dei Benincasa, cartografi anconetani." *Bollettino della Società Geografica Italiana* 73 (1936): 485-510.

SALINARI, M. "Notizie su di alcune carte nautiche di Grazioso Benincasa." *Rivista Geografica Italiana* 59 (1952): 36-42.

SPADOLINI, E. "Il portolano di Grazioso Benincasa." *La Bibliofilia* 9 (1907-1908): 58-62, 205-234, 294-299, 420-434, 460-463.

TASTU, J. "Observations relatives à des cartes des quatorzième et quinzième siècles." *Bulletin de la Société de Géographie*, series 2, vol. 6 (1836): 239-246.

VIETOR, A.O. "A Pre-Columbian Map of the World, Circa 1489." *Yale University Library Gazette* 37 (1962). Reprint. *Imago Mundi* 17 (1963): 95-96.

We cite separately the writings listed below about the mappamundi of Fra Mauro Camaldolese because of the importance of this work, even though it is outside the Ligurian tradition:

ALMAGIÀ, R. "Introduction." In *Il Mappamondo di Fra' Mauro*, edited by T. GASPARRINI LEPORACE. Rome: Istituto Poligrafico dello Stato, 1956.

CERULLI, E. "Fonti arabe nel mappamondo di Fra Mauro." *Orientalia commentarii periodici Pontifici Instituti Biblica*, new series 4 (1935): 336-338.

CRONE, G.R. "Fra Mauro's Representation of the Indian Ocean and the Eastern Islands." *Atti del Convegno Internazionale di Studi Colombiani, Genova 1952*, 3: 57-64.

GASPARRINI LEPORACE, T. *Il mappamondo di Fra Mauro*. Rome: Istituto Poligrafico dello Stato.

SANTAREM, M.F. "Note sur le mappamonde du cosmographe Fra Mauro." *Bulletin de la Société de Géographie*, series 3, vol. 5 (1846): 251-252.

WINTER, H. "The Fra Mauro Portolan Chart in the Vatican." *Imago Mundi* 16 (1962): 17-28.

ZURLA, P. *"Il Mappamundo" di Fra Mauro Camaldolese, descritto ed illustrato*. Venice, 1806.

The following works, on the other hand, have to do with the question of the map attributed (without foundation) to Paolo dal Pozzo Toscanelli:

BIASUTTI, R. "È stata ritrovata a Firenze la carta navigatoria di Paolo dal Pozzo Toscanelli?" and "Reply." *Rivista Geografica Italiana* 48 (1941): 293-301; 49 (1942): 44-54 (see entry below).

BIASUTTI, R. "Il mappamondo del 1457 non è la carta navigatoria di Paolo dal Pozzo Toscanelli." *Rivista Geografica Italiana* 49 (1942): 44-54.

CARACI, G. "Beffa al Toscanelli." *Leonardo* 12 (1941): 152-161.

CARACI, G. "Per l'identificazione della carta che serví a Colombo." *Leonardo* 12 (1941): 262-264.

CARACI, G. "Paolo dal Pozzo Toscanelli ed il Planisfero Palatino del 1457." *Il Giornale di Politica e Letteratura* 18 (1942), fasc. 7-8, 1-24.

CRINÒ, S. "La scoperta della carta originale di Paolo dal Pozzo Toscanelli che serví di guida a Cristoforo Colombo per il viaggio verso il Nuovo Mondo." *L'Universo* 22 (1941): 379-405.

CRINÒ, S. "Ancora sul Mappamondo del 1457 e sulla carta navigatoria di Paolo dal Pozzo Toscanelli." *Rivista Geografica Italiana* 49 (1942): 35-43.

DAINVILLE, F. "Cartes et contestations au XVe siècle." *Imago Mundi* 24 (1970): 99-121.

MAGNAGHI, A. *Tutto è chiaro finalmente!* Turin: Artigianelli, 1941.

MAGNAGHI, A. "Ancora intorno alla carta attribuita a Paolo dal Pozzo Toscanelli: brevi chiarimenti." *Rivista Geografica Italiana* 49 (1942): 141-154.

TAVIANI, P.E. *Cristoforo Colombo. La genesi della grande scoperta.* 3rd. ed., vol. 1: 177-185; vol. 2: 189-193. Novara: I. G. De Agostini, 1988.

UZIELLI, G. *La vita e i tempi di Paolo dal Pozzo Toscanelli.* Raccolta Colombiana, pt. 5, vol. 1. Rome, 1894.

WAGNER, H.R. "Die Rekonstruktion der Toscanelli-Karte von Jahre 1474." Nachrichten von der Königlichen Gesellschaft der Wissenschaft zu Göttingen (1892): 541-572.

GENOA AND CULTURE AT THE TIME OF COLUMBUS

The topic of Columbus's education and cultural level (it would be better to speak of Christopher and Bartolomeo Columbus when dealing with cartographic cultural knowledge and output) has also been discussed by many authors. First of all we cite here some writings about medieval Genoa as a center for culture and especially for cartographic production.

Besides REVELLI'S *Cristoforo Colombo e la scuola cartografica genovese*, which was mentioned earlier, it will suffice to list certain essential works, some classic, others more recent and abounding in new contributions.

AIRALDI, G. "Colombo e la Spagna, Colombo e la patria genovese." In *Storia d'Italia. Comuni e signorie nell'Italia settentrionale: il Piemonte e la Liguria*, 432-442. Turin: UTET, 1966.

AIRALDI, G. *Genova e Spagna nel secolo XV.* Fonti e Studi, vol. 9. Genoa: Istituto di Paleografia e Storia Medioevale, Università di Genova, 1966.

AIRALDI, G. "Diplomazia, diplomatica e cultura tra Genova e Spagna nel Quattrocento." *Atti del III Convegno Internazionale di Studi Colombiani, Genova 1977*, op. cit., 91-99.

AIRALDI, G. "La cultura del mercante." In *Cristoforo Colombo nella Genova del suo tempo*, 185-209. Turin: ERI, 1985.

AIRALDI, G. *Genoa e la Liguria nel Medioevo.* Turin: UTET, 1986.

AIRALDI, G. "Quattrocento ispano-genovese tra ideologia e politica." In *Scritti in onore del prof. P.E. Taviani*, vol. 3 (*Temi Colombiani*): 5-12. Genoa: Facoltà di Scienze Politiche, Università di Genova, 1983-1986.

BAROZZI, P. "Qualche ombra di troppo tra Genova e Colombo." *La Casana* 30 (1988): 50-55.

BAROZZI, P. "Cristoforo Colombo fra Medioevo e Rinascimento." *Novinostra* 3 (Novi Ligure 1990), facs. 3, 3-13.

BAROZZI, P. "Genova e il genovesato." In FERRO, G. *La Liguria e Genova ai tempi di Colombo*, op. cit., 105-124.

BELGRANO, L.T. *Della vita privata dei Genovesi.* Genoa: Tip. R. Ist. Sordo-Muti, 1875.

BRAGGIO, C. "Giacomo Bracelli e l'Umanesimo dei liguri nel suo tempo." *Atti della Società Ligure di Storia Patria* 23 (1890): 5-206.

CONTI, S. "Aspetti storico-geografici degli insediamenti italiani in Andalusia." *La presenza italiana in Andalusia nel basso Medioevo, Atti del secondo Convegno, Roma 1984*, 115-123. Bologna: Cappelli Ed., 1986.

DE NEGRI, T.O. *Storia di Genova*. Milan: A. Martello (E. Sormani), 1968.

DE SIMONI, C. "Intorno all vita e ai lavori di Andalò di Negro matematico e astronomo genovese del secolo decimoquarto." *Bollettino di bibliografia e di storia delle scienze matematiche e fisiche* 7 (1874): 1-66.

D'ARIENZO, L. "Mercanti italiani fra Siviglia e Lisbona nel Quattrocento." *La presenza italiana in Andalusia nel basso Medioevo...*, op. cit., 35-49.

GATTI, L. *Maestri e garzoni nella società genovese fra XV e XVI secolo*. Centro di studi sulla storia della tecnica, no. 4. Genoa, 1980.

Genova e Siviglia, l'avventura dell'Occidente. Genoa: SAGEP, 1988.

GROSSI BIANCHI, L. and E. POLEGGI, Una città portuale del medioevo, Genova nei secoli X-XVI. Genoa: SAGEP, 1979.

HEERS, J. *Gênes au XVe siècle. Activité économique et problèmes sociaux*. Paris: SEVPEN, 1961. Reprint. Paris: Flammarion, 1971. From this was derived *Genova nel Quattrocento. Civiltà mediterranea, grande capitalismo e capitalismo popolare*. Translated by P. MASTRAROSA. Milan: Jaca Book, 1984.

HEERS, J. "Urbanisme et structure sociale à Gênes au Moyen-Age." In *Studi in onore di A. Fanfani* 1: 369-411. Milan: Giuffrè, 1962.

KOLHER, C. "Traité du recouvrement de la Terre Sainte adressé vers l'ans 1295 à Philippe le Bel par Galvano de Levanto médecin génois." *Revue de l'Orient latin* 6 (1898): 343-369. In this work can be found a partially edited version of *Liber sancti passagii christianorum contra Sarracenos pro recuperatione Terrae Sanctae Galvani de Levanto Ianuensis*.

LUZZANA CARACI, I. "Genova e Colombo." In *Scritti geografici di interesse ligure*, 227-255. Pubblicazioni dell'Istituto di Scienze Geografiche 39. Genoa, 1984.

MARTIGNONE, F. "Politica ed economia in Genova sulla fine del Quattrocentro." *Studi Genuensi* 5 (1964): 99-125.

MOLLAT DU JOURDIN, M. "Culture et religion des gens de mer à la fin du Moyen Age et au début de l'Epoque Moderne." *Atti del II Congresso Internazionale di Studi Storici. Rapporti Genova-Mediterraneo-Atlantico nell'Età Moderna*, 35-45. Pubblicazioni dell' Istituto di Scienze Storiche Università di Genova 6. Genoa, 1985.

MUSSO, G.G. "La cultura genovese fra il Quattro e il Cinquecento." In *Miscellanea di Storia Ligure* 1: 121-187. Genoa: Istituto di Storia Medioevale e Moderna, Università di Genova, 1958.

MUSSO, G.G. "Per la storia degli Ebrei nella Repubblica di Genova tra il Quattrocento e il Cinquecento." In *Miscellanea di Storica Ligure* 3: 103-125. Genoa: Istituto di Storia Medioevale e Moderna, Università di Genova, 1963.

MUSSO, G.G. "Politica e cultura in Genova a metà del Quattrocento." In *Miscellanea di Storia Ligure in onore di G. Falco*, 315-354. Fonti e Studi 12. Genoa: Istituto di Paleografia e Storia Medioevale, Università di Genova, 1966.

MUSSO, G.G. "Genovesi e Catalogna nell'ultimo Medioevo: documenti d'archivio." In *Mostra documentaria Genova-Catalogna*, 7-64. Genoa, 1969.

Musso, G.G. *Genovesi e Portogallo nell'età delle scoperte*. Studi e Testi, geographic series, vol. 1. Genoa: Civico Istituto Colombiano, 1976.

Musso, G.G. *La cultura genovese nell'età dell'umanesimo*. Genoa, 1985.

Pandiani, E. *Vita privata genovese nel Rinascimento*. Genoa: Sambolino, 1915.

Petti Balbi, G. "Deroghe papali al devetum sul commercio con l'Islam." *Rassegna degli Archivi di Stato* 32 (1972): 521-533.

Petti Balbi, G. "Libri greci a Genova nel Quattrocento." *Italia medioevale e umanistica* 20 (1977): 277-302.

Petti Balbi, G. "Il libro nella società genovese del secolo XIII." *La Bibliofilia* 80 (1978): 1-48.

Petti Balbi, G. *L'insegnamento nella Liguria medievale. Scuole, maestri, libri*. Genoa: Tilgher, 1979.

Petti Balbi, G. "Società e cultura a Genova tra Due e Trecento." *Atti della Società Ligure di Storia Patria* 29 (1984), fasc. 2, 123-149.

Pistarino, G. "Genova medievale tra Oriente e Occidente." *Rivista Storica Italiana* 81 (1969), fasc. 1, 45-73.

Pistarino, G. "Il Medioevo in Cristoforo Colombo." *Saggi e Documenti*, 453-477. Studi e Testi, historical series, no. 8. Genoa: Civico Istituto Colombiano, 1985.

Pistarino, G. *Genovesi d'Oriente*. Studi e Testi, historical series. Genoa: Civico Istituto Colombiano, 1990.

Revelli, P. *La cultura dei mercanti genovesi e Cristoforo Colombo*. Genoa: Comit. Citt. Celebr. Colomb., 1951. Republished in *Atti Accademia Ligure di Scienze e Lettere* 8 (Genoa 1952): 6-35.

Ruiz Domenec, J.E. "Genova e la Spagna nel Basso Medioevo." In *La Storia dei Genovesi (Atti del Convegno di Studi sui Ceti Dirigenti della Repubblica di Genova, Genova 1984)*, 49-64. Genoa, 1985.

Vitale, V. *Breviario della storia di Genova*. 2 vols. Genoa: Società Ligure di Storia Patria, 1955. Facsimile reprint, 1989.

Zazzu, G.N. "Genova e gli Ebrei. Incontro di due culture." In *Cristoforo Colombo nella Genova del suo tempo*, op. cit., 209-235.

COLUMBUS'S GEOGRAPHICAL IDEAS

Here we indicate the most important of those works that, while discussing the ideas and intuitions that led Columbus to plan for and prepare his enterprise, address the cosmographical, geographical, and cartographical concepts well as he believed in and expressed in his writings as his voyages.

Almagià, R. "Pietro d'Ailly e Cristoforo Colombo." *Rivista Geografica Italiana* 38 (1931): 166-169.

Almagià, R. "Gli Italiani primi esploratori dell'America." *L'Opera del genio italiano all'estero*. Rome: Libreria dello Stato, 1947.

ALMAGIÀ, R. "Cristoforo Colombo davanti alla scienza." *Scientia* (1948): 51-59. Republished in ALMAGIÀ, R. *Scritti Geografici*. Rome: Cremonese, 1961.

ALMAGIÀ, R. "Christophe Colomb et la science moderne." In *Les conséquences de la découverte de l'Amérique par Christophe Colomb*. Paris, 1951.

ARMAS, A. RUMEU DE. *Libro Copiador de Cristóbal Colón. Correspondencia inédita...* 2 vols. Madrid: Testimonio Comp. Ed., 1989. Also contains references to Columbus's activity as a cartographer and to his ideas.

BALDACCI, O. "Il segreto di Colombo: solo le rotte atlantiche del primo viaggio?" In *Scritti in onore del prof. Paolo Emilio Taviani*, vol. 3 (Temi Colombiani): 13-50. Genoa: Facoltà di Scienze Politiche, Università di Genova, 1983-1986.

BALDACCI, O. "Teoria e sperimentazione nella scienza di Colombo." *Bollettino della Società Geografica Italiana*, series 9, vol. 7 (1990): 159-169.

BAROZZI, P. "Le postille colombiane al Milione." In *Scritti in onore di A. Sestini*, 53-65. Florence: Società di Studi Geografici, 1982.

BAROZZI, P. "Il computo dell'età del mondo nelle postille colombiane ai trattati di Pierre d'Ailly." *Miscellanea 1*, 155-173. Pubblicazioni dell'Istituto di Scienze Geografiche 40. Genoa, 1986.

BAROZZI, P. "Colombo ed Esdra." *Atti IV Convegno Internazionale di Studi Colombiani, Genova 1985*, 169-180. Genoa: Civico Istituto Colombiano, 1987.

BOSCOLO, A. "Ricerche su Cristoforo Colombo e sulla sua epoca." *Atti del III Convegno Internazionale di Studi Colombiani, Genova 1977*, 51-58. Genoa: Civico Istituto Colombiano, 1979.

CARACI, G. "A proposito delle *Postille Colombiane*." *Pubblicazioni dell'Istituto di Scienze Geografiche* 18, 3-15. Genoa, 1971.

CRINÒ, S. *Come fu scoperta l'America*. Milan: Hoepli, 1943.

DE LOLLIS, C. "Postille." *Scritti di Cristoforo Colombo*. Raccolta Colombiana, op. cit., pt. 1, vol. 2, 289-570. The entire text of the Postille is given here.

DE LOLLIS, C. *Chi cerca trova ovverossia Colui che cercò l'Asia e trovò l'America*. Rome: Pubblicazioni dell'Istituto Colombo, 1925.

DE LOLLIS, C. "Gli sconsacratori di Colombo." *Giornale d'Italia*, 7 April 1925.

GALLIANO, G. "Forma e dimensioni della Terra nelle postille colombiane." *Miscellanea 1*, op. cit., 175-191.

GIL, J. "La correspondencia con Toscanelli." In *Cartas de particulares a Colón y Relaciones coetaneas*, 129-141. Madrid: Alianza Universidad, 1984.

GIL, J. *Introducción a el libro de Marco Polo*. Madrid: Testimonio Comp. Ed., 1986.

GIL, J. *Mitos y utopias del Descubrimiento*. Vol. I: *Colón y su tiempo*. Madrid: Alianza Editorial, 1989.

LUZZANA CARACI, I. "La postilla B 858 e il suo significato cronologico." *Atti del Convegno Internazionale di Studi Colombiani, Genova 1975*, 197-223. Genoa, 1977.

LUZZANA CARACI, I. "Colombo e le longitudini." *Bollettino della Società Geografica Italiana*, series 10, vol. 9 (1980): 517-529.

Luzzana Caraci, I. "La cultura di Colombo." *Atti IV Convegno Internazionale di Studi Colombiani, Genova 1985*, 2: 209-228. Genoa, 1987.

Luzzana Caraci, I. "La cultura nautica di Colombo." *La Storia dei Genovesi. Atti del Convegno di Studi sui Ceti Dirigenti della Repubblica di Genova, Genova 1989*, 71-90. Genoa, 1990.

Luzzana Caraci, I. "Scienza, cultura ed esperienza nella genesi del progetto di Colombo." *Mare Liberum* 1 (Lisbon, 1990): 143-151.

Luzzana Caraci, I. "In tema di cartografia colombiana." In *Studi in onore di Osvaldo Baldacci*, 105-114. Bologna: Patron, 1991.

Magnaghi, A. "I presenti errori che vengono attribuiti a Colombo nella determinazione delle latitudini." *Bollettino della Società Geografica Italiana*, series 6, vol. 5 (1928): 459-494, 553-582. Republished in *Questioni Colombiane*, 35-125. Naples: Loffredo, 1939.

Magnaghi, A. "Ancora dei pretesi errori che vengono attribuiti a Colombo nella determinazione delle latitudini." *Bollettino della Società Geografica Italiana*, series 6, vol. 7 (1930): 459-515. Republished in *Questioni Colombiane*, op. cit., 125-132.

Manzano Manzano, J. *Cristobal Colón. Siete años decisivos de su vida, 1485-1492*. Madrid: Ed. Cultura Hispanica, 1964. Published in Italian translation in Nuova Raccolta Colombiana, 10, cited earlier.

Muro Orejon, A., ed. *Pleitos Colombinos*. 4 vols. published thus far. Escuela de Estudios Hispanos-Americanos, 1964-1989. These volumes contain many references to Columbus's ability to make and use maps.

Nunn, G.E. "Marinus of Tyre's Place in the Columbus Concepts." *Imago Mundi* 2 (1938): 27-36.

Nunn, G.E. *The Geographical Conceptions of Columbus: A Critical Consideration of Four Problems*. New York: American Geographical Society, 1924. Republished in Freeport, NY: Books for Library Press, 1972 and New York: Octagon Books, 1977.

Taviani, P.E. *Cristoforo Colombo. La genesi della grande scoperta*. 2 vols. Novara: Istituto Geografico De Agostini, 1974. Latest edition 1988.

Taviani, P.E. *I Viaggi di Colombo. La Grande Scoperta*. 2 vols. Novara: Istituto Geografico De Agostini, 1984. Latest edition 1992. As with the preceding work, there are various editions in foreign languages. English translation by L.F. Farina and M. Beckwith.

Taviani, P.E. "Si perfezionò in Castiglia il grande disegno di Colombo." *Presencia Italiana en Andalucía. Siglos XIV-XVII. Actas del I Coloquio Hispano-Italiano 7-9 de junio 1983*, 11-20. Seville, 1985.

Taviani, P.E. "Brevi cenni sulla residenza di Colombo in Andalusia." *La Presenza italiana in Andalusia nel basso medioevo...*, op. cit., 7-12.

Taviani, P.E. "Ancora sulle vicende di Colombo in Castiglia." *Presencia Italiana en Andalucía...*, op. cit., 221-248.

Taviani, P.E. "Come Cristoforo Colombo maturò la grande idea." *Columbus 92*, 2 (1986), no. 10: 27-31.

Taviani, P.E. "La personalità e gli intenti di Cristoforo Colombo nella scoperta delle Americhe." *Convegno I diritti dell'uomo e la pace nel pensiero di F. de Vitoria e B. de las Casas, Roma 1986*, 15-30. Milan: Massimo, n. d.

Taviani, P.E. *Cristoforo Colombo. The Genius of the Sea*. Rome: Ministero per i Beni Culturali e Ambientali, 1990. Other editions in Spanish, Portuguese, and French.

More specifically we cite here certain writings that have expanded our understanding of the problem of the influence that his knowledge of the cartographic works of Henricus Martellus, with their retention of Ptolemaic notions, may have had on Columbus's ideas, while his possible relationship with Martin Behaim must have been much less certain. The following references relate to these topics:

Almagià, R. "I mappamondi di Enrico Martello e alcuni concetti geografici di Cristoforo Colombo." *La Bibliofilia* 42 (1940): 288-311.

Davies, A. "Origins of Columbian Cosmography." In *Studi Colombiani* 2: 59-67. Genoa: Civico Istituto Colombiano, 1952.

Davies, A. "Behaim, Martellus, and Columbus." *The Geographical Journal* 143 (1977): 451-459.

De Gandia, E. "Claudio Ptolomeo, Colón y la exploración de la India americana." *Investigaciones y Ensayos de la Academia Nacional de la Historia* 3 (1972): 35-87.

Gallez, P.J. "Les grandes fleuves d'Amérique du Sud sur le Ptolomée londonien de Henry d'Hammer (1489)." *Erdkunde* 29 (1975): 241-247.

Luzzana Caraci, I. "L'opera cartografica di Enrico Martello e la *prescoperta* dell'America." Rivista Geografica Italiana 83 (1976): 335-344.

Luzzana Caraci, I. "Il Planisfero Enrico Martello della Yale University Library e i Fratelli Colombo." *Rivista Geografica Italiana* 85 (1978): 132-143.

Nunn, G.E. *The Columbus and Magellan Concepts of South American Geography*. Glenside: Privately printed, 1932.

Ravenstein, E.G. *Martin Behaim, His Life and His Globe*. London: G. Philip & Son, 1908.

Vacca, G. "Martin Behaim e il suo globo." *Rivista Geografica Italiana* 16 (1909): 787-790.

All that has been said must be placed in the general context of geographical knowledge derived from the explorations of the Atlantic in the fifteenth century. Related essential works that also discuss cartography are:

Babcock, W.H. "Legendary Islands of the Atlantic: A Study in Medieval Geography." *American Geographical Research* 8 (1922): 196 ff.

Broc, N. *La géographie de la Renaissance*. Paris: Les Editions du C.T.H.S., 1986.

DE GANDIA, E. "Viajes marítimos anteriores a Colón." *Historia de la Nación Argentina*, 237-238. Buenos Aires, 1939.

FERNANDES COSTA, M. *As navegaçoes atlanticôs no seculo XV*. Lisbon: Institut de Cultura Portuguesa, 1979.

FERNANDEZ-ARMESTO, F.R. "Atlantic Exploration before Columbus: The Evidence of Maps." *Renaissance and Modern Studies* 30 (1986): 12-34.

HARRISSE, H. *The Discovery of North America*. London, 1892.

MAGALHAES GODINHO, V. *Os descobrimentos e a economia mundial*. Lisbon: Arcadia, 1983.

RAMOS PÉREZ, D. *Los contactos transatlánticos decisivos como precedentes del viaje de Colón*. Vallodolid: Casa Museo de Colón, 1972.

RAMOS PÉREZ, D. *Los viajes españoles de descubrimiento y de rescate*. Valladolid: Casa Museo de Colón, 1981.

RANDLES, W.G. "Le Nouveau Monde, l'Autre Monde et la Pluralité des Mondes." *Actas Congr. Intern. Hist. Descobrimentos, Lisboa 1961*, 4: 347-382.

CHRISTOPHER AND BARTOLOMEO COLUMBUS, CARTOGRAPHERS

The Columbus brothers' activity as cartographers is barely documented, yet that of Christopher in particular is mentioned, usually cursorily, in many, indeed in almost all, of his biographies and in works of a general nature devoted to his life and undertakings. In addition to the citations included in the volumes of the Nuova Raccolta Colombiana, mentioned earlier, we indicate here some of the main works of this kind, especially those addressing major problematical points:

ARRANZ, L. *Don Diego Colón, Almirante, Virrey y Gobernador de las Indias*. Madrid: Inst. Gonzalo Fernández de Oviedo, 1982.

LUZZANA CARACI, I. *Colombo vero e falso*. Genoa: SAGEP, 1989.

LUZZANA CARACI, I. "El verdadero y falso Colón." *Boletín de la Real Academia Sevillana de Buenas Letras* 18 (1990): 91-107.

MORISON, S.E. *Admiral of the Ocean Seas: A Life of Christopher Columbus*. Boston: Little Brown and Co., 1942. New ed., 1951. Italian translation by A. BALLARDINI, *Cristoforo Colombo Ammiraglio del Mare Oceano*. Bologna: Il Mulino, 1962.

MORISON, S.E. "Columbus as a Navigator." *Atti Convegno Internazionale Studi Colombiani, Genova 1951*, 2: 39-48. Genoa, 1952.

MORISON, S.E. *Christopher Columbus, Mariner*. Boston: Little Brown, 1955. Italian translation by A. LANDI. *Cristoforo Colombo*. Milan: Mondadori, 1958.

THACHER, J.B. *Christopher Columbus: His Life, His Work, His Remains as Revealed by Original Printed and Manuscript Works*. 3 vols. New York: G.P. Putnam & Son, 1903-1904.

VIGNAUD, H. *Histoire critique de la grande entreprise de Christophe Colomb*. 2 vols. Paris: Welter, 1911.

With regard to the maps of the Columbus brothers in particular, or rather to the ones attributed to them or inspired by them and believed to be derived from their works, especially the famous map in the Bibliothèque Nationale in Paris, the following should be consulted:

ALMAGIÀ, R. "Una carta attribuita a Cristoforo Colombo." *Rendiconti della R. Accademia dei Lincei, Classe di Scienze Morali, Storiche e Filiologiche*, series 6, vol. 1 (1925): 749-773.

ALMAGIÀ, R. "Il mappamondo di Piri Reis e la carta di Colombo del 1498." *Bollettino della Società Geografica Italiana* 71 (1943): 442-449.

ALTOLAGUIRRE Y DUVALE, A. DE. "La carta de navegar atribuida a Cristóbal Colón por M. de La Roncière historiador de la marina francesa." *Boletín de la Real Sociedad Geogr. Madrid* 65 (1925): 325-341 and *Boletín de la Real Academia de la Historia* 87 (1925): 439-453.

BALLESTREROS BERETTA, A. "Una carta inédita de C. Colón." *Revista de Indias* 9 (1949), no. 37-38: 489-506.

CARACI, G. "Una carta attribuita a Colombo." *Rivista Geografica Italiana* 33 (1925): 280-286.

CARACI, G. "Sulla data della pretesa carta di Colombo." *Atti X Congresso Geografico Italiano, Milano 1927*, 1: 331-335. Milan, 1927.

CARACI, G. "Cristoforo Colombo e la scuola cartografica genovese." *Civiltà Moderna* 6: 455-465. Florence, 1938.

CARACI, G. "In tema di cartografia colombiana." *Memorie Geogr. dell'Istituto Sc. Geogr. e Cart., Facoltà di Magistero, Roma* 7 (1961): 223-263.

CLAPAREDE, A. DE. "Une carte de géographie faite par Christophe Colomb." *Le Globe. Bulletin de la Société de Géographie de Genève* 5 (1894): 45-47.

DE LOLLIS, C. "La carta di Colombo." *La Cultura* 4 (Rome 1924-1925): 749-775.

FERRO, G. "Le carte di Colombo." *Ulisse 2000*, supp. to nos. 33-34 (Rome, 1986): 36-38.

GALLOIS, L. "Cartographie et géographie médiévales. Une carte colombienne." *Annales de Géographie* 34 (1925): 13-209.

GARCÍA GALLO, S. "Sobre un Portulano de 1500. Lo dibujó Colón?" *Revista General de Marina* 158 (Madrid 1960): 27-29.

GRAVIER, G. "Découverte d'une carte de Christophe Colomb." *Bulletin de la Société Normande de Géographie* 16 (Rouen 1894): 24-31.

HENRIQUEZ Y CARVAJAL, F. "El mapa de Colón." *Cuba contemporanea* 36 (Havana 1924): 24-31.

ISNARD, A. "La carte prétendue de Christophe Colomb." *Revue de Questions Historiques* 6: 317-335; 7: 297-321 (Orléans 1925). Republished in Orléans: Tip. Loiret, 1925.

KAHLE, P. "Piri Re'is, und seine Bahriye." *Beiträge zur Hist. G. Kulturg. vornehmlich des Orients* (1929): 60-76.

KAHLE, P. "Impronte colombiane in una carta turca del 1513." *La Cultura Moderna* (1931): 774-785.

KAHLE, P. "A Lost Map of Columbus." *The Geographical Review* 23 (1933): 621-638.

KRETSCHMER, K. "Die verschollene Kolumbuskarte von 1498 in einer türkischen Weltkarte von 1513." *Petermanns Mitteilungen* 80 (Gotha 1934): 48-50.

LALOY, E. "Une Carte de Christophe Colomb." *Mercure de France* (Paris 1926): 5-14, 101-110.

MANFRONI, C. "La carta di Colombo." *Rivista Marittima* 58 (1925): 705-713.

MANFRONI, C. "Di una presunta carta di Colombo." *Atti R. Istituto Veneto, Scienze, Lettere ed Arti* 84 (1924-1925), pt. 2: 361 ff.

PEUCKER, C. "Discovery of a Map by Columbus." *The Geographical Journal* (1894): 44-45.

PIERSANTELLI, G. *Lo schizzo cartografico di Colombo e il S. Cristoforo nella carta del suo pilota.* Genoa: Civico Istituto Colombiano, 1955.

REVELLI, P. "Cristoforo Colombo cartografo." *Comptes Rendus du Congrès Interna/tional de Géographie (Amsterdam 1938)*, 2: 194-195.

RONCIÈRE, C. DE LA. "Une carte inspirée par Christophe Colomb." *La Géographie* 41 (1924): 598.

RONCIÈRE, C. DE LA. *La carte de Christophe Colomb par Charles de La Roncière... texte en français et en anglais.* Paris: Les Editions Historiques, 1924.

RONCIÈRE, C. DE LA. "Colombo, sua carta illustrata." *Rivista Geografica Italiana* 32 (1925): 120.

RONCIÈRE, C. DE LA. "Le livre de chevet et la carte de C. Colomb." *Revue des Deux Mondes* (Paris 1931): 423-441.

SKELTON, R.A. "The Cartography of Columbus' First Voyage." In *The Journal of C. Columbus*, edited by C. JANE and A. VIGNERAS. London: A. Blond and Orion Press, 1960.

STANTON, S.M. "The Admiral's Map: What Was It? And Who Was the Admiral?" *Isis* 22 (1935): 512-515.

TAVIANI, P.E. *Cristoforo Colombo, la genesi della grande scoperta.* Op. cit., 1: 198-211; 2: 235-256.

VENTURA, A. *Gli Stati Italiani di Piri Re'Is. La cartografia turca alla corte di Solimano il Magnifico.* Lecce: Capone Ed., 1991.

VIGNAUD, H. "Les cartes et sphères attribuées à Colomb." In *Histoire critique de la Grande Entreprise de Christophe Colomb*, app. 3. Paris: Welter, 1911.

Literature specifically about Bartolomeo Columbus and his cartographic work, on the other hand, is scarce:

ALBONICO, A. "Bartolomeo Colombo, adelantado mayor de las Indias." *La Presenza italiana in Andalusia nel basso medioevo...*, op. cit., 51-70.

ALMAGIÀ, R. "Intorno a una carta di Bartolomeo Colombo." *Rivista Geografica Italiana* 42 (1935): 29-53.

ALMAGIÀ, R. "Intorno a quattro codici fiorentini ed uno ferrarese dell'erudito veneziano Alessandro Zorzi." *La Bibliofilia* 38 (1936): 313-343.

BIGELOW, J. "The So-called Bartholomew Columbus Map of 1506." *The Geographical Review* (1935): 643-656.

NUNN, G.E. "The Three Maplets Attributed to Bartholomew Columbus." *Imago Mundi* 9 (1967): 12-22.

WIESER, R.V. "La carte de Bartholomé Colomb concernant le quatrième voyage de l'Amiral." *Bulletin de la Société Royale de Géographie d'Anvers* 19 (1894): 5-21. Review by CUELENEER, M. "Die Karte des Bartolomeo Colombo über die vierte Reise des Admirals." *Revue de l'Instruction Publique en Belgique*, 37, no. 5 (Ghent 1894).

Finally, with regard to the handwriting and the vocabulary used in the writings of the Columbus brothers, including the *Postille*, and their reflection in the maps attributed to them, see the following:

ARCE FERNÁNDEZ, J. "Problemi linguistici inerenti il diario di Cristoforo Colombo." *Atti del Convegno Internazionale Studi Colombiani, Genova 1973*, 53-75. Genoa, 1974.

BECCARIA, G.L. "Tra Italia, Spagna e Nuovo Mondo nell'età della Scoperta: viaggi di parole." *Lettere Italiane* 2 (Florence 1985): 177-203.

BERTONE, G. "Appunti sugli italianismi linguistici di Colombo." *Columbeis II* (Genoa 1987): 17-29.

CARACI, G. "Il presunto *lusismo castiglianizzante* della lingua di Colombo." In *Tra Scopritori e Critici*, 147-205. Rome: De Sanctis, 1963-1964.

CARACI, G. and I. LUZZANA CARACI, "Il latino di Colombo." *Atti I Conv. Int. Studi Amer., Genova-Rapallo 1974*, 87-93. Genoa, 1976.

CHIARENO, O. "Postille linguistiche al *Diario de a bordo* di Cristoforo Colombo." *Bollettino dell'Istituto di Lingue Estere* (Genoa 1973): 147-156.

CHIARENO, O. "Recenti studi sulla lingua scritta di Colombo." *Atti I Conv. Int. Studi Amer., Genova-Rapallo 1974, 107-117. Genoa, 1976.*

CONTI, M. "Le postille di Cristoforo Colombo alla Naturalis Historia di Plinio il Vecchio." In *Scritti in onore del prof. Paolo Emilio Taviani, 3 (Temi Colombiani)*: 75-92. Genoa: Facoltà di Scienze Politiche, Università di Genova, 1983-1986.

DAMONTE, M. "Le lingue di Cristoforo Colombo." *Columbeis II* (Genoa 1987): 9-18.

FERRO, G. "Termini geografici e marinareschi nel *Diario di Bordo* di Colombo." *Actas del II Coloquio Hispano-Italiano, Presencia italiana en Andalucía, siglos XIV-XVII...*, op. cit., 143-163.

STREICHER, F. "Die Kolumbus-Originale. Eine paläographische Studie." *Spanische Forschungen der Gorresgesellschaft* 1 (Münster 1928): 195-249.

TAVIANI, P.E. "Un breve commento sul tema della lingua di Colombo. 'Le lingue di Colombo. Tavola Rotonda.'" *Columbeis II* (Genoa 1987): 37-42.

As for Columbus's instruments, the issue of the use of the Taoleta de Martelojo has been recently discussed by the following:

BALDACCI, O. "Una *Taoleta de Marteloio*, fatta da Cristoforo Colombo." *Pubblicazioni dell'Istituto di Geografia, Università di Roma "La Sapienza"*, series B (1985): 1-22.

BALDACCI, O. "La *Taoleta de Marteloio*, dal Mediterraneo all'Atlantico." *Presencia Italiana en Andalucía, siglos XIV-XVII...*, op. cit., 361-375.

THE FIRST DEPICTIONS OF AMERICA AND THE NAUTICAL CHARTS OF THE SIXTEENTH CENTURY

The literature about the first depictions of America and the nautical charts of the end of the fifteenth and early decades of the sixteenth century is copious. Of these we will limit ourselves to citing the following:

ALMAGIÀ, R. "Le prime conoscenze dell'America e la cartografia italiana." *Atti XXII Congr. It. Americ. (Rome, 1926)*, 2: 589-592. Rome, 1928.

ALMAGIÀ, R. "I mappamondi di Francesco Roselli." *Rivista Geografica Italiana* 46 (1929): 90-92.

ALMAGIÀ, R. "The Atlas of Pietro Coppo." *Imago Mundi* 7 (1950): 48.

ALMAGIÀ, R. "On the Cartographic Work of Francesco Rosselli." *Imago Mundi* 8 (1951): 27-34.

BARREIRO MEIRO, R. "Algo sobre la carta de Juan de la Cosa." *Revista General de Marina* 183 (1972): 3-8.

BELLIO, V. "Notizia delle più antiche carte geografiche che si trovano in Italia riguardanti l'America." *Raccolta Colombiana*, op. cit., pt. 4, vol. 2: 108-111.

CHIAPELLI, F., ed. *First Images of America*. 2 vols. Los Angeles: University of California Press, 1975.

CRINÓ, S. "Schizzi cartografici inediti dei primi anni della scoperta dell'America." *Rivista Maritima*, supp. to fasc. of November 1930.

CRINÓ, S. "I planisferi di Francesco Rosselli dell'epoca delle grandi scoperte geografiche. A proposito della scoperta di nuove carte del cartografo fiorentino." *La Bibliofilia* 41 (Florence 1939): 381-405.

DE PALMA, M.T. "Immagini del Nuovo Mondo da fonti cartografiche. Illustrazioni." In *Iconografia Colombiana*, op. cit., 421-458. In addition to the many beautiful reproductions this work includes a rich and careful bibliography.

DEGRASSI, A. "Di Pietro Coppo e delle sue opere." *L'Archeografo Triestino*, series 3, vol. 11 (1924): 319-373.

DEL BADIA, J. "La bottega di Alessandro di Francesco Rosselli merciaio e stampatore." *Miscellanea Fiorentina di Erudizione e Storia* 3 (1894): 24-30.

DERBY, O.A. "The Egerton Map of Early American Discoveries." *Geographical Journal* 38 (1911): 494-504.

DESTOMBES, M. "Nautical Charts Attributed to Verrazano (1525-1528)." *Imago Mundi* 11 (1954): 57-66.

DIMITROV, B. "Carta nautica di Andrea Benincasa, Ancona 1508." In *Manoscritti slavi, documenti e carte riguardanti la storia bulgara della Biblioteca Apostolica Vaticana e dell'Archivio Segreto Vaticano (IX-XVII secolo)*, vol. 29, Plate LXXII. Sofia, 1979.

DURO, C.F. "Mapamundo e Juan de la Cosa." *El Centenario* 1 (1892): 245-255.

DURST, A. *Carta nautica di Andrea Benincasa (Borgiano VIII) 1508*. Milan: Jaca Book, 1986.

ERRERA, C. "Di Pietro Coppo e della sua opera *De toto orbe* (1520)." *Atti Acc. Ist. Cl. Scienze Mor. Rend.*, series 3, no. 8 (1933-1934): 26-27.

FERRO, G. Introduction to the volume *Le "Tabulae" di Pietro Coppo (1524-1526)*. Izola, Yugoslavia: Casa di Cultura di Isola, 1986.

FERRO, G. "Pietro Coppo e la sua opera cartografica." *Rivista Geografica Italiana* 97 (1990): 243-249.

GALLOIS, L. "Une nouvelle carte marine du XVIe siècle. Le portulan de Nicolas de Caverio." *Bulletin de la Société de Géographie de Lyon* 9 (1890): 97-119.

HEAWOOD, E. "The World Maps Before and After Magellan's Voyage." *Geographical Journal* 57 (1921): 431-478.

HEAWOOD, E. "A Hitherto Unknown World-map of A.D. 1506." *Geographical Journal* 62 (1923): 279-293.

JOHNSON, A. *America Explored: A Cartographical History of the Exploration of North America*. New York: Viking Press, 1974.

KISH, G. "The Mural Atlas of Caprarola." *Imago Mundi* 10 (1953): 52 ff.

KRETSCHMER, K. *Die Entdeckung Amerikas in Ihrer Bedeutung für die Geschichte des Weltbildes*. Berlin, 1892.

KUNSTMANN, F. *Atlas zur Entdeckungsgeschichte Amerikas*. Munich, 1859.

LAGO, L. "Le conoscenze geografiche di un mondo in transizione nell'opera di Pietro Coppo (1469-1566). *Atti del IV Convegno Internazionale di Studi Colombiani, Genova 1985*, 2: 437-468. Genoa, 1987.

LAGO, L. "Nota introduttiva a *Il Portolano* (1528) di Pietro Coppo." *Speculum Orbis* 1: 1-44. Trieste: Ed. Lint, 1985.

LAGO, L. and ROSSIT, C.L. *Pietro Coppo. Le "Tabulae" (1524-1526). Una preziosa raccolta cartografica custodita a Pirano. Note e Documenti per la storia della cartografia*. 2 vols. Collana degli Atti del Centro di Ricerche Storiche di Rovigno 7. Trieste: Ed. Lint, 1984-1986.

MAGNAGHI, A. "La prima rappresentazione delle Filippine e delle Molucche dopo il ritorno della spedizione di Magellano nella carta costruita nel 1522 da Nuno García de Toreno, conservata nella Biblioteca di S.M. il Re in Torino." *Atti X Congresso Geografico Italiano, Milano 1927*, 1: 293-307. Milan, 1927.

MARTINEZ, R.C. "Aportación al estudio de la carta de Juan de la Cosa." In *La Géographie du Moyen Age...*, edited by M. PELLETIER, op. cit., 149-162.

MILANESI, M. *Tolomeo sostituito. Studi di storia delle conoscenze geografiche nel XVI secolo.* Milan: Unicopli, 1984. Also includes the second half of the century.

MILANESI, M. "La cartografia del Cinquecento e la nascita della tradizione colombiana." In *Iconografia Colombiana*, op. cit., 71-98.

NUNN, G.E. *Mappemonde de Juan de la Cosa: A Critical Investigation of Its Date.* Jenkintown: George H. Beans Library, 1934.

REVELLI, P. "Un cartografo genovese amico a Cristoforo Colombo: Nicolò Caveri." *Rendiconti Accademia dei Lincei, Classe di Scienze morali, storiche, filologiche*, series 8, no. 2 (1947): 449-458.

ROTH, C. "Judah Abenzara's Map of the Mediterranean World, 1500." *Studies in Bibliography and Booklore* 9 (1970): 116-120.

ROUKEMA, E. "Some Remarks on the la Cosa Map." *Imago Mundi* 14 (1959): 38-54.

STEVENSON, E.L. *Maps Illustrating Early Discovery and Explorations in America 1502-1530.* New Brunswick, NJ: 1903-1906.

For what concerns Ligurian cartography in particular, it is useful to keep in mind the bibliography about the Maggiolo dynasty:

ASOLE TERROSU, A. "Su una carta nautica di tipo medioevale realizzata nel 1575 da Giovan'Antonio da Maiolo." In *Studi in onore di Osvaldo Baldacci*, op. cit., 145-160.

AVEZAC, M.A.P. D'. "Encore un monument géographique parmi les manuscrits de la Bibliothèque d'Altamira: atlas hydrographique de 1511 du génois Vesconte de Maggiòlo." *Annales des voyages, de la géographie, de l'histoire et de l'archéologie* 3 (1870): 20-32.

CARACI, G. "Un Atlante sconosciuto di Vesconte Maiollo (1548)." *L'Universo* 7 (1926): 4-7.

CARACI, G. "Carta nautica di Giovan'Antonio da Maiolo quondam Visconte, 1577." *La Bibliofilia* 28 (1926): 40-44.

CARACI, G. "Di un atlante poco noto di Vesconte Maggiolo." *La Bibliofilia* 36 (1935): 1-29.

CARACI, G. "Sulla data del Planisfero di Vesconte Maggiolo, conservato a Fano." *Memorie Geogr. Fac. Magistero Roma* 2 (1956): 109-128.

CARACI, G. "La produzione cartografica di Vesconte Maggiolo (1511-1549) ed il nuovo mondo." *Memorie Geogr. Fac. Magistero Roma* 4 (1958): 221-289.

FERRETTO, A. "I cartografi Maggiolo oriundi di Rapallo." *Atti della Società Ligure di Storia Patria* 52 (1924): 55-83.

GROSJEAN, G., ed. *Vesconte Maggiolo, "Atlante nautico del 1512": Seeatlas vom Jahre 1512.* Dietikon and Zurich: Urs Graf, 1979.

PAMPALONI, C. "1561, Jacopo Maggiolo. Carta nautica raffigurante il Mediterraneo e i mari adiacenti." Entry in *Carte nautiche da musei e biblioteche della Liguria*, edited by G. FERRO, op. cit., 38.

PAZ Y MELIÁ, A. "Una mapa de Vizconde Maiollo de 1535." *Revista de archivos, bibliotecas y museos* 12 (1908): 170-171.

RUGE, W. *Älteres Kartographisches Material in deutschen Bibliotheken*. Königliche Gesellschaft des Wissens. Nachrich. Phil.-hist. Klasse 1911. Contains a brief, but exact, description of the Atlas of Vesconte Maggiolo.

The following writings on Battista Agnese are also worth consideration:

ALMAGIÀ, R. "Una carta del 1514 attribuita a Battista Agnese." *Rivista Geografica Italiana* 56 (1949): 167-168.

Atlante nautico e terrestre. L'Atlante manoscritto della scuola di Battista Agnese conservato a Bergamo. Clusone: Banca Popolare di Bergamo, 1984.

CARACI, G. "Di due carte di Battista Agnese." *Rivista Geografica Italiana* 35 (1928): 227-234.

FERRO, G. "L'Atlante manoscritto della Scuola di Battista Agnese conservato a Bergamo." *Rivista Geografica Italiana* 81 (1984): 501-520.

KRETSCHMER, K. "Die Atlanten des Battista Agnese." *Zeitschrift der Gesellschaft für Erdkunde zu Berlin* 31 (1896): 362-368.

MAGNAGHI, A. "L'Atlante manoscritto di Battista Agnese della Biblioteca Reale di Torino." *Rivista Geografica Italiana* 15 (1908): 65-77, 135-148.

MALAVIALLE, L. "Notice sur un portulan manuscrit de Battista Agnese conservé à la Bibliothèque de l'Université de Montpellier." *Bulletin de la Société Languedocienne de Géographie* 31 (1908): 7-88, 141-203.

PAMPALONI, C. "Seconda metà del secolo XVI. Battista Agnese (o scuola), *Tavola di atlante nautico raffigurante il Mar Nero*." Note in *Carte nautiche da musei e biblioteche della Liguria*, edited by G. FERRO, op. cit., 52.

WAGNER, H.R. *The Manuscript Atlases of Battista Agnese*. Papers of the Bibliographical Society of America 25 (1931).

WAGNER, H.R. "Additions to the Manuscript Atlases of Battista Agnese." *Imago Mundi* 4 (1947): 29-32.

WINSOR, J. "Battista Agnese and American Cartography in the XVI Century." *Proceedings of the Massachusetts Historic Society* (1897): 372-385.

The following works are about other sixteenth century cartographers, either Ligurian or in some way related to the Ligurian tradition, and about other issues pertinent to this period:

ASTENGO, C. "Spionaggio e cartografia nel XVI secolo." *Annali di Ricerche e Studi di Geografia* 42 (1986): 1-6.

ASTENGO, C. "Le carte nautiche manoscritte conservate presso la Biblioteca Universitaria di Genova." *Annali di Ricerche e Studi* (1981): 11-21.

DE GRAZIA, P. "L'Atlante di Bartolomeo Olives (1561)." *Atti IX Congresso Geogr. Ital., Genova 1924*, 2: 308-311.

DURO, C.F. "Atlas inédito de Juan Olives (1592)." *Boletín de la Sociedad Geográfica de Madrid* 27 (1889): 287-289.

ENRILE, A. "Di un atlante nautico disegnato in Messina nel 1596 da Giovanni Oliva e conservato oggi nella Biblioteca del Comune di Palermo." *Bollettino della Società Geografica Italiana*, series 5, no. 4 (1905): 64-75.

IOLI GIGANTE, A. "Le officine di carte nautiche a Messina nei secoli XVI e XVII." *Archivio Storico Messinese*, series 3, no. 30 (1979): 103-113.

MONGINI, G.M. *Una singolare carta nautica "doppia", a firma di Joannes Oliva (Livorno 1618)*. Pubblicazioni dell'Istituto di Geografia, Series B (Geographical History), 5. Rome: Facoltà di Lettere e Filosofia, Università di Roma, 1975.

PAMPALONI, C. "1557, Ibanet Panades, Carta nautica raffigurante il Mediterraneo e il Mar Nero." Note in *Carte nautiche da musei e biblioteche della Liguria*, edited by G. FERRO, op. cit., 34.

PAMPALONI, C. "1571, Joan Martines, Carta nautica raffigurante il Mediterraneo orientale e il Mar Nero." Note in *Carte nautiche da musei e biblioteche della Liguria*, edited by G. FERRO, op. cit., 40.

PAMPALONI, C. "1571, Joan Martines, Carta nautica raffigurante il Mediterraneo centrale e il Mar Adriatico." Note in *Carte nautiche da musei e biblioteche della Liguria*, edited by G. FERRO, op. cit., 42.

PAMPALONI, C. "1571, Joan Martines, Carta nautica raffigurante l'Oceano Atlantico e le coste occidentali dell'Europa." Note in *Carte nautiche da musei e biblioteche della Liguria*, edited by G. FERRO, op. cit., 44.

PAMPALONI, C. "1571, Joan Martines, Carta nautica raffigurante l'Oceano Atlantico e le coste nord-occidentali dell'Africa." Note in *Carte nautiche da musei e biblioteche della Liguria*, edited by G. FERRO, op. cit., 46.

PAMPALONI, C. "1590, Joan Martines, Carta nautica del Mediterraneo." Note in *Carte nautiche da musei e biblioteche della Liguria*, edited by G. FERRO, op. cit., 48.

PAMPALONI, C. "Matteo Prunes, Carta nautica raffigurante il Mediterraneo." Note in *Carte nautiche da musei e biblioteche della Liguria*, edited by G. FERRO, op. cit., 50.

PAMPALONI, C. "Seconda metà del secolo XVI, Girolamo Costo, Carta nautica raffigurante il bacino del Mediterraneo, con tratti dell'Atlantico e del Mar del Nord." Note in *Carte nautiche da musei e biblioteche della Liguria*, edited by G. FERRO, op. cit., 54.

PAMPALONI, C. "Seconda metà del secolo XVI, Atlante nautico di tredici tavole." Note in *Carte nautiche da musei e biblioteche della Liguria*, edited by G. FERRO, op. cit., 56.

PERSANTELLI, G. *L'atlante di carte marine di Francesco Ghisolfi e la storia della pittura in Genova nel Cinquecento*, 1-7. Genoa, 1947.

LIGURIAN CARTOGRAPHICAL DOCUMENTS
FROM THE DECADENCE PERIOD

There are few important works specifically about nautical cartography of the seventeenth century apart from the writings already mentioned by G. GUARNIERI, G. CARACI, and A. IOLI GIGANTE.

For Monno in particular, the following should be mentioned:

ANDRIANI, G. "La Liguria nel *Portolano* di Giov. Francesco Monno (1633)." *Atti della Società Ligustica di Scienze Naturali e Geografiche* (Genoa 1916): 105-106.

PAMPALONI, C. "1633, Giò Francesco Monno di Monaco, *Arte della vera navigazione...*" Note in *Carte nautiche da musei e biblioteche della Liguria*, edited by G. FERRO, op. cit., 66.

PUNCUH, D. *I manoscritti della Raccolta Durazzo.* Genoa: SAGEP, 1979. Includes mention of a "Portolano" by G.F. Monno.

RAINERO, R.H. "L'*Arte della vera navigatione* di Giovanni Francesco Monno e la sua importanza." *Imago et mensura mundi...*, op. cit., 71-80.

The following works, on the other hand, have to do with Saetone:

BENISCELLI, G. "Custodito nel Comune di Albissola Marina un antichissimo *portolano* del Mediterraneo." La Casana 3 (1975): 22-30.

FERRO, G. "L'Atlante portolanico di Guglielmo Saetone conservato ad Albissola." *Bollettino della Società Geografica Italiana*, series 7, no. 10 (1957): 457-477.

STRADA, E. "Di due sconosciuti atlanti nautici manoscritti di Guglielmo Saetone." *Atti XV Congresso Geografico Italiano, Torino 1950*: 787-790. Turin, 1952.

The following works offer evidence about the possible Ligurian ancestry of the Cavallini family:

ALMAGIÀ, R. "Note intorno alla tradizione della cartografia nautica a Livorno." *Rivista di Livorno* (1958): 304-312.

ASTENGO, C. "Giovanni Battista Cavallini cartografo genovese." *Annali di Ricerche e Studi di Geografia* 43 (1987): 1-25.

CALEGARI, A. "Carte nautiche eseguite in Livorno da Giovanni Battista e Pietro Cavallini." *Bollettino Storico Livornese* 3 (1939): 1-5.

CARACI, G. "Giovanni Battista e Pietro Cavallini." *Bollettino Storico Livornese* (1939): 380-388.

GUARNIERI, G. "Livorno e il tramonto della cartografia nautica medievale." *Bollettino Cons. Prov. Econ. Corp.* (Livorno 1932): 1-6, 716-739. Republished in *Scritti geografici...*, op. cit., 179-195.

GUARNIERI, G. *La scuola livornese di cartografia nautica.* Pisa: Ed. Giardini, 1975.

MAGNAGHI, A. "Carte nautiche esistenti a Volterra." *Rivista Geografica Italiana* 4 (1897): 34-40.

PAMPALONI, C. "1639. Giovanni B. Cavallini. Carta nautica raffigurante il bacino nel Mediterraneo con il Mar Nero." Note in *Carte nautiche da musei e biblioteche della Liguria*, edited by G. FERRO, op. cit., 68.

PINNA, M. "Sulle carte nautiche prodotte a Livorno nei secoli XVI e XVII." *Rivista Geografica Italiana* 84 (1977): 279-314.

Finally, the following are other writings about the history of cartography in the seventeenth century in Liguria, including map makers from outside the region who may have worked and left traces there:

ASTENGO, C. "Una carta nautica inedita di Placido Caloiro e Oliva nella Biblioteca Civica di Savona." *Atti e Memorie della Società Savonese di Storia Patria* 15 (1981): 167-170.

CONTI, S. "Una carta nautica inedita di Placido Caloiro et Oliva del 1657." *Pubblicazioni Serie Geostorica, Istituto Geografia, Facoltà di Lettere, Università di Roma.* Rome, 1978.

CONTI, S. "Un'originale carta nautica del 1617 a firma Placidus Caloiro et Oliva." *Geografia* (1986): 77-86.

PAMPALONI, C. "1639, Placido Caloiro e Oliva. Carta nautica raffigurante il Mediterraneo con qualche tratto costiero dei mari adiacenti." Note in *Carte nautiche da musei e biblioteche della Liguria*, edited by G. FERRO, op. cit., 70.

RONCHETTA, T. "Una carta nautica di Placido Caloiro e Oliva del 1639." *Annali di Ricerche e Studi di Geografia* 41 (1985): 157-180.

INDEXES

The index compilation system was designed and implemented by the Cultural Activity Division of the Italian Encyclopedia Institute – founded by G. Treccani – Rome.

INDEX OF NAMES

MAGGIOLO, GIACOMO: 140, 142, 143

MAGGIOLO, GIOVANNI ANTONIO: 140, 142

MAGGIOLO, GIOVANNI ANTONIO the younger: 142

MAGGIOLO, NICOLO: 142, 143

MAGGIOLO, VESCONTE: 139-143

MAGNAGHI, A.: 22-3, 31, 50-52, 54, 70, 145

MAIOLO, see MAGGIOLO

MALFANTE, ANTONIO: 56, 154

MALIPIERO, DOMENICO: 104

MALOCELLO, LANZAROTTO: 57

MANDEVILLE, JOHN OF: 18

MANFRED, KING OF SICILY: 64

MARCHENA: ANTONIO DE: 102

MARINELLI, G.: 152

MARINUS OF TYRE: 13, 38, 105, 126, 129

MARTELLUS, HENRICUS GERMANUS: 90, 91, 122, 124-128, 157

MARTINELLI, FRANCESCO: 148

MARTINEZ (Martines), JOAN: 63, 132, 136, 146

MECIA DE VILADESTES: 78

MEDICI, DE', family: 35, 57, 74

MERCATOR, G. (Gerhard Kremer): 132, 146, 155

MOLLAT DU JOURDIN, M.: 71

MONNO, GIOVANNI FRANCESCO: 148, 149

MORALES, FRANCISCO: 103

MOTZO, B. R.: 74

MUSAMELIDUS: 82

MUSSO, G. G.: 61

NICHOLAS V (T. Parentucelli): 82

NICOLINUS DE SANCTO PROSPERO: 59

NICUESA, DIEGO DE: 116

NORDENSKIÖLD, A. E.: 21, 35, 52, 117

ODERICO, NICOLÒ: 138

OLIVES (Oliva), family: 132, 136, 146

OLIVES, BARTOLOMEO: 133

OPICINO DE CANISTRIS: 29, 52

ORTELIUS (Ortelio, Oertel), ABRAHAM: 79, 147

OVIEDO Y VALDES, GONZALO FERNANDEZ: 98, 100, 116

PAGANI, L.: 30, 34, 66, 67, 106

PANDIANI, E.: 120

PARETO, BARTOLOMEO DE: 60, 81, 82, 137

PARMENIDES: 17

PELLETIER, M.: 21, 112

PERESTRELO, BARTOLOMEO: 97

PERRINO VESCONTE: 67

PESCHEL, O.: 21

PETER MARTYR OF ANGHIERA: 79, 118-9

PETRUS PEREGRINUS: 46, 54, 62

PETTI BALBI, G.: 58-60, 79

PICCOLOMINI, ANDREA SILVIO: 61

PIERSANTELLI, G.: 67

PINZÓN, MARTÍN ALONSO: 99, 100

PIRI RE'IS: 103-4, 119

PIUS II (Enea Silvio Piccolomini): 105, 126, 127

PLINY THE ELDER: 127

POLO, MARCO: 24, 29, 36, 41, 90, 110, 125, 127, 152, 156

PRESTER JOHN: 31

PRUNES, family: 134

PTOLEMY: 13, 14, 36, 37, 39, 41, 42, 62, 75, 83, 84, 87, 97, 105, 110, 122, 124-126, 129, 133, 141, 143, 145, 149, 152, 154, 157, 158

PYTHAGORAS: 11

QUAINI, M.: 16, 21, 34

RAFFAELINO: 79

RAMUSIO, G. B.: 154

RANDLES, W. G. L.: 12, 17, 21, 42, 83

RAVENNA COSMOGRAPHER (anonymous): 47

REGIOMONTANUS: 91

REVELLI, P.: 5, 21, 25, 29, 30, 32, 33, 35, 40, 46, 56, 57, 64, 67, 68, 70, 75, 79, 99, 103, 106, 107, 109, 137, 138

RIBES, JAIME (see also CRESQUES, J.): 76

RIVAROLO, FRANCESCO: 138

ROBERT OF ANJOU: 59

ROSELLI, PIETRO: 80

ROSSELLI: 80, 125, 137

RUFFINO: 59

RUMEU DE ARMAS, A.: 102

SAETONE, GUGLIELMO: 147, 155

SANTÁNGEL, LUIS DE: 100

SANUDO, MARINO: 28, 38, 41, 66

SCOTTI, FRANCESCO: 146

SCOTTO, GIACOMO: 146

SENAREGA, BARTOLOMEO: 96

SILVANO, BERNARDO: 125

SIMONE DA GENOA, see CORDO

SIMONE DA SARZANA: 79

SKELTON, R. A.: 16, 21, 31, 76

SOLER, GUGLIELMO: 74

INDEX OF PLACES

INDEX GENERAL

PRINTED IN THE SECURITY PRINTING PLANT
OF THE ISTITUTO POLIGRAFICO E ZECCA
DELLO STATO, IN ROME, 1997, ON
SPECIAL WATERMARKED PAPER
PRODUCED BY CARTIERE
MILIANI FABRIANO
PAPERMILLS

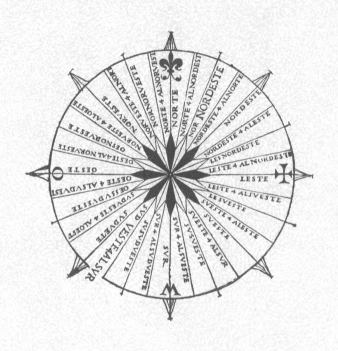